Be a Goddess!

Be a Goddess!

A Guide to Celtic Spells and Wisdom for Self-Healing, Prosperity, and Great Sex

Francesca De Grandis

HarperSanFrancisco
A Division of HarperCollinsPublishers

Material in this book has appeared, perhaps in different form, in *Green Egg; Reclaiming Newsletter; Green Consensus;* The Third Road® training material; *Quest; The Wiccan and Faerie Grimoire of Francesca De Grandis* (an online publication); *Her Winged Silence: A Shaman's Notebook;* and in lectures throughout the United States and Britain. The Third Road® is a registered service mark owned by F. De Grandis.

The true stories in this book are about people who gave their permission to have their stories herein. The rest is fiction. No matter how much it sounds like you.

Use of this book implies full responsibility by the user for its results.

HarperCollins Web Site: http://www.harpercollins.com

HarperCollins®, 🦅 ®, and HarperSanFrancisco™ are trademarks of HarperCollins Publishers Inc.

FIRST EDITION

Library of Congress Cataloging-in-Publication Data
De Grandis, Francesca.
   Be a goddess! : a guide to Celtic spells and wisdom for self-healing, prosperity, and great sex / Francesca De Grandis, – 1st ed.
    p. cm.
   ISBN 0-06-251505-5 (pbk.)
   1. Magic, Celtic. 2. Goddess religion. I. Title.
BF1622.C45D4 1998   97-43302
133.4 3 089916–dc21   CIP

98 99 00 01 02 ❖/RRD 10 9 8 7 6 5 4 3 2

To my parents, Antoinette Marie De Grandis Stafford and William Winston Stafford, who gave me my love of learning, tendency toward constant reading, creativity, psychic gifts, ability to see potential in something broken, independence, and necessary stubbornness.

To my spiritual ancestors, some of whom helped people like me and Dominic Romani not regret the past.

And to my teachers, Cora and Victor Anderson, who bless me and give their whole beings to healing people and cosmos.

Great Goddess, who created all things, through every way this book is used, be with us, guide us, and take care of us. Help us love you and give to you joyfully, the way a happy child gives to a loving parent.

God, help us love and give to you; we need to. Lord of the Dance, help us celebrate. Warrior God, protect and uphold us. Dian-y-glas, be with us throughout this book, your constant presence a strength and joy.

Contents

First Week's Lesson:
The Old Gods Bless Everything We Do

Second Week's Lesson:
Love Your Body and Be Cleansed in Spirit

Third Week's Lesson:
To Be Truly Human Is to Be Truly Divine

Fourth Week's Lesson:
An Altar Is a Place of Power

Rituals

*There are untitled rituals in this text not included in this list.
Everything in life—a journal entry about your lover,
for example—is a ritual.*

Be a Goddess!

From My Book of Shadows
(Magical Journal)

A Fey sorceress, I am a myth and have lived outside of human comings and goings, human circles, human history, until this lifetime. So why tonight do I remember, in a time long ago, a circle of women making quilts? They whisper magical spells, their socializing a disguise for rites holy to the Goddess, rites to keep their farmlands fertile and their families healthy. Why this memory if I never hid my magic in a circle of needles?

I also remember a woody glen further back in time. Two lovers anoint their foreheads with dirt to dedicate their love to the Old Celt Gods. They tumble laughing onto a bed of leaves, where he murmurs a foolishly lewd suggestion in her ear. I sigh with pleasure at the sight of the lovely fleshy belly of the earth beneath them, their bodies dense with the spirit's power, and with the sexy drive the Old Gods have bestowed on all of humankind. I did not suckle at the woman's breast, nor feel the man's body against mine, so why do I remember this tryst?

I remember an even older age, a woman in a cave, her magic hidden and safe from the condemning eyes of her village. She realizes she cannot use a fire to heat her sacred cauldron; the smoke would draw attention. She smashes her fist into the cave wall. How can she do a spell to learn the powers of divination without the fire? She beats her fist against the stone again, cursing her desire for the Old Wisdom that drew her to magic.

Why do I remember these things, when I was not part of them? I remember but was not part of Irish peasants, their lusty magical chants casting off chains of servitude.

I was never fully in the realm of humankind, not part of human history. I was circling a star, learning its song, imitating its grin. I was tumbling like a seal in the ocean bottom, a mermaid amiably mocking my attempts at water ballet. While humans were in circles of quilt making, lovemaking, bread baking, I was circling alone within an atom, in dance with a dream, in pursuit of wish.

Until this lifetime, in which, drawn to the human men and women, I become as them, and, now part of human history, discover that once again my job is to teach the Fey magic to the human race. And I do.

My memory of those past lifetimes becomes clearer. The women making quilts don't remember me, but I went to the eldest of them in a dream and taught her the spells they use when they sew. The woody glen with the two lovers was blessed by me; my unseen rite made that clearing a vortex of pleasure for all who passed through it. The frustrated woman in the cave meets me when I take on flesh for seven years to teach her the basics of the Old Wisdom. The Irish learned their chant from me. It cast an illusion to shield them from the view of the landowners. Their spell keeps them safe.

Throughout the ages I have taught humans magic, humans who later said of me, "Faeries? They are a myth!" Only their teacher, never their companion, I stayed apart from the human rites, and lovemaking and feasts. Besides, no one ever sees a Faerie unless the Goddess kissed their mother's eyelids at the moment of their conception, or Fey salve was put on their eyes. Or they themselves are Fey blooded.

So while I now join mortal history, I am still myth, unseen. Circling around a star, within an atom, in dance with a dream, yours or mine.

My Experience with the Faerie Tradition, in This Lifetime

The college I attended had two campuses, separated by a forest. I often had to walk through those woods at night, and the path was not lit. I was terrified. I believed Faerie Folk lived in the woods, so I would run as quickly as I could, thinking they wanted to abduct me, and treat me cruelly.

Little did I know that the Fey Folk are a kind race, and that I was a witch with Fey blood in my veins. The Faeries in those woods must have been calling me, and I feared the call because I knew no better. But later I completed a rigorous and rare seven-year training with Victor Anderson, to become a Celtic shaman, by being adopted into Victor's family, which had kept Celtic shamanism—also called Faerie Tradition—intact. Faerie Tradition is a Wiccan branch specifically devoted to deep inner transformation, and it forms the basis of this book.

By the way, since most folks do not know who Victor Anderson is: he is an expert on Celtic and Hawaiian shamanism, who has rather quietly trained some of the most seminally influential practitioners of the Goddess movement. If asked what qualifies him to do this, Victor might point out that studying shamanism doesn't earn one a college degree. Victor's wisdom speaks for itself: you can find his name in the acknowledgments or dedication section of many a spiritual book, or mentioned as a source in the main body of a text.

Everything I say about magic or Wicca in this book is specific to Faerie Tradition. Anything I say in this book, period, is about *my* tradition. In addition, I am writing only about the particular branch of Faerie I was taught, and/or the branch I developed. I will use the terms *Celtic shamanism, Wicca, Goddess Spirituality, the Old Religion, the Old Ways, witchcraft,* and similar terms as synonymous. I will generally treat words like *witch, pagan, shaman, priest, mystic,* and *magician* the same way. The following overview of Faerie Tradition includes some of its dominant traits.

Faerie Tradition has been lightly touched by the Fey Folk both spiritually and magically. Still, *Faerie Tradition* is something of a misnomer, a contemporary name for something that was once nameless. The magic that a Faerie Tradition witch practices is still very human, and is Fey only to lesser or greater degrees, depending upon one's personal inclination and teacher. In this book you will rarely find me talking directly about the Little People, though their morals and magic are woven throughout. The Faerie magic must be subtle or it becomes a parody of itself.

Faerie Tradition is the shamanism once practiced by the village witch, and has been passed down from generation to generation within families. Although it is inherently feminist and builds psychological health, its origins are far older than, and distinct from, those two twentieth-century developments, and it is a process and paradigm unto itself.

Celtic shamans honor both the Goddess and the God without elevating gender stereotypes into a sacred cosmology.

Most Wiccan traditions insist one cast a magic circle before doing any magic. Practical Faerie Tradition does not agree with this practice. If I am to use magic as did the ancient Celt—as a natural part of my day, throughout my day, while getting my dishes washed—I can't cast a circle for every bit of magic I do.

In the same vein, the practices are often done without external trappings such as magic wands and ritual gesture. If magic and spirituality are to be really applied to life, you must be able to use them right *in* that life. You can't very well do a discreet ritual on a bus if it necessitates lifting your arms skyward, yelling, "Goddess, be here now" at the top of your lungs, then hitting the middle of your forehead with a magic wand. Celtic magic can be used right when you need it, and the sensuality and majesty that might seem lacking when a rite is simple and direct may be all the greater because bit by bit the magic becomes internalized, completely a part of your body and soul.

Celtic shamanism emphasizes personal purity as a primary, regular, and ongoing practice. Crystals, ritual cups, and incense are not only worthless but dangerous unless the primary tool—oneself—is fit. Don't get me wrong: I love props as much as the next witch—I'm American—but when getting ready for a big ritual, after I put on my red velvet full-length gown with its Renaissance train and sacred tasseled collar with fake pearls and rubies, I make sure my head's on straight! Any spell we cast out into the universe first travels through our own beings, and whoever we are shapes that spell. Magic is like any work of art; the artist's character is indelibly printed on it. So it is with a spell: if you are not fit, neither will the spell be. Purification work is also an essential part of Faerie Tradition's approach to inner growth.

Faerie Tradition is also the bard's path. Celtic shamans who taught the Old Religion through song, story, myth, and poetry were called bards. The Faerie Bard also writes rituals.

Finally, Celtic shamanism focuses on building technical skill with psychic matters. As you will come to see, the tradition in this book is Fey touched and a primal form of witchcraft. So we tap into a wilder power, making more magical training the custom.

A Re-creation of an Ancient Practice

The Faerie training I received was safe only for people with a certain temperament and psychic makeup. For example, a student needs both a strong ego and ease with the mystic poetry of unseen worlds. Such a student is not threatened when, in a vision, he sees the huge distance between stars. (Psychic astronauts need to have no fear of large empty spaces.) Faerie Tradition offers a drastic training, appropriate only for the desperate seeker who can gain the healing and power he needs in no other way.

In 1986, I approached Victor Anderson with an idea for a novel way of teaching Faerie Tradition that would be safe and suitable for the general public. I wanted to teach people how to do what the average person of ancient times did: live close to the earth, use magic in a simple, practical way, and apply the mystic to the everyday. My new system would offer the benefits of Faerie Tradition noted earlier. I would include rituals Victor had taught me, traditional Faerie teaching modes, new rituals, and a new system of working with energy in order to do magic, interwoven with carefully constructed theological and cosmological paradigms appropriate to that magic. These parts would make up a whole different from anything I had seen, yet everything new would be on some level old. With Victor as my consultant, I re-created an ancient practice, and a curriculum still touched by the Fey Folk and as traditional as always.

I called my curriculum The Third Road®.[1] Instead of the either/or answers offered by most religions, I needed a middle way—a midway, if you will—that brought so-called opposites together; for instance, discipline is a key to personal freedom. And mysticism *can* be practical: good magic gets your house cleaned!

I also teach that one must have both self-respect and humility—a difficult balance, but necessary if the Fey path is to be safe. For example, a practitioner with the self-confidence to wield immense power will nevertheless have no unhealthy cockiness that might cause him to put himself and others in danger by attempting spells beyond his ability.

And though the shamanic journey is an ecstatic path, ecstatic is not the same as sloppy, undisciplined, or unethical. For example, one of my students did a purification ritual regarding an ethical dilemma. The purification opened her up so much that she had a spontaneous orgasm while listening to an opera! Travelers of The Third Road can dance with wild magic because we are so disciplined that we do not lose our footing.

While brainstorming with me for a name for my work, Aidan Kelly quoted lines from the poem "Thomas, the Rhymer": "There's the road to heaven, and there's the road to hell, and

---

[1]The Third Road, and variations on it, are a registered service mark owned by Francesca De Grandis.

there? That's the road to Faerie." Since the Fey Folk embrace opposites, and encourage people to be themselves, I felt that calling the latter road "The Third Road" would create an image of freedom from the usual absurd dictums and nonsensical dualities. A bard creates her own lore. I hadn't heard the term "The Third Road" until it came out of my mouth. I am not an academic, and so hadn't read a lot of obscure books on the topic. Ten years later I was told that "Thomas, the Rhymer" refers to ancient Celtic shamanism, proving that imagination, logic, and intuition are as good a way to research history as any.

Part of the system presented here is adapted from the curriculum of The Third Road, whose popularity over the past twelve years has allowed me to be one of only five people in the United States privileged to earn their living as a witch. The rest I created specially for this text. I am also a psychic counselor. The tools for change that I use with my clients influenced my text. Henceforth, I will use terms like *Faerie Tradition* and *Fey magic* as synonymous with The Third Road, unless I am referring specifically to the earlier family system of Faerie Tradition, in which case the meaning will be clear. As I said earlier, the comprehensive nature of Faerie Tradition is such that *Celtic shamanism, Wicca, Goddess Spirituality, the Old Religion, the Old Ways, witchcraft, Faerie Tradition, Fey magic,* and similar terms are generally interchangeable, at least for our purposes.

The Veil Between the Worlds

A fortune-teller once told me that my work during this lifetime is to bring Faerie magic to the human race. She told me of a lifetime long ago when I was a half-breed: half human, half magical being.

Unknown to her, when I was given that psychic reading, I was celebrating my five-year anniversary of teaching The Third Road.

Long ago, the Celtic god Dagda drew a veil between humans and the Fey Folk. In our time, the Goddess has charged me to help bring the Fey magic back through that veil so that we humans can be renewed by the starry-eyed mysticism of the Little People, by the passion and wisdom of the poet in love with the Goddess, and by the wild integrity of the dark and dangerous Faerie Folk.

Today, people are dying body and soul for want of the poetry of the Fey Folk. Faerie magic is not a poetry on the page but a living, breathing poetry, the poetry of ritual, the poetry of waking each morning to the Mother's embrace, the art of walking with Her on the way to work. I try to offer my students a Faerie glimmer, to touch their DNA with my Faerie breath so their blood will remember just a little bit how it flowed when humans were first touched by the Fey.

Every day I am privileged to know this magic: the Goddess walks with me wherever I go. And I truly can feel Her presence; She is not a belief, but an actual, tangible presence in my life that comforts and guides me. As She will guide you in the training ahead.

Preparing for
an Ecstatic Journey

What You Will Gain
from Walking the Shamanic Path

Wicca celebrates passion, sexuality, and unique individuality. In the twelve years I have taught shamanism, innumerable students have confided: "For the first time ever, I feel I have permission to . . . " (quit an unsatisfying job, enjoy sex, write poetry, stand up to an overbearing parent, travel to Europe, come out of the closet, or any number of other things). My students feel they can be fully themselves and live the life they yearn for.

Wicca is a means to change yourself and your life in ways you might have thought impossible up to now. Anyone can gain the wild, natural power of Goddess Spirituality.

Wiccans—those who practice Wicca—have a loving and compassionate Goddess and God, who embrace all humankind as their children and offer us vitality as their sacred gift. Unlike religions that teach us to be ashamed of ourselves and our desires, Wiccan instruction will show you how to achieve self-love, attain personal goals, and find joy in living. My goal as a teacher is to be a kind and gentle guide for personal growth.

My student Marion wanted to be a professional artist, but didn't act on this dream, because "art might not pay the bills." When I taught Marion a myth in which the Goddess creates the universe out of her sexual union with God, Marion discovered the real reason she chose practicality over passion. "My parents taught me," she confessed, "that passion ruins life, that if I reach for my dreams with my whole body and soul, there'll be a disaster. But you're telling me that the Goddess's passion created *all* life." Because of her family's long, harsh history of poverty and alcoholism, her parents had no trust that life is good, or that things can improve. They taught this distrust to Marion.

Marion felt ashamed of her inability to produce art. The love of the Goddess can dissolve unhealthy shame. I suggested that Marion repeatedly use her imagination to pretend she was in the presence of a deity who was a gentle, supportive mother figure instead of a scary scowling judge with a white beard. During this ritual, Marion actually experienced a kind Goddess whom she could trust to take care of her if she risked pursuing her dreams. She now sells her gorgeous, pricey paintings.

You can see that Wicca stresses practical application and improving our daily lives. The more you use this book for internal growth, the more you'll clear the way for abundance to manifest on the physical plane. This book will also teach you spells to acquire the "good things in life": fun, romance, cars, fine food, and other material goodies.

Are you asking what material bounty has to do with a spiritual path? The Goddess is a very down-to-earth deity. She wants us to enjoy ourselves the way any good mother wants her children to have fun, prosperity, and personal satisfaction . So She gave us the material world as Her sacred gift and, in another measure of Her practicality, made sure we had tools—magical spells—to make the most of Her gift.

You will also find that love and sex—ecstasy—are at the heart of the Craft. In this book, we will explore the sexual mysteries of Celtic shamanism, and I will show you how to achieve healthy romance and sexuality through a step-by-step approach. Near the end of our lessons we will focus on a love spell, because, again, witches are concerned with getting concrete results.

Unlike religions that tell us how to think and behave, Wicca teaches us to figure out for ourselves what is moral and good. This is a two-edged sword: with personal freedom comes personal responsibility. The consequences and morality of your acts cannot be foisted onto someone who tells you what to do. We Wiccans might turn to psychic consultants and priests more advanced than ourselves, but in the final analysis we are all priests to our own souls, to our community, and to the land. The training in this book supports your personal freedom while helping you develop your own integrity, ethics, and ability to serve others.

Once you have changed inside, you can be an effective agent for change in your community and for the planet. More and more, physicists discover things that the ancient shaman knew all along, including the long-held magical principle that what happens to one atom anywhere affects every atom everywhere. When I sneeze, atoms on the other side of the planet move. All of life is an interweaving mystery. So if you make yourself healthier, everything in proximity and *in the universe* becomes healthier.

My student Francis was a diligent Roman Catholic when he was young. He longed for a spiritual way of life and to be a good person. As a child, he enjoyed feeding stray cats. As a teenager, he was the confidant of confused peers. By his senior year in high school, he wanted to somehow fight injustice to women. However, his father told him, "They can take care of themselves. Stick to your studies and make us proud."

By age twenty-five, Francis had dutifully taken his master's degree in business administration and begun working in the family business. One day he looked down to see his hands shaking uncontrollably. His legs felt so unstable he feared he would fall, and his mouth became dry with fear. He had several similar episodes, until every morning he woke in a sweat. Was he going crazy? What if someone noticed? What if he lost control and hit someone? What if he humiliated his parents? Sheer willpower got him to work, but though the panic attacks ended, he was so worried about the possibility of another attack that his work suffered. His parents' constant complaints about his job performance only added to his fear and guilt.

Through Wiccan rituals Francis was able to give up the false goodness his parents had forced on him, and to get in touch with what was healthy and sacred for *him*, including his innate goodness. In one such ritual, he wrote down all the lies he had been taught about what "good" is, then burned the list in a cauldron. In another rite, he wrote down all the things inside himself that kept him from self-love. He burned that list also. Rites finished, Francis trained a friend in the family business (who did a far better job at it than Francis ever could). That responsibility taken care of, Francis did the Spell for Self-Acceptance discussed in lesson 10. The last time I saw him was on the opening day of a new health clinic for low-income mothers that Francis was instrumental in setting up; Francis manages its finances while studying to become a doctor. So Wicca helped Francis directly improve both his own life and the life of others in his community.

One of shamanism's most precious gifts is that it teaches us how to develop our full personal potential while honoring society and the cosmos. Wicca helps us affect more than just ourselves. For example, as we destroy forests and water supplies through our greedy consumerism, we actually get further from the real abundance and happiness we are seeking. The lessons ahead will show how this is so and how we can reverse this trend.

If all this sounds deadly serious, it is. But remember also: Wicca is an ecstatic path. We do rituals because we enjoy them and the Old Gods. (By *Gods*, I mean both Male and Female Deity.) If you want to not only change your life, but also find revelry and mirth, come be blessed by walking with the Old Gods.

What to Expect on a Shamanic Journey

This is a how-to book whose primary goal is deep inner transformation through the religion and science of Wicca. In this book are fifteen self-help lessons, each a chapter long, that will lead you through a shamanic journey. Readers—women or men—can do rituals to remove the things inside themselves that are keeping them from prosperity, peace of mind, romance, and happiness. They can also do rituals to achieve an internal sense of self.

Unlike a Wiccan "cookbook" that contains spells for random use, this book embodies a traditional shamanic training. Each week's lesson builds on the one before to develop psychic skill, much as an athlete builds skill through sequential exercises. This step-by-step approach also opens you, the student, to profound personal change, as well as helping you achieve shamanism as an actual spiritual lifestyle.

A shaman does not teach everything about a topic in one sitting, as if reading from an encyclopedia entry. When training others for shamanism as an actual practice or lifestyle, a shaman teaches themes, tenets, and goals in layered increments so that through ongoing experience the student can absorb these teachings into daily life. Few students can absorb advanced shamanic material on a given topic unless earlier lessons on that and other subjects have been explored through ritual and other pertinent assignments, and lived with for at least a week. So initially I'll probe a topic just enough for you to actually put it into practice. Use what's there, and then I'll give you more.

Each week's chapter also contains sub-lessons. A ballet student simultaneously learns exercises to become limber, exercises to increase ankle strength, exercises to gain grace, and so on. Actual dancing can be done at class's end because the building blocks are all in place. Just so, you can start the shamanic dance.

This is a *doing* book, a guide for hands-on learning instead of lots of theory. The ability to parrot a teacher's theory reflects only "head" knowledge. Knowledge of shamanism is embodied knowledge. It is a fairly modern assumption prevalent in academia that to talk about something is equivalent to being able to do it. Although theory is important, Wicca is basically understood through doing. Learning consists of listening to the teacher's lectures, which contain little theory, and doing ritual. A shamanic teacher's lectures are fanciful and include stories, anecdotes, images, and poetry.

This method of instruction is part of the complex weave that I talk about throughout the book. Although it might seem illogical to your rational mind, go with the flow, and you will feel the deep holistic logic involved.

Training involves repetition. Like the tai chi student using physical muscles, we must use our psychic and spiritual muscles over and over, working on the same truths until they are no longer concepts but part of our personal dance. Furthermore, when we hear and practice these truths in many contexts, they become woven into the texture of our lives. There is also the cumulative effect of repetition: one automatically has a magical, joyful day.

A shamanic lesson is a complex, nonlinear dance. Bring your whole being to the experience and dance with me. Use your mind, heart, intuition, and gut feelings. Layers upon layers will be revealed to you simply by doing the rituals.

Having your whole being involved in your rituals and daily life is an essential goal of shamanic training. Nowadays we tend to do things with only sections of ourselves. A jogger runs, but doesn't fully enjoy it because his mind is a million miles away at a business meeting that happened yesterday. A devoted lover is cut off from emotions, so she can't be intimate with her partner during sex.

The Celts recognized that just as humans have a physical anatomy, we each also have a psychic anatomy. Together these make our whole being. Culture after culture has discovered the same truths about our psychic anatomy: each person is composed of three parts, three "souls."

There is the *conscious* self, the part of ourselves of which most folks are most aware. In this culture, it's the part of us that we most often identify as ourselves.

There is the *Godself*, the most sound, whole, and perfect part of each of us.

And there is the *unconscious*. The Portuguese have no word for this. Instead they speak of the *in-conscious*—a wise choice, because *unconscious* is an inaccurate way to describe a part of ourselves that has enormous awareness.

The Hawaiians have a term, *Uhane Kahikolu me ke kino mea,* that means "whole being"—the three souls plus the physical body. When we bring this whole, rich being harmoniously into our ritual and daily lives, everything inside ourselves and our lives falls into place. We are also freed from political, religious, and personal tyranny. Because when *Uhane Kahikolu me ke kino mea* is harmoniously operative in our lives, we find the power, guidance, and authority within ourselves to live in happiness and freedom.

A shaman learns to honor and draw on *every* aspect of the three souls and body in daily life; there is no part of ourselves that is shunned. At times, emotions are as intelligent as logic, full expression of sexual passion as moral as restraint, and bright, hot anger as holy as meek acceptance.

I will explore in depth the three souls and *Uhane Kahikolu me ke kino mea* in later lessons. And more and more will be revealed to you about your whole being simply by doing the rituals, for it is only by full participation that we come to understand certain things.

I use terms like *spell, ritual, rite, meditation, working, exercise,* and *prayer* interchangeably a great deal of the time.

How to Use This Book

During many of the years that I have taught shamanism, I have lived a solitary and contemplative lifestyle. I joke with my friends about it, because in those years I am so typically a shaman that I am a parody of myself. Like the archetypal hermit in her isolated cave or hut, I stay in my home for days, spinning my world of magic, a place of my own design in which I can live as I please. Seekers come for an hour or for several hours to share my world. I give them lessons and psychic readings. I have little reason to leave my hut.

Each lesson in this book is structured as though you and I were having a weekly visit in my hermit's dwelling, during which I lead you through the lesson. During each meeting, I give you assignments to do outside of class. I might also ask you to do an exercise, meditation, or written work right then and there. For instance, during a lesson I might stop the lecture and lead you through a ritual before moving on with more instruction.

Always *do* each exercise, meditation, and ritual. What might seem like very little on the page can transmute into glorious revelation, experience, learning, or inner growth when actually done. As previously noted, personal growth, the spiritual and mystical joys of a ritual, and an understanding of the science of Wicca are gained only through the participation of our whole self, not just by analyzing words on a page.

When you pray or do a rite, put as much of yourself into the act as possible. Include your healthy cynicism, which helps balance an open mind with a discerning eye.

Some folks think the only way to pray is to get on one's knees, hands pressed together palm to palm with the fingers pointing skyward, while reciting the Lord's Prayer. Although that can have great power, it puts a lot of folks off. The Celts viewed prayer in a broader sense. Prayer can mean any number of things. Be open to the specific way in which I am using the word in each instance. In one case that might mean giving you specific words to say to the Goddess, in which case you can be assured there are no postures you have to take unless you want to.

Or I might use the word *prayer* to mean telling the Goddess whatever you need to tell Her, in whatever way you think works best. You can talk to Her in your own words, whether they be plain, everyday words or formal prayers of your own composition. Or you can read the Goddess a poem you found that expresses a request you have for Her. Or you can silently dance what you want to tell Her.

Another time, I might speak of casting a spell for a car as *praying* for a new car. There are endless possibilities, and no formulas by which you will be dominated. Just go with the spirit of each way in which I use the word.

For each weekly meeting, read the lecture in that lesson even if you have already peeked ahead. Each week's lectures and rituals are woven together to make up a ritual unto themselves. Furthermore, as noted earlier, part of the experiential quality of this training derives from it sequential nature. Each lecture, when read in sequence and as part of the appropriate lesson, will bring revelations more splendid and far-reaching than if perused out of context. This also means you shouldn't do a ritual before you have done the preceding ones.

Another reason to do the rituals and lectures in the order and manner given is to ensure safety. Magic is neither a toy nor a metaphor. Shamanic rituals are powerful, and each lesson prepares you safely for the next. For instance, unless you've done the needed preparatory work, you might not be able to handle the emotions generated by a particular ritual or exercise. Do the rituals in the order given, and without adaptation.

The latter might seem odd advice, since magic respects diversity, and many self-help books encourage readers to tailor exercises to their personal style. However, this is a powerful training, derived from a system taught only by qualified mentors. In this sense it is like tai chi. The goals of tai chi include a healthy, power-ful flow of energy in the practitioner, and flexibility of body and mind. Over thousands of years, exact means—precise exercises—have been developed to reach these goals. Just as an adaptation of tai chi exercises doesn't help students gain tai chi's power and benefits, neither will adapting the rituals and exercises in this book help you gain their power. But as with tai chi, sticking to the provided format will instill in you a free flow that eventually will allow you to go with your own unique style in a larger sense. Also, variations can allow magical power to backfire; it would be pretty silly to adapt exercises done in preparation for a trapeze act, wouldn't it? I don't want you to be morbidly fearful: adapt when you absolutely must, as would a trapeze artist. As the lessons progress, I will help you develop a sense of the cautions needed for the particular work you are about to do. So please accept my guidance as a teacher, and fly powerfully and safely.

You may want to work through this book in the company of others. Though not always an option, or even the ideal—I really enjoy working alone—group training can be valuable. (A group of witches who meet regularly to work together is called a *coven*. A witch who works alone is called a *solitary*.)

If you meet as a group, you may want to share thoughts or feel-ings about the text or rituals. Or you may find that you have noth-ing to express, especially at first. If working alone, you can write down your feelings. Discussion can be at the heart of the Craft. Wiccans think for themselves. Reflection and discussion help this thoughtfulness and build our inner authority. And coming to authentic moral decisions is easier through thoughtfulness and with the help of others. As is coming to a good understanding of the science of magic—as when Cora Anderson was teaching me herbal medicine and I foolishly said, "This is fine, but what I'm *really* interested in is the *magical* use of herbs." She responded, "Francesca, if it's good for your body, it's magic."

Reflection and discussion also have a magic of their own. Think how electric a room feels during a spirited (!) debate. That electricity is a real power that feeds the people in the room. And what about the gentle, calm buzz you sense in a room after you've been writing in your personal journal? That's another sort of power, one that calms the soul. These energies also help a magical or spiritual experience blossom and deepen.

Do the work at the pace at which it is given, neither rushing nor lagging. I will explain later. However, don't be neurotic about it. For instance, if a particular week's visit is too lengthy for you, divide the material up into two visits, made over two weeks' time.

Shamanic Discipline and Self-Defeat

Another term for spiritual practices might be *discipline*. We do something over and over until we get good at it, just as athletes practice for their games. For people who are looking for an alternative to the harsh, restrictive religions they were raised with, *discipline* can be a scary word. It's no wonder. Discipline is often abused in this culture, used as a tool to destroy a person's individuality and passion. Yet true discipline gives us freedom. Dancers know that if they do the necessary stretches first, they can dance joyfully, without restraint. Just so, the discipline of Wicca can be the key to true personal freedom and joy. By applying the lessons in this book, you will build skills so that when you finally learn

The Spell Itself, my name for the quintessential ritual that can be used to get just about anything—boom! flash of smoke!—it'll really work, and safely. A witch's discipline entails the following:

You pursue a steady application of the rituals. I will guide you in this with weekly assignments—tools to celebrate life.

You do assignments. Assignments can be as scary a word as *discipline.* When I was in high school classes, I would get excited about a question that would come to mind, raise my hand, and wildly wave my arm back and forth in my enthusiasm. I was always instructed to calm down. Homework was so boring that its only relevance to *me* was that I would get into trouble if I didn't do it. It seemed homework's sole purpose was to stultify my mind and suppress my natural instinct to live fully. Remind yourself that your weekly assignments can reverse the effects of oppressive school assignments.

You continue on your spiritual path despite any self-defeating inner voice that tries to sabotage you. The voices of discouragement, fear, and resistance are as much a benchmark of a legitimate spiritual journey as are revelation, self-improvement, mystical visions, and faith.

At first the very idea of doing magic might spark the imagination and generate excitement, but then the initial excitement can give way to many forms of self-sabotage, some of which are subtle. Perhaps you will tell yourself, "I have to face this alone; that's too hard." Throughout the text I offer guidance so you don't feel alone, and I discuss other ways to get support should you need it. You will also have your inner guide and the Goddess to help you navigate your life, and this training. You are not alone.

You may hear a voice that says, "It's too much work." Yet many students have completed shamanic trainings. Or you may hear,

"I've never been good at studying." I will lead you through this study step-by-step. You might also ask for pointers from friends who have successfully used workbooks. Maybe you think you will never grow, but you will.

You might also tell yourself, "People will laugh at me," or ask yourself, "How will I find the time?" If these are legitimate concerns instead of manufactured excuses, remember that obstacles are part of any spiritual path, and can be overcome if one clings to one's path.

Ask the Goddess in your own everyday words how to overcome your obstacles. She will give you the help you need. Her guidance might come as an inner voice, a friend's feedback, a magazine article, a song on the radio.

I suffer more self-defeating thoughts than almost anyone I have ever met. To make matters worse, most of the time no matter what I do, I can't get rid of a negative belief. But I can *act* as if I believe otherwise. As long as I do that, I am moving toward my goal. No matter what negative thought or feeling comes to you, keep on moving down the road. If you fall, take a nap. And then just keep on going.

You never use Wicca and its discipline as a vehicle for self-abuse. For instance, avoid criticizing yourself for taking time to achieve a goal. Change and right living can take a long time. One day I realized that my baby steps, which seemed too small to count, had taken me across the universe.

Nor should you chastise yourself if you can't always get your assignments done, or if you have not accomplished what you thought you should in an exercise. It's enough to do the best you can.

Nor should you shame yourself for shortcomings that are only human. The goal of Wicca is not sainthood, but happiness.

Many spiritual systems are based on shame, self-incrimination, and fear of a punishing God. You can pursue *this* spiritual path without that. The Old Gods are not cruel, but love us for who we are.

You keep going through hard times. It's worth it. One night halfway through class, my student Etta started fidgeting and biting her lip. She practically held her breath for about ten minutes, until she burst out, "Francesca, just now when you told us that the Goddess loves us for who we are, not for our fancy cars or nice clothes, I realized that I accepted a husband who married me only for my money because I'm afraid to be alone. I finally got the courage to leave him, but I've been divorced two weeks and it makes me just as miserable as my selfish husband did."

She was about to dive into another inappropriate relationship. I suggested that instead she stick to her shamanic disciplines because through them she could learn why she chose a husband who hurt her, and how to enjoy solitude. It was a struggle, but hard times turned around. Etta found someone who could love her and treat her as she deserved.

For the Advanced Practitioner

By *advanced practitioner* I mean someone with six years or more of serious study in Wicca. Serious study *can* consist of self-taught magic.

If you are experienced in other Wiccan traditions, you might find premises in this book that contradict what you have learned.

Simply follow Faerie Tradition rules when practicing The Third Road, and what is traditional in your other forms when you practice them. There are different goals, rules, and warm-ups for baseball than for basketball.

If I say, "To meet the Old Gods safely one must be pure of intent and respectful," and you disagree, I won't argue with you. Magic respects diversity. If you do all the exercises, however, you might find that our Gods are different from those you know, despite identical names and descriptions.

I have often had very advanced practitioners join my beginner groups. For most of them it has been a truly enriching experience. But to learn from a peer takes a certain amount of humility and a willingness to "sit on your hands." In other words, the experienced students who benefited from working with me in a beginner context had to be able to put their sometimes formidable knowledge and experience aside to some extent, and come to my classes much as a child would. In that spirit they could gain much.

For the advanced practitioner and novice alike, it is only by using this text in the order, pace, and manner given, and with one's whole being, that one can obtain the benefits exclusive to Faerie Tradition and gain gut-level knowledge of a path with subtle differences from other Wiccan traditions.

Some of our visits will end with a section called "For the Advanced Practitioner." Advanced practitioners can use these sections to help bring more of their expertise to the lessons, and to provide options if they want to work at a faster clip (the first such option is to work on the fourth week's lesson, the altar section, as soon as you want; the information in that section can be pursued at length).

☾ ☾ ☾

A few last details:

Faerie Tradition uses some terms differently than do other Wiccan traditions.

At the end of this book is "Supplementary Magical Resources," a guide to resources that can support and expand your Wiccan work.

Finally: look forward to having earned the "Certificate of Completion," which is also at the end of this book.

The Old Gods Bless Everything We Do

Blessing Your Work

Following the pagan path means that we are blessed at all times not only by the Old Gods' protection and guidance, but by their joy and tender love.

To gain this benefit, do the following: whenever you practice Wicca, dedicate your Wiccan work to the Old Ones—the Gods of the Old Religion—in the manner shown below. This helps the Gods protect and guide you in your work, whether that work involves receiving your weekly lesson from me or doing your assignment.

Another benefit of invoking the Gods before any of your work is that you will become more and more aware of the love with which they surround us in our daily life.

Wicca is ancient, and easily misunderstood by a modern person. For instance, when first studying Wicca, I thought parts of it were metaphor for helping me understand my psyche. Now I know that magic is *real*, not a metaphor, so I try to avoid mishaps in my spells. The following ritual not only protects against mishaps, but helps us gain an ancient witchy perspective.

First, read through the ritual once to get the gist of it. Then, after gathering the few easily found objects you will need, do the ritual to the best of your ability, silently or out loud, as a way of starting our first week's visit. As with all the rituals in this book, do each numbered step before going on to the next.

The phrase "so mote it be" in the prayers simply means "It *shall* be as I have just said" or "What I have prayed for will surely happen, without doubt."

RITUAL
Blessing the Path

Tools and Ingredients

☾ Water in a small bowl, shell, or whatever container you have on hand. If you want, the container can be something especially sacred or meaningful to you.

☾ A pinch of dirt added to the water. The dirt can be potting soil, dirt from your backyard, or dirt from a site that is sacred or special to you. If neither water nor dirt is easily available, a nominal amount of your saliva can be used.

Step 1. Say the Prayer to the Great Mother:

> Lady, from you all things emerge,
> and unto you all things return.
> Please bless this work I do now,
> that I may feel it flowing from your pleasure and bounty
> and boundless intelligence.
>
> Lady, from you all things emerge,
> and unto you all things return.
> So now I give this work to you.
> For though all is yours,
> it is possible to run from your love.
> Instead I raise my face,
> like the child's to the mother,
> that I may live in your pleasure, bounty,
> and boundless intelligence.
> So mote it be.

Step 2. Say the Prayer to the Lord of the Dance:

> Most holy sacrament of Selfhood,
> Who forever lifts His divine head
> to be blessed and to bless,
> please be with me now.
>
> You are Her chosen one, Her anointed one.
> Bring me these mysteries.
>
> It is all pleasures to love you.
> Make me smile with these pleasures.

You see the futures our Mother breathes life into.
Bring me your vision.

You reside in myself,
so that I shine with my own unique divinity,
and am in myself and of myself a God.

Bless this work.
So mote it be.

Step 3. Anointing your forehead with the water-and-earth blend, pray:

> *Goddess, bring the body of God into my being*
> *that like Him I may shine and be loved by you.*
> *Lend me earth and water, air and fire—*
> *fill me with these elements, these powers of creation,*
> *that I may tend them because they are your garden,*
> *and that I may be safe in this work,*
> *and happy and one with you.*
> *So mote it be.*

Once you have done this rite a fair number of times, a quick touch to the forehead without even a prayer will pull in the same energy as would using the earth-and-water blend and prayer. This is useful for when you want to do an unseen rite at the office. Just don't give up using the earth-and-water blend and prayer altogether, or you will lose the impact.

Love Is a Science, Science Is Mysticism

Witches are scientists, though they are unlike many modern scientists who believe nature and science are at odds. Science *can* be used in harmony with nature. Furthermore, Wiccans don't believe in a spiritual life divorced from scientific laws, or from nature. Witchcraft is a nature religion. Nor do we believe in a spiritual life divorced from our bodies.

Magic is a science through which we change reality by the psychic manipulation of atoms, as you will learn to do.

Our spiritual beliefs, our magic, and often our myths do not contradict the most contemporary knowledge. The more contemporary the physics, the more it expounds the same laws that are part of the magical art.

All the cosmos weaves in a scientific, mystical dance in which are myriad forms, endless diversity; each thing created is unique but dancing with all other things. This is an unusual concept for people who believe, consciously or unconsciously, that the cosmos is based on a few basic blueprints—as if there were one best way to be—or a few linear processes, or a polarity-based reality.

We see the Goddess and God in nature. And we see them within the laws of nature (physics), within the motions of physics. This does not mean that our Lord and Lady are only personifications of nature; the Gods are spirits with spirit bodies. There's a Hawaiian saying, "God is self and self is God and God is a person like myself." To quote further, Victor once told me that the Gods personify nature the same way *we* do: though *we* personify nature, we still exist as beings in our own right.

The Goddess is in all things. No, let me rephrase that. She is not "in" them, She *is* each tree, plant, and animal. If you pick up a rock, you hold the Goddess in your hand.

She, and hence He, is *all* things. Whenever I mention Her, He is included, for the Lord has never left Her side. Repeatedly where there have been found relics of the Mother, nearby have been found His symbols.

Even a car is the Goddess, offering to transport us through our day. I try not to refuse Her aid, in any of Her manifestations. A witch really sees the Goddess in everything.

You can bring the mysteries of the above lecture further into your life with the following prayer.

Sincere prayer is powerful magic. Empty prayer is just that—empty. Put as much of yourself as you can into your prayer. But if you are only trying this prayer as an experiment, that is great! A prayer made by someone who does not believe, yet is trying anyway, has its own magic. Besides, I advise prayer for those who do not believe in it: an answered prayer can change one's mind.

Now say the prayer, out loud or silently. Do this before you read any further, because it is part of our visit.

🌙

PRAYER
The Laws of Nature

I know the Laws of Nature are you, Lady.
Keep me mindful that I step upon your body,
with your feet,
that my sorrows are your sorrows,
and that a healthy priest(ess) makes all things sound.
I feel your breath in the wind, and your hand in mine.
Keep me sincere.

Give me your work,
which is to be joyous and to tend all things,
because all things live,
of themselves,
and with your spirit.
Your will through mine, so mote it be.

Having made the prayer, if you are working with a group or partner, you might now want to discuss your experience or your thoughts about it. Or about anything that has happened so far in our meeting this week. If working alone, you may want to pause and write something for yourself or to share with a friend later. After you have finished your discussion or note taking, read on.

A Healthy Priest(ess) Makes All Things Sound

"A healthy priest(ess) makes all things sound." That means a lot of things.

Without any magical training, any of us can be a minister of the Old Gods by being of service to our friends, our community, and the land. Any of us can be priest and teacher to all those around us, whether we teach by overt instruction or by the examples of our own behavior.

We become healthy and prosperous as individuals only if we help the rest of humankind become so. For instance, scientific studies have shown that a lack of being loved promotes heart problems. A man who is so focused on earning money and prestige that he neglects his family eventually suffers an overwhelming emptiness and loneliness. He does not receive or give the love needed to be healthy.

Each of us is also part of the family that is animal, plant, and rock. We are also part of a planet and universe. All these things weave with, interact with, and impact us. Destruction of our earth, in a scramble for so-called abundance, actually robs us of the abundance and happiness we desire; environmental diseases are hurting, even destroying, many people's lives.

Just as you can often tell a person by the company she keeps, so humans are defined by that which surrounds them. A bleak city housing project seeps into the pores of its tenants until they carry themselves with a dismal posture in which their shoulders are hunched up to protect the back of the neck. All of life is a sometimes subtle weave.

"A healthy priest(ess) makes all things sound" thus translates into: witches recognize their obligations to family, friends, community, and nature.

It also translates into: a witch recognizes her obligation to herself. Many in our culture were raised to believe that we are not important in and of ourselves. As we got older, in keeping with this teaching, we neglected our needs for love, relaxation, positive feedback, satisfying careers, maybe even healthful food. Often the excuse was that we were busy helping others.

But every person's first responsibility is to himself or herself. If you do not take care of yourself, you are doing no one else any service. Alan, for example, works full-time managing a restaurant. He also takes culinary classes three days a week because he wants to become a chef. So Alan needs weekend mornings to sleep in. But his friend Greg needs help with a move, so, thinking he is doing Greg a favor, Alan forgoes his weekend rest to helps Greg pack his possessions, load up Greg's car, and transport all the boxes to Greg's new apartment.

As the following week passes, Alan becomes tired, irritated, and sloppy at work. The restaurant owner criticizes him because a customer was shortchanged. The customer is none too pleased about it either. Alan burns himself because in his fatigue he becomes careless in class. Worst of all, he comes to resent Greg for having accepted his help, and that puts distance between them. When Alan continues to neglect himself in the name of friendly assistance to Greg, the resentful gap between the two widens until finally one day Alan explodes in a tirade against Greg.

No one is helped in this scenario. Because Alan didn't think it was important to take care of himself before anyone else, he, the restaurant manager, the customer, and Greg are *all* shortchanged.

On the other hand, self-care can have an enormous, wonderful impact on those around you. For example, the long-suffering wife of an alcoholic finally says, "You can drink yourself to death, but I'm not hanging around to be dragged down with you any longer." Her leaving, an act of self-love, is *the* thing that finally compels him to get sober. Perhaps the couple even gets happily back together.

Of course, thoughtless use of natural resources and negligent acts that hurt friends are not excused by the phrase "Well, gee, I was *only* taking care of myself." But if we tear ourselves down with self-neglect in the name of charity, we are also tearing down the fabric of the community and the universe. "Taking good care of yourself is a way to take good care of the entire world" is another way of saying, "A healthy priest(ess) makes all things sound."

Assignment

1. Say the prayer "The Laws of Nature" three mornings over a week's time. You can then use it after this week whenever it seems

suitable. It is an excellent prayer to say before a ritual or mundane event.

2. If you want to do more, apply the prayer by doing something beneficial for yourself that you would usually find difficult. I find it hard to take enough breaks when I'm writing, so taking more breaks would be a good way for me to do this assignment. As would going to the beach, which makes me feel serene and in touch with the Goddess, but which I don't do as often as I would like. Maybe you find it hard to let your answering machine get the phone when you're trying to rest; if so, ignoring that insistent ring would be a good piece of homework for you. Maybe doing *any* act of self-love is hard for you. In that case, any way, large or small, in which you can be nice to yourself would be great. Often we have to acknowledge our needs and limited resources to the exclusion of others' needs. There are times in our day, week, and life that we must devote exclusively to self-care. And though I say we are excluding others by doing this, actually we are loving them.

If it's harder for you to do something beneficial for others, do that instead. Bring your girlfriend flowers. Help a buddy clean his garage. Or just spend five minutes listening to a boring friend recite the contents of last night's TV dinner.

3. If you want to do still more, explore another practical application of one other line of the prayer. Clean a beach. Buy better shoes if your feet—the Goddess's feet—are getting sore in shoes you've worn down to thin leather. Try to have a sense of humor about trouble at work. A mystic lives her prayers! Use your imagination to decide what's a good application for you.

RITUAL
Blessing the Path, Part 2

At the beginning of this chapter you learned how to dedicate your work to the Old Ones whenever you practice Wicca. The other part of that dedication is to end your Wiccan sessions with a devocation and a closing prayer. *Invocation* is from the Latin for "calling in"; *devocation* implies the opposite. It is a good-bye.

Devocation to the Gods

Holy Mother, thank you for your gifts and blessings.
Blessed be.
Lord, thank you for your presence and love.
Blessed Be.

Closing Prayer

Mother, Keep me mindful.
Stay with me in the union of all things.
So mote it be.

The Blessing the Path ritual is part of The Magic Formula, a format that, for now, you will use for all Wiccan work. Bit by bit you will learn all the parts of The Magic Formula. Whenever I tell you to use The Magic Formula, you need only use as much of it as you have learned.

Love Your Body and Be Cleansed in Spirit

The Healing Light of Love

A Prayer That You May Love Your Body and Be Cleansed in Spirit

Read the prayer, then its accompanying lecture, before you actually use the prayer.

Tools, Ingredients, and Options

☾ Optional: A body lotion or oil applied to the body as the prayer is recited. If you like scents, pick one you find sensual, such as musk.

☾ Optional: Deepening the impact of this or any other prayer in the book by using your imagination. Pretend that one or all lines of the prayer are true, and that you experience them as such. For instance, when you get to "My veins run with Her red," ask yourself what it would feel like to actually have the blood of the Goddess flow through you, then imagine you feel that. Don't worry if you don't feel successful in your attempt. Doing the best you can makes any rite effective—in the case of this prayer, transforming you in and of itself.

I am the Goddess's beloved.
My lungs take in Her breath.
My veins run with Her red.
Blessed are the feet
that have walked my path
of trials and pleasure.
My hands are Her hands.
I am God as surely as
I created the universe at the beginning.
I need bow down before no one
nor before any deity.
My body is Her body,
glistening with the sweat of stars.
My tears and my sex are Her gifts;
I bestow these as I will.

Goddess within and without,
fill me with the light
that exposes evil;
fill me with the light
that evil flees from;

fill me with the light
that illuminates me in my hiding,
that I may come from hiding
and bathe in the joy of the light.

God, within the context of this prayer, is meant to imply both the male and female Deity. If you are a man, still use the feminine deity genders where they appear in the prayer. That might seem odd, but, as I said in the first lesson, the Deities are not metaphors. They are real. So to change a gender is to miss a specific function of the prayer.

Furthermore, as the Craft expression says, "First we meet the Goddess, then we meet the God." Once you have taken Her energy in, you will come to let in the love of the Horned One in a way that you never could without Her tutelage.

When I refer only to Her, He is implicitly spoken of and stands by Her. We will explore this important, far-reaching truth later in more depth.

It is easy to assume from this prayer that light and evil are opposed in a mechanistic way throughout all time and space. But darkness is loving, not evil. Witches believe that God made nothing that was evil. Life is in no way a war between the powers of evil and the goodness of light. There is good darkness and bad, there are good lights and bad. This particular prayer just happens to be about a good light, and a darkness that at the time is hurting someone. Unless that is clear, it would be easy to codify this prayer into an entire theology or science, especially since it appears early in this book, and since most religious systems are based on the concept of light versus darkness. The Third Road views darkness differently from how it is usually seen, and as the greatest healer of all. Later we will deepen an understanding of

the true and loving nature of darkness, and its deep healing powers. For now it is sufficient to have introduced ideas that shift us
away from notions of darkness as a consistent evil without any
ability to heal. It is in the dark that we rest and recover from illness. It is in the dark that we sleep to dream our sorrows away.

Having touched on this matter of darkness and light, we can
understand the rest of the notes on this prayer in a much truer
fashion.

The light invoked in this prayer is a literal light—not a
metaphor—actually existing on the etheric plane. It is a specific
light—not a generic white light—from which evil flees. It is very
bright and beautiful, and it is often white. Evil cannot stand expo-
sure to it.

It would be easy to interpret that portion of the prayer to
imply that we ourselves are evil. Yet we are the literal children of
the Gods, so how could we be anything but sacred? *This prayer
should in no way be used to make you feel bad about yourself!* Instead,
you are praying for this light to remove any malicious energy or
spirit around you.

Later in the prayer, where it says, "Fill me with the light that
illuminates me in my hiding, that I may come from hiding and
bathe in the joy of the light," I am referring to the fact that many
people are filled with an unhealthy shame. In our shame we often
hide from the Goddess like Adam and Eve in the Garden.

When you do something that you feel is wrong and then hide
from the Gods, they cannot heal you.

Hawaiians say, "If there is no hurt, there is no sin." It is not a
sin to enjoy life as long as there is no unnecessary hurt. We
should not be shamed by false accusations of sin when we enjoy
sex or pursue our heartfelt dreams.

However, we sometimes do sin by hurting ourselves or others.

Perhaps you have criticized someone in a way that was unnecessarily hurtful. Or maybe you have been sexually irresponsible. You deepen that sin, and your own pain, if you deny yourself the care of a nonjudgmental, nonpunitive Goddess. Without this gentle care we cannot change the things in ourselves that are hurtful. We then continue to hurt ourselves and others.

Shame, which makes us hide from the Gods, and punishment do not heal us. And it is *not* healing to get tossed out of the Garden. And it is *not* healing to be told to toil in pain and suffering. Love heals. We can be given that love when we do not run from the light of the Gods that is prayed for in this prayer. We are sacred and worthy of love, caring, and gentleness in the guidance we need when we make a mistake. After all, the Goddess created us out of love; why then should we feel as if we were anything other than pieces *of* Her love, and worthy of all the goodness and kindness there is?

The Gods welcome our errors as long as we are trying.

Many of us can come up with lots of excuses as to why we are not worthy of the love and care of the Gods. No matter *what* you have done, throw away your excuses. And if you think you are not trying hard enough to change yourself, that's *all the more reason* to get the Gods' help. Use the prayer!

It is a sin to deny yourself a good life. We deserve to treat ourselves as the holy children of the Great Mother of all things. Part of this good life is basking in Her love, which shines within the light of this prayer.

You deserve Her love all the time. An eight-year-old child may climb up into his mother's lap when he is upset. But he also wants love and warmth whenever he can get it, and so will climb into his mom's lap any old time. Seek the Goddess's love for the sheer pleasure of it; you don't have to wait until you have a problem. If you want and are able to, use this prayer for the sheer joy of communing with Her.

Strive to be willing to be illuminated, not hiding, so that this actual beautiful psychic light can be shed upon you and heal you, and fill you with joy. When you are filled with this light, things inside you that need to be cleansed will be.

Now go back and, with this lecture in mind, use the prayer, right now, saying it out loud, or silently to yourself. When you have finished, you might want to take a moment to sit quietly. Then continue reading.

The Great Mother Brings Life and Death

The Goddess has within Her all powers and potentialities. We can turn to Her for anything. If we need compassion She will show us Her aspect of a loving, forgiving parent. If we need the kind of strength a warrior has, She will come to us as Athena, the warrior mother, and will stand at our back while we fight! And She will come to us as Aphrodite, goddess of love, when we need to bring the wiles and ways of spring pleasure into our lives.

Though She has many other aspects, She was often referred to by the Celts as the threefold deity. In this understanding of the Goddess we bring Her into our lives as Maiden, Mother, and Crone.

The Maiden is the seven-year-old goddess Nimuë. Nimuë is mischievous. And She is turbulent. And She embodies unspoiled freedom.

Nimuë also embodies, to paraphrase a traditional Wiccan expression Victor told me, a wild ethics, known only in the hearts of children and small animals. This ethic is outside the laws of society, yet is a true and pure way nonetheless.

Assignment

Although I often give homework at the end of each chapter for quick reference, some homework will be given immediately after the related lecture. Hearing an assignment with the shamanic lecture often adds more power and effectiveness to the ritual when it is finally done. So, read assignments that appear midvisit before going on with the week's meeting, but understand that any section labeled "Assignment" is homework.

You can best understand Nimuë at a gut level if you try to imagine nature in the hands of an intelligent seven-year-old. This will show you Her place in the universe. Sometime this following week, between this week's lesson and next week's, write a bit about that. Even if it is only a line or two.

Because children in this society have so few rights, it is hard to see Nimuë as a powerful deity. Nimuë embodies the purest love, yet She is not to be trifled with; She is as fierce, wild, and dangerous as all the Old Ones. Survivors of sexual and other childhood abuse can pray to Her for healing and retribution. She is God Herself.

As Ana, the Goddess shows Herself to us as the Crone. She, like any old woman, can be many things. She can be the wise guide for us in our times of confusion, or a comfort like a grandmother. Like Nimuë, She is turbulent. The Crone also embodies death, and transformation.

Death is a scary word. But sometimes death is not literal; it is, rather, the death of an old way so that we can be new people. It is *this* death, as well as the literal one, that Ana, the Crone, brings to us. She teaches us lessons we need in order to change our lives; sometimes She acts gently, the way an elder does when quietly and lovingly speaking to a youngster. If She is not listened to, Her ways of helping us can be very difficult, for the Crone will *make* us confront our lives and change them. A friend of mine got cancer, years ago. He told me that the cancer made him realize he had been wasting his life, and that he didn't want to die without having "done something." Ana's hand had touched him, and though the cancer was a horror that I would never wish on anyone as a way to grow spiritually, he was ready to live fully as a result. After a year of struggle, the cancer was healed. It is best to listen to Her the first time around when She is teaching us with gentle words rather than later, with the harsher of life's lessons.

It is easy to forget when talking about aspects of a God that within each aspect is the whole deity. The Goddess is not divided, She is whole. So if you look deep into the eyes of the Crone you will see the Mother and the Maiden.

An example: if you are a waitress you probably do not wear the same clothes for work that you do to go on a date. Yet you are the same person in both situations. And certain aspects of you come more to the foreground at work, but *all* of you is present and accessible. So if last night's date shows up at your workplace, the romantic part of you might emerge to blow your sweetie a surreptitious kiss. Your whole self is always present. So it is with the Gods, and with the Crone.

This wholeness of being is not reflected in how we treat the elderly. According to societal perceptions they are not, for example, supposed to be romantically and sexually inclined. Nor are they supposed to need to be productive as would a younger person. Yet within the Crone, as within an elderly man or woman, are all things: creativity, sexuality, the need for hugs and fulfilling work, humor, passion, and anything else you can imagine.

Assignment

Optional: Over the next week, watch for an old woman, whether on the street or in your office or family. Try to imagine her as a younger woman. In the older woman, the young woman still resides, vital, intelligent, and needing and able to give love. This exercise will help you realize the powers of an old woman. Within her, as within the Crone, are *all* aspects of the Goddess.

The Goddess is ultimately known in Her Mother aspect: Mari, the Great Mother, or Mater Magna. Like most females, Mari is misunderstood. Because sexism has narrowly defined women's roles for hundreds of years, Mother, as an archetype, is usually thought of only as the raiser of children and she who gives nurture. By the same measure, the Goddess becomes the giver of life, grain, nurturance. Although these are crucial roles that will be explored later in this book, they are limiting.

In reality Mari is the *Great* Mother, Mother of all things, creator of life and of *all* things.

I have a friend who is a dynamic, high-income businesswoman. A pagan, she knew that upon becoming pregnant with a much-wanted child she was entering the Mother phase of her life. She became confused and resentful because she thought coming into motherhood restricted her to home and family. But motherhood means coming into full fruition as a woman, and encompass all aspects of the mature woman's life: home, business, society, politics, the arts, and whatever else she might desire to involve herself in.

Furthermore, as the mature woman—Mother—moves into each of these arenas, it is not simply as the nurturer or support system—for instance, the secretary who fetches coffee or does the paperwork so the executive can do the *interesting* parts of the job. Rather, when a woman comes into her full-blown womanhood, she is the Mother of *all* things. She is the visionary, entrepreneur, city planner. She is the mover and shaker, the congresswoman, the political activist, the visual artist, the movie producer, the potter, not always the caretaker (nurse) but also the hospital administrator. When a woman comes out of her Maiden phase into Motherhood she is maturing into a fullness of being. Like a fully bloomed rose. That blooming includes her deepening capacity to nurture children, but a woman in the Mother phase of her existence is at the height of her capacity in every aspect of her life: the community leader, the mentor.

She is also at her *sexual* peak. (Which blows the whole concept of choosing between being a good wife/mother and being a sexy woman! Next time your hubby says, "You're a great mom," smile mysteriously, bat your eyelashes, and say, "D'ya wanna find out *how* good?") Mother is the woman at her sexual peak and height of desirability, like a wine aged to its full maturity, with richness and depth.

Charlotte Perkin Gilman in her novel *Herland* portrays a utopian society, the motivating force of which is motherly concern for the children of generations to come. This concern creates profound technology, sound ecological practices, excellent education, and high morals. Motherly concern and instinct, if not narrowly defined, can be a greater force for our society.

Each woman who creates is a Mother whether she bears children or not. She is truly a reflection of Mari, who is creator of life and of all things. Each woman who engages in self-healing, in the healing of the planet, in being a carpenter or a plumber or an advertising executive, is a mirror of Athena, whom even the patriarchal Greeks recognized as the creator of cities and technology, and who, before she was dethroned by the Greeks, was considered the Great Mother. (Which is why she was considered the creator of cities, originally. Clever mom that She was—aren't moms great?—She managed to stay in the game by adapting herself to Grecian ways.)

A narrow definition of Mother debases us. My daughter is one of the greatest gifts of my life, but no man would be so narrowly defined by parental love that he would be expected to forsake all but the immediate child-care tasks. As a father he would be expected, ideally, to care about the community he lives in and take an active part in making the world decent for his children. His role as father is akin to the role of the mother in Herland.

When we bring ourselves to an understanding of the Great Mother, when standing before Her to be touched by both Her enormous power and Her great compassionate love and gentleness, it is important that we not misunderstand who She really is. She is not God's little housewife but God Herself. This needn't imply that being a housewife is a bad thing, nor that the Male Deity is a lesser being. But our Goddess is a Mother, and we must truly understand what Mother is as a God and as a human in order to find our true power as women and men. The Great Mother is God Herself, creator of all things.

Here's an exercise to do right now, to get a break from all these concepts, and to experience firsthand some of what has been talked about. Reminder, do each numbered step before going on to the next. With any ritual that employs imagination and visualization, take some time to do each step before moving on to the next. It is best to read the exercise through once before doing it. Men should see themselves as a female deity in this rite, just as in following lessons women will work the Male Deity along with the men. This is important.

RITUAL
Becoming the Goddess

Step 1. Get in a comfortable, relaxed position, then close your eyes.

Step 2. Using your powers of imagination, picture yourself as a female deity.

Step 3. Keeping that sense of being a deity, see yourself with breasts and all aspects of a feminine being. Whether your skin is dark or light, you might picture it as quite dark, like a black woman's, or like a blue-black night sky shimmering with stars.

Step 4. Keeping that sense of feminine deity, imagine yourself to be all-powerful.

Step 5. Imagine that you created everything that exists; imagine what it feels like to be able to do that.

Step 6. Imagine that within yourself are *all* powers, potentialities, and forms of nature. Imagine that there is nothing you need that is not within yourself.

Step 7. Imagine that you are as vast as all of creation.

Step 8. Imagine that you, a female god, reside within all things—each person, plant, rock.

Step 9. Become aware of your breath. Simply take note of it, without analyzing it, judging it, or trying to change it.

Step 10. Become aware of your clothing against your skin. Again, simply take note of it.

Step 11. With your eyes still closed, become aware of the chair or floor you are sitting against.

Step 12. Eyes still closed, become aware of the room you are sitting in; think of what is in it, what colors the walls are, what the temperature is like—anything you can notice or remember.

Step 13. When you're ready, open your eyes.

Step 14. Take a few minutes to stretch your body all over. Do not be perfunctory about this; it is important that all parts of you get a bit of a stretch.

Step 15. Take a few minutes to gently, with the palm sides of your hands, slap your body all over. Again, do not be perfunctory about this. It is important to ground yourself, and to use this way to do it, so that the exercise is done safely. When you get to your face and head, instead of using the palms, gently tap with your fingertips.

I dedicate the above section on the Mother to my daughter.

A Book of Shadows

Part of being a magical practitioner is writing in a notebook about the things that happen to you. I will sometimes refer to it as your Book of Shadows. Entries needn't be more than a line or so, but *do* keep a journal if possible. The writing assignments in this chapter would be kept in such a journal.

When you have read a lecture in this book, or after you have done an exercise or assignment, you might want to write a few lines for yourself. You may also want to add thoughts that occur to you during the course of the week, those amazing realizations that occur to one while doing the dishes or walking to work. Or while making love. (Yup, makes you smile, maybe chuckle, doesn't it, that seemingly incongruous pairing of sex and revelation?) You needn't, of course, use The Magic Formula every time you want to jot something down. It's hard enough to extract yourself from a comfy bed after lovemaking so that you can scribble a few lines in your journal without having to make a production number out of it. Though I say, "Always use The Magic Formula," use common sense in applying that dictate.

Writing will deepen your understanding of your process. By *understanding* I mean not only an intellectual realization but a down-to-the-bones understanding. Journal writing also helps you find yourself, and Wicca is a religion of self-realization. Journal writing is a magical and transformative tool.

This writing needn't be fancy or "poetic." As a matter of fact, the best way to keep a shamanic journal is to write in the language you speak in. After all, it's *your* journal, so it can be in *your* language, and don't be bothered by any stick-in-the-mud who thinks otherwise. My writing style is not a contradiction of this: I am a natural storyteller/poet and am as likely to speak in a poetic mode as to say, "George, pass me the mustard."

When you do this writing, don't try to be someone other than yourself: use your own language, and write about what *really* is going on. For instance, if an exercise does nothing for you, don't be ashamed to write just that: "I woke up in a really bad mood today. I broke up with Frank yesterday and am feeling hopeless. So I did my morning ritual but I don't feel any better."

A magical journal chronicles a *spiritual process*. Folks tend to see spirituality as joy, revelation, love, healing, and personal achievement. But a legitimate spiritual journey is equally about setback, disillusionment, fear, personal shortcomings that are ruining your life yet seem eradicable, and sometimes not seeing that you have made a lot of headway. Anyone whose so-called spiritual journey is all joy and freedom is either a far better person than I or a liar to themselves and others. Most of the time it will be the latter. OK, maybe *a liar* is too harsh. How about *delusionally psychotic?*

I suspect that there is only one saint on this planet, and that's my cat. Well, there might be a second: there was an ant trail at my picnic yesterday, and the third ant in line obviously had no need for further personal development. Anyway, write about your actual journey. For example, if you are experiencing doubts about your path, write about that: "Gee, I wonder if this is really for me. . . ." These honest entries will serve not only as an outlet for your problems but as a catalyst for growth.

A man attended a workshop I taught about magical journal writing because he had writer's block. He shared a profound journal entry. Its sincerity reflected deep experiences we all had gone through. Informed of this, he replied, "Oh, I have notebooks and notebooks of this junk." Junk? His ability to use his own words to talk about what was actually happening to him had produced a beautifully crafted, publishable piece. He didn't have writer's block. He had a low estimation of his writing. If you want to share your journal but fear doing so, remember what my writing teacher, Kush, told me: "The deepest part of you is the deepest part of everyone else."

Throughout this book there will be specific writing assignments, plus occasional reminders to do magical journaling in general.

The Process of Change

I will offer helpful hints, both in sections called "The Process of Change" and throughout the text, about the shamanic pitfalls, quandaries, and challenges that my students have asked me about over the years, or that I have encountered myself. In these sections I will also add any other necessary or helpful hints that could not be added to the body of the lessons.

After years of traveling the shamanic path, both personally and as a shamanic guide, I have come to know the path's pitfalls well. One bit of self-sabotage I used to engage in was to ask God for guidance about a challenge I was facing, only to then say, "Thanks very much for the input, God, now get out of my way." Of course, since I wasn't following Her guidance, I kept falling flat on my headstrong face, and didn't even get anything accomplished for it!

When traveling on a spiritual path, it is common to try too hard, or to get discouraged, or to go off on *wild-goose changes*—my term for moving spiritually in a direction that is self-destructive, or a waste of time, yet feels like a direction in which you are growing and really going somewhere.

A helpful hint for this week's lesson: Are you feeling intimidated about continuing the work in this book? Good! That shows you are normal. It is scary to grow and change. One might be plagued with thoughts like "Oh, I'm not understanding magic well enough" or "If I keep trying to improve my life, my father will get angry with me." But if you put one foot in front of the other, and remember that the Goddess and the Horned One are carrying you, gently cupped in their hands, toward your goals, you will find your dreams possible. You might tell a friend, "Gee, I am nervous about this work." The Gods often give you their encouragement through a few heartfelt words from one of your buddies.

Assignment

This following week, say "A Prayer That You May Love Your Body and Be Cleansed in Spirit" on at least three and at most six days. Take one day off per week from most disciplines. (When I mentioned writing that last line to a friend, she quipped, "That in and of itself is a discipline." Smart gal.)

For the advanced practitioner: If you want to move at a faster pace, say the prayer every morning this week but one, and the prayer from last week every evening but one.

To Be Truly Human Is to Be Truly Divine

A God of Life

God: a loaded word for those of us who were taught to fear His harsh punishments and judgments. Many people gravitate toward the Goddess because She is not so scary.

But the Wiccan Male Deity is a God of life, vitality, joy, celebration, and fertility. And He is loving. When we say that our God is loving, we really mean it. A cruel parent might strike a child brutally, saying, "I am doing this because I love you." Our God does not use the word *love* as an excuse for cruelty. We are never tortured by a pagan deity in the name of "this is in your best interest. You may not like it, but you will grow from it." That is nonsense. The Old Ones are parents who truly love us. Therefore, they would never torture us by burdening us with disasters in life "for our own good."

Our God is horned, but He is not a rank, defiled, immoral beast. He is horned like a proud stag. The Gods are glorious animals. Though religion, as I learned it growing up, focuses mostly on *transcendence*—which means "to rise above the material world"—the earth is sacred, so to always transcend it desecrates it. We are the animal children of the Gods, and to become Godlike means to become fully human and fully animal.

An animal has integrity. Our God exemplifies this integrity, and it is also in ourselves. Think of the nobility of a wild stallion, or the fierce protective parenting of some animals. There are many vile things in life, and in nature, but that's different from saying that life and nature are *inherently* vile. Someone once said (was it me?) that the latter belief implies that the only solution is nuclear destruction, which often seems the logical conclusion of transcendence.

Transcendence can be very healthy and moral, and is an important part of paganism. But in most contemporary religions, transcendence is practiced in ways that are abusive, punishing, and oppressive. We pagans, by contrast, anoint our foreheads with dirt because the material world is a sacred gift from the Gods that we honor by taking pleasure in it. (One of my students calls The Third Road® "the cult of the muddy forehead.")

The biblical creation myth tells us that God stood outside and looked into the darkness, saying, "I think I'll make something." A god without a body. So some men believe that to be in God's image they must emotionally castrate themselves. Stripped of their true potency, robbed of their unbound fire and passion, they are left instead with machismo and rage.

Faerie lore tells us of an ancient God whose name translates into "Self-fire." This is the God of the witches. What is this "Self-fire"—the fire within each of us—that post-pagan societies rejected, squelched, often all but put out? It is a holy integrity, a holy passion. It is the burning in a man or women to embrace life fully, to laugh hard, cry hard, love hard, and fight hard for our rights.

Instead, modern men are told they have no innate worth, that they must earn it by bringing in the bacon, or dying on a field of war. And the sacred fire within a man has been ridiculed and bastardized: "Fire when you see the whites of their eyes."

Men are told to keep their fire dulled. Women, too. We are told, "It is a sin to rejoice in the breath of your body." And we live in a world where passion is equated with war or rape or rage, where every man, woman, and child is supposed to be tamed, just as the land and all of nature is to be subdued.

But Self-fire is an untamed God, glorying in the holy passion of life; life is sacred. His untamed power resides in all of us, and in the land society tries to subdue. His powers flow through storm, and horn, and grape, and leaf. They flow through our sex, and our dancing, and our love of our children, in a joyous, healthy weaving of and union with all things in harmony.

In *Her Winged Silence: A Shaman's Notebook*, I wrote, "He is a God of feeling, both physically and emotionally, of unbound passion coupled with integrity."

Our God does not stand outside all of creation. He is in all things, including ourselves. Note that I just used the word our*selves*. As in the God *Self*-fire. It is in the fire of self that we find the God within. So Wicca is a religion of selfhood. Individuality is a reflection of the Goddess and of the God. The Goddess gave each of us unique talents, unique desires, unique *selves*—and not so we could forsake such gifts. We are each a microcosm of the universe, in and of ourselves.

Assignment

Do this assignment sometime this week before your next class.

RITUAL
An Honor Candle

When you have worked hard at something, this ritual is a way to honor yourself and your work. Another translation of Self-fire's name is "Ego-fire." Witches strive to respect themselves (*selves*, self-fire) and to have healthy egos. Sometimes it is hard to see the merit in what we accomplish. We affect false modesty, and don't give ourselves the nurturance of ego-feed.

Witches know that without a healthy ego, people fall back on a false ego, a false pride. With low self-esteem they often try to bolster their false ego by buying the "right" car or wearing the "right" clothes. In making these prestige purchases they try to fill a gap that can be filled only by self-respect.

This first time, use the ritual to honor the work you have done so far with this book. This includes whatever it took to even get *started* with the book, which is in itself an accomplishment. Then use the ritual anytime you want to honor any work you've done.

A reminder: when you do this assignment, use both parts of the Blessing the Path ritual. (The list of rituals following the table of contents makes the rituals easy to find.)

Tools and Ingredients

☾ A candle of any color. You may want to use an orange one; orange is a good ego color because it is proud and almost calls attention to itself, saying, "Aren't I something?"

☾ An incense that is very lovely and pleasant to your senses. I enjoy amber or rose.

Step 1. As you light the candle, say "The Honoring Chant":

> *I light this fire in praise and recognition of myself.*
> *As it sends its heat to the heavens,*
> > *it honors my work, that which I have done*
> > *and that which I am doing,*
> > *and that which I will do.*

Step 2. Light the incense and say "The Honoring Chant" again.

Step 3. Take a moment to contemplate this song of praise, and anything else upon which you want to reflect. While you do so, you might be able to hear the candle flame and incense smoke sing your praises!

Step 4. Go about your day, washing the dishes or getting dressed for work. From time to time, should the candle catch your eye, take a quick moment to honor your work. For instance, it's sufficient to tell yourself, "I did a great job!"

Step 5. Burn the candle until the flame is gone. If you are going to bed or leaving home, put out the honor candle. When you are home again, relight it. You needn't repeat the chant unless you want to. For fire safety, burn candles only when you are at home.

While you are doing this rite, if you have a self-praising thought, don't follow it with negative remarks like "Yeah, well, *anyone* could have done this" or "Well, it really wasn't that much to accomplish."

Such remarks invalidate any praise we give ourselves, and thus sabotage our *self*-esteem.

If you balk at doing this ritual, don't berate or scold yourself. Lovingly and gently tell yourself it is not surprising you balk. All our lives we hear remarks like "Don't be *self*ish—give your baby brother that toy of yours," as if you were cruel to want something all your very own. Or remarks like "Why are you so into your new job? What about me? You're so *self*ish." The new job might be your *self*-fulfilling destiny, and when we fully realize our unique God-given dreams and potential, we *truly* serve our community and family.

With negative ideas about selfhood drummed into us over and over, it is OK to procrastinate a bit about doing this rite. If you are gentle with yourself, you will get the assignment done.

Mythic Lessons

Faerie Tradition Creation Myth no. 1

The Mother Before Creation is walking in the outer darkness. Her steps touch nothing, Her steps touch Herself, who is all things. She uses space as a mirror. This mirror is known as the Mirror of Darkness. In it, the Mother Before Creation is as vast as a starless universe, like sleep without dreams, like sleep in which all dreams reside. She draws the image from the mirror into space and calls Her "Miriel," which means "Beautiful One from God." Each is virgin: unspoiled sexuality in all its freshness. Yet old beyond time, each kissing the other with all the ripeness and experience of a dying courtesan. They make love, each desiring the other as much as they desire the Self.

Then Miriel moves away from the Mother Before Creation, so dark emptiness lightens to cobalt blue as She becomes Dian-y-glas, the Blue God. The Great Mother says to Him, "They shall never take you from me. Whatever form you take, because you are my word, my hammer, and my seal, you shall return to me in your present form. And this our love shall be forever. And through our sexual union all things shall be created and are created, all things which were and are not, and are yet to be."

Victor told me the above myth, which I substantially embellished, adapted, and otherwise changed in the above retelling. A bard alters the old tales, for if a story is unchanged, its wisdom dies.

Learning from the Myth: The Nature of Darkness

One mystery revealed in this myth is the true nature of darkness, embodied in the universe as the Mother's mirror. In the Christian creation myth, God looked into the darkness, into the void, and decided to make something to fill it. And henceforth He remained separate from that which He created, outside of nature and humanity. The theological implication is that God is too good to be a part of nature, and thinks the material world evil.

How much more sense it makes that the Goddess saw Herself *as* that void, that darkness, and from that loving, vital, dark womb all things were created. Instead of condemning the material world, She not only saw it as Herself, but loved and embraced it, just as She embraces us whenever we call on Her. The belief that the Goddess is within us and all of nature is called *immanence*, and implies that nature is good and sacred.

This society usually uses the term *dark* only in pejorative, racist ways: "Oh, that person has such a dark personality," or "It is always darkest before the dawn." But the darkness of Celtic shamanism is not evil; it is the darkness of spring nights when lovers court, of the rich soil from which our food is grown. It is the darkness that a child finds when snuggled under the covers at night while a mother whispers tender words of loving reassurance.

The Goddess's dark immanence also makes sense in terms of physics: past the lighted atmosphere of earth is mostly darkness. The cosmos is not, as some would have it, a balance of light and dark, but mostly darkness. Furthermore, most of an atom is empty space; there is very little *matter* to the material world. Existence consists mostly of the emptiness between the particles of the atom. In fact, if you took the whole planet and condensed it to the actual bulk of the matter therein, it would all fit into my apartment. So most of reality is dark and empty. But just as the dark is not evil, so this is not an evil emptiness. This emptiness is the Mother Herself, replete with Her love and fecundity. Sweet mirror of darkness! O luminous darkness.

The contemporary lack of respect for darkness is subtle when darkness is viewed as a *necessary* evil, as in "You can't appreciate the light without the dark." That's like saying a beautiful night sky has worth only because it helps us appreciate the day sky.

To consider darkness, or anything else, only in terms of its relationship to something else is limiting, not to mention racist, sexist, and downright nonsensical. And just as most of reality is neither light nor a balance of light and dark, existence is not a balance between good and bad, man and woman, leader and follower, the powerful and the powerless. There is no consistently balanced, natural order of things that we all must strive for. To look for such an order would be unrealistic, not the strived-for goal of a truly witchy mind. To always dichotomize is to live merely by an intellectual construct. It is better to trust what your experiences and common sense tell you, so you can observe the true nature of things in your magical science and in your everyday life.

The prayer of last week's lesson said, "Fill me with the light that exposes evil; fill me with the light that evil flees from; fill me with the light that illuminates me in my hiding, that I may come from hiding and bathe in the joy of the light."

I said in that lesson that although this particular prayer is about a good light and a hurtful darkness, there are good and bad lights, good and bad darknesses. An analogy: some plants need the shade that might kill sun-loving plants. For shade-loving greenery, the bright sun is not an illuminating, loving force but a relentless agent of death. Witches, like gardeners, must honor the rules of nature.

Sweet mirror of darkness! I fear a city street if it is unlit and deserted, because an attacker might hide there. But darkness per se? Never! Darkness is not only our shadow, but also the mirror through which we find our essential and beautiful selves. Our quiet bedrooms offer privacy at night in which to love a beloved; the dark brown eyes of an infant reflect our own beauty and innocence back to us. When in darkness, it is crucial that we not hide in it, but face its gift and its challenge. Especially there, we need to be true and authentic! O luminous darkness.

Learning from the Myth: The Goddess and Her Lover

Dian-y-glas, the Blue God, forever stays close by the side of the Goddess, in joy and pleasure. This does not imply subservience on either of their parts; they simply love each other so much that they never separate. If you call upon the Goddess, Dian-y-glas is there, even if unseen. Hence it is eventually necessary to embrace both Goddess and God if you are to walk the Faerie path.

I support women who want no contact with a male deity. There are sound reasons for such a choice, only one of which is that Jehovah can be a real sexist pig. But some women find healing through the love of a good God. And though hearing "Lesbianism can be cured by the love of a good man," makes me want to spit at the speaker (temper, temper, Francesca), the knowledge that love, however it's packaged, is improved by the support of a good God fills my very bones with smiles.

Many men, on the other hand, reject a female deity because they fear that to accept such a deity would be substituting one dominating, oppressive deity for another. Yet many men come to their full power as a man by welcoming the Mother of All Things into their lives. And it eventually becomes too dangerous to work with the Male Deity of the Fey Folk without Her love and guidance.

The Goddess is at the heart of both the poetry and the science of magic. To ignore Her makes practicing that science dangerous. Besides, what comfort and power is in a Goddess who is mere metaphor? If you are a man who is perplexed by Her, ask Her in your own words to help you understand Her better, and then be patient with yourself.

If you are like many of my students, both male and female,

who struggled for years to find peace with the Goddess's consort, be patient with yourself.

If you choose, for now, to relate to only one deity or the other, don't worry. Focus on growing in other areas and on finding the joy life offers. Do only what you want with this section's material on embracing both deities. Only after practicing The Third Road for many years does it become necessary to embrace both deities. The Gods are our patient parents, who will not punish us if we slowly find our own, unique answers with faltering steps—even if that means choosing another Wiccan path that focuses on only a male or female deity. If you are truly seeking the Fey path, you will eventually find and sincerely love both the God and the Goddess.

Endless Purification

My students joke about an expression I use in class: *endless purification.* Shamanic training, with its focus on personal transformation, demands precisely that. I constantly send even adepts (advanced practitioners) home to do yet another purification ritual on themselves.

There is an old Welsh myth about a witch called Cerridwen that is relevant here. In tales older than even this Welsh telling, she is revealed to be not a witch, but a goddess. By the time she is recorded in the Welsh myth, she has been demoted in the lore to a mean, spiteful woman. Many of the myths of the Old Religion were bastardized like this, with the Old Ones portrayed as cruel or demonic so as to discredit the religion.

In the Welsh myth, Cerridwen boiled herbs in a cauldron for a year and a day. After the year and a day passed, her cauldron offered up three drops that gave the poet Gwion Bach the knowledge of soothsaying and all other knowledge. He was transformed into a magical being. All the rest of what was left in the cauldron was poison. It is a tale of a Celtic shaman's training.

We are, ourselves, Cerridwen's cauldron, a vessel of magic and of change. As her cauldron, her cup of delight, her vessel of change, we must be worthy. The magic of the Goddess should not be done by the unfit. Hence the extensive purification work. And to be purified down to those essential three drops of wisdom, poetry, and magic, we must free ourselves of the emotional, spiritual, and psychological toxins that are also in the cauldron. Each of us is our own primary magical tool, and as such must become a fit tool.

I'm not using words such as *worthy* and *fit* in the uptight, judgmental, oppressive ways they are often used, so please don't shrink from the page, or feel inadequate or guilty. This is a religion of loving-kindness. Part of being worthy is simply being a seeker. Being worthy also means that you're *willing* to grow and change. And it means being willing to learn to celebrate yourself as a divine being; remember: "To be truly human is to be truly divine." To embrace your humanness, to trust that anger and instincts are Goddess given, to know that your desires and needs for fulfilling work and happy lives are sacred, to believe that sex is sacred, to believe that sweaty sex is sacred—all this is spiritual, worthy. To be *worthy and fit* means to try to be cleansed of the blocks, complexes, unhealthy fears, unhealthy anger, and false ego that not only interfere with magic but also make you unhappy. And as we are cleansed, each of us becomes a priest whose health makes all things sound.

Being worthy means becoming our truly human selves, who

we are *naturally*. Most of us, having been raised in an oppressive society, are in a state that is far from natural and need "endless purification" to be fully human and fully magical beings.

For those who first experience any authentic spiritual path, the new experience automatically washes away inner blocks, at least temporarily. As such, you have started the process already. Many personal-growth systems stop there. But now that you have experienced an initial cleansing, you are ready to cleanse yourself in a direct manner. Please do the Purification by Earth ritual now as part of this week's visit. Read it through once before doing it.

RITUAL
A Purification by Earth

The purification rituals in this book, like material in any spiritual text, are only a start. If you move more deeply into the Craft, you, like my students, will find yourself rolling your eyes and moaning, "Endless purification." Even a Master of the Art has to clean away complexes and fear; as each layer of the onion is peeled away, another reveals itself.

With each layer comes growth, joy, and self-fulfillment. Doing the cleansing work in this book will make you freer than you have ever been. Though my students moan about this work, they do so joyfully!

Tools and Ingredients

☾ Optional: a brown candle

Step 1. Optional: Light a brown candle to symbolize the healing power of the earth; or find a patch of earth to stand on.

Step 2. Spend one to two minutes taking deep breaths—nothing fancy, just deep, natural breaths, as if you were at the beach breathing in fresh ocean air. Focus on nothing but these breaths. If you find yourself yawning, that is good; yawning opens up the chest and throat so you can breathe freely.

Step 3. Are there concerns that are distracting you from this ritual? Perhaps you are worried about a family member, or you have a health problem, or you are worried if "he" or "she" is *ever* going to give you a call. If you have concerns about daily living that are "sticking to your brain," then imagine your worry, fear, and anxiety settling out of you into the earth, our Mother. Let our Mother take these unpleasant feelings.

It is not the issue itself that you are pouring into the earth but rather your unhealthy preoccupation with it. When the exercise is over you can go back to thinking about these issues, but this rite is a time to focus in a different way.

Step 4. Choose one thing inside yourself that needs to be cleansed away. Perhaps it is fear of asking your boss for a raise. Maybe you are plagued by a resentment toward your father. Maybe you want to write a book or take a class or ask someone special out to dinner but you just can't do it. Perhaps you are terrified of something that seems small to others: some people would be surprised to hear of fear about asking a boss for a longer lunch hour, but for others it can be terrifying to ask for anything at all. Imagine that fear, that resentment, that being-stuck-ness, or that "disproportionate" terror draining away into the earth.

You can also do this with a negative obsession, such as spending all your time worrying about finances or your weight. Or use the rite to be rid of a defeating belief, crippling indecision, depression, or any other negative attribute. The "disproportionate" terror in and of itself could be removed.

Step 5. Pray to the earth and to the Gods that this attribute be transformed within the darkness of the underground into pure life force, and then returned to you as whatever positive attribute the Gods think you need instead of that which has plagued you. For example, if the fault is fear of your boss, perhaps it will be returned as courage and compassion when dealing with him or her. If you cannot ask someone out on a date, perhaps you will find yourself being forthright yet courteous.

You might be surprised at the results of this rite. That it is effective can be amazing to someone who is new to witchcraft. You might also find that it works toward a different but better end than you expected. For instance, if the fault was that you couldn't start writing a book about Brazil, perhaps you will find yourself writing instead a book of poems, which makes you happier than writing about Brazil ever could. Sometimes what we envision as best is not the most productive, healing, giving, fun thing we could be doing. Be open to the unexpected gifts the Goddess sends.

A *reminder*: After doing this ritual, you might want to write a few lines or more in your magical journal, your Book of Shadows, about what it was like for you. For example, was it freeing? Empowering? How well could you feel your inner block leaving during this first attempt at a cleansing rite? Maybe the ritual even felt silly. New things often do. Perhaps you ended up comparing this rite to other religions' attitudes toward inner blocks. If you are working with a partner or group, you might want to stop and share these thoughts and feelings, discuss them, and perhaps discuss what you have read so far.

The Process of Change

I have insisted that, if at all possible, you move through the material at the pace suggested. I have also stressed that the pace is effective, safe, and powerful, both for the novice and for the advanced practitioner. Let's look at why, so you can better decide whether or not you want to follow my suggestion (even though *everyone* thinks themselves an exception to the rules).

Most adepts in my beginner classes have been greatly rewarded for their humility and patience. They have found an abundance of material to learn, challenges to face, and personal growth to gain. Fey magic is unique—Wicca 101 is not Third Road 101—so a beginner's pace is needed for the advanced magician, to whom I strongly suggest you try my pace for a few more visits and see what you can see. To go faster will not speed up the process; it will instead cause you to *miss* the process. Besides, any master worth her salt occasionally restarts from the ground up.

Also, Faerie Tradition demands more safety considerations than most other Wiccan forms of magic. For instance, the Faeries love to help humans respect themselves, but in our society ego gets out of hand; strong-minded folks trample those with less gumption. If you try that with the Fey powers, you're the one that gets trampled. I mean, can you imagine an uptight, look-down-the-nose, pursed-lipped preacher possibly winning a face-off with one of the Little People? He'd be magical mincemeat. So one safety factor is helping the student find bit by bit the harmony between strong ego and humility that I spoke of earlier. Another is the pacing in this book, which has you deal with powers only when your ego structure is ready. Also, Faerie magic might, superficially, seem like other types of power, but an in-depth training touches one's bones. Like yoga, shamanic training works at a deep level, making you flexible and opening up the flow of good energy inside. The pacing helps this happen bit by bit so that it's safe.

Both personal growth and the development of magical skill are slow, evolving processes that demand pacing. Like the skills learned by a ballet student, these things cannot be rushed. The pace in these lessons makes for a loving, gentle pattern of improvement.

Trying to rush can, at best, discourage you. Impatience also might injure you. A ballet student who tries to leap before he has stretched out his body can end up with a torn muscle. So trying to leap past what you are emotionally or magically "stretched" out for can hurt you.

Working with a Group

Have you found that no one has anything to share after you do an exercise or read a lecture? Great! It doesn't matter. Don't force yourselves. Some folks are naturally silent, and though they may need to learn to express themselves a bit more, it is not everyone's goal in life to be talkative. Some people find power in silence.

Assignment

1. Do the Honor Candle ritual.

2. Optional: Contemplate "Faerie Tradition Creation Myth no. 1" over this next week. Focusing on only a few lines, then perhaps writing

about them in your magical journal, can unfold many things to you; there is much contained within each bit of the myth. By writing in this lesson on darkness and the relationship of the God and Goddess, I shared what I personally gained from the myth. Myths that spring from oral tradition are often densely packed with information and themes to be discovered on your own. We're not used to this. The media is dense in another way, as in a highway laden with billboards, and provides a different sort of stimulation, often giving us much stimulus but little information or transformation. On the other hand, oral tradition's densely packed sentences and paragraphs contain much information and transformation, and are full of the mysteries of shamanism.

If you have a working partner or group, you might want to discuss your writing about the myth next week as part of that week's meeting.

3. Do the Purification by Earth ritual once or twice more this week. Each time, clear away another internal block. Enjoy the results!

In next week's lesson about altars, I write that first and foremost *we* are each our own altars. Now you will be a cleaner, fitter altar at which to worship the Gods and yourself.

An Altar Is a Place of Power

Find Your Inner Altar

The Celtic Altar

The *Oxford English Dictionary* says that the word *altar* likely comes from the Latin word for "high place." Maybe this is because in ancient times a shaman would climb high hills and mountains to be close to the Gods and to nature.

This elevation is not to remove us from the world, to make us "above all that." Magical religions realize that our material world is sacred. The elevation of mountain, cliff, or hill brings us *closer* to the natural elements. On a high cliff we truly feel the power of the wind. On a mountain, we see the full scope of what the Gods have created for us to live in. The high place was sought because it was a place *of the world*, a place of *power*, a place where we could get closer to the grandeur and holiness of nature, as opposed to the concept of altar as a place *removed* from the world. In some cultures the altar is dug out in the ground; one descends to the altar, reminding us of the sacredness of our own depths.

To understand the pagan altar you must understand the ancient Celtic shaman's sense of *place*. Living in harmony with the land, she understood that we are not distinct from what is around us. Think of the depression that might have settled on you when you visited a friend at the hospital. Modern hospitals are usually cheerless places, stripped of humanity despite valiant attempts by staff members. They are depressing places. And think of how you feel in a bar: many bars, if not dismal enough, are at least boring enough to make you *want* to drink.

Magic is about being in harmony with place, and finding, or creating, harmonious environments. In other words, a Celtic shaman worked both to create a happy, fertile, healthy home, farmland, and planet, and to obtain harmony with and power from these environments. Nowadays your office might be the farmland, its crop your paycheck.

So the concept of altar is not an artificial one. It is natural. An altar is a constructed place of power, where we become closer to the Old Gods and nature.

An altar is a consecrated place for religious practices of love and worship, and a place to meditate, just as ancients would meditate in sacred forest groves and caves, on mountains and high hills.

An altar is a place that, just by standing at it, gets you in touch with your spiritual objectives and needs, similar to the way a favorite beach makes you feel.

Pagans love to place natural objects on their altars, but if the shells that you have chosen to grace your altar have been gathered at great cost to the ecology of the area from which they were harvested, your altar won't help you be more in touch with your spiritual needs as an earth-loving witch.

Assignment

An altar will not work well as a power spot if its consists of things hurting natural power spots. Without being a perfectionist about it, check your source of altar supplies. Find out how those beautiful shells were harvested before you buy them. This is an ongoing assignment, part of a shaman's life. If you're not good at it at first, don't worry: you have time to improve.

The shamanic altar is also a place to take in God (male or female) just as a Catholic receives the host while kneeling at a cathedral altar. If you seek to receive God's divine energy and spiritual sustenance from crystals, here's another example of the above assignment. Some crystals are mined by dynamiting mountains. We cannot receive God's grace through a practice that threatens Her well-being, the health of the planet.

An altar is also a workbench for the magician. It is all the things I have mentioned, and all of them at once, in harmony, because shamans make no division between the sacred and the mundane, nor between the religion of Wicca and the science of Wicca.

As a workbench, it is a focus of attention magically and spiritually, a focus of magical energies, and a means of empowering your working.

Making the Celtic Altar

So, how do *you* make such a place as I have described above? The following are some traditional practices.

A clean altar is a sign of respect to the Gods and to ourselves. And since the altar is a mirror of self, an extension of self, and a powering of self, your altar needs that clarity. I've noticed that when I have been disorganized and confused, so has my altar.

Your altar can be as fancy as an old Chinese cabinet or simply a portion of your bedside table. It can be a permanent fixture or put together only when you feel like it. When you first set up your altar space, you might want to give it a thorough cleaning: dusting, washing—whatever is appropriate to the surface you are about to use as a sacred space. If you so desire or feel it necessary, you may even sprinkle the surface with water into which you have placed sea salt. This sprinkling will cleanse the altar spiritually.

The Celts saw power in everything: the power of a strip of beach to calm, the power of a crying child to get us to meet his needs, the power of a problem in our lives to cause us to grow. Just so, each object we see, hold, touch, and encounter has power. You might look around your home, your neighborhood, and wherever you go to find things to bring power into your altar. Here are some thoughts about that.

Consider all those objects that have been gathering dust on your knickknack shelf. You've kept them all these years because they mean something to you. So elevate them to their proper status.

Maybe go through that drawer that you have always filled with "stuff" that you never quite knew why you were saving. You know what "stuff" I'm talking about. An antique marble, a crumpled paper doll from childhood, a frayed scrap of fabric that was part of your father's military uniform, a feather you thought pretty, and all those other objects you've gathered over the years because you felt you *had* to have them. They speak to the part of you that is a dreamer and a poet, trusting in magic and needing inspiration.

What objects bring you closer to nature? Perhaps flowers or tree branches or an earthenware bowl filled with water will do the trick. Maybe you have a rock that you found on a beach at a moment when you truly felt the power of the ocean.

Also ask yourself if any objects focus you into the sacred. For some people these might be shells, crystals, pictures of people who are role models, a picture of a loving God(dess), a photo of a place that "takes you away."

Finally, be creative. What objects embody power for *you*?

A candle may be placed on the left side of the altar, for the Goddess, and one to the right, for the God. These are lit when calling on the deities for a ritual or an event. Notice that I used the word *event*. The altar is not used only during ritual. The pagan has a *daily, ongoing* experience of the sacred. Wicca is a religion of love and devotion that is *lived*. Therefore, if you desire, the altar can be part of your daily life.

A simple heartfelt prayer, in your own words, asking the Gods to join us, help us, and watch over us in our ritual or endeavor is a perfectly good substitute for the longer invocations in lesson 1.

The Goddess is invoked, and Her candle lit, first because all things, including Him, come from Her. At the end of the ritual or event the candles are put out as the Lord and Lady are thanked for the help, love, and support that they have just given you in the ritual or event. At that time, also thank them for whatever else they added to your undertaking. This can be done formally or by natural, direct words such as "Dear Lord and Lady, thank you for the power, love, and caretaking you gave to me in my ritual [or event] tonight." The Lady is thanked last because She is not only the beginning of all things but also the end of all things.

You might want to place representations of the Gods by their respective candles. The Goddess figure can be a miniature Greek-goddess statue, a shell, a flower, a drawing of Wonder Woman, or whatever else works for you. It is a matter of personal choice. Even a photo of yourself can be used, to remind you that you yourself are imbued with Her spirit.

Sometimes I choose a Goddess image appropriate to the spell or event I am lighting the candles for. Before a self-healing ritual that I am afraid to face, I might put a figure of Quan Yin, the Chinese goddess of healing, mercy, and compassion, by the Goddess candle. Quan Yin helps us change in a gentle way. If a friend who needs to be comforted is about to visit, I might call on Diana, whom Italian witches pray to as the Great Mother, creator of all things. She is very comforting.

Sometimes I put a Goddess on my altar who is appropriate to the period of life I am in. The Goddess image can be used without the candle; I either just ask that particular deity for what I want—no devocation needed, though thanks are always appreciated—or just let Her image on the altar work its magic on me. If I am dealing with lots of professional matters that demand that I be very assertive, I might have a picture of a different aspect of the goddess Diana on my altar. Diana is also the independent and assertive goddess of the hunt. If I am puzzled about how to write a chapter in a book on witchcraft, I might keep an image of Aradia, goddess of the witches, on my altar until my confusion is over. (If you ever have trouble getting your witch homework done, you can ask Aradia for help.)

Long before the airplane existed, migration, war, and far-traveling merchants created a degree of cultural exchange that people often think happens only nowadays. The wise Celts borrowed from different cultures whatever suited them, including Gods. In that spirit, I do the same.

An image of the God is chosen in the same manner as the Goddess image. A photo of a horned animal, a drawing you make, a picture of your boyfriend, a photocopy of a picture you found in a book, an acorn, an ear of corn. You can be creative; once my altar God was a photo of a political demonstration. The people in the photo were joyous and rich with life—a reminder that God is within *all* of us, that we are all Gods.

You may also focus on specific aspects of Him. You can invoke the Horned One, who is one and the same as Self-fire, when you want to be in touch with that which is wild and free in you. Or perhaps you are a man desiring a man's freedom but you don't want to be trapped by going to extremes; you might place something that is cobalt blue by the candle, for that is the color of Dian-y-glas, who is fully virile and free yet close to the Goddess. Or if you are working on an ecological project, you could invoke the Green Man. He is lord of all the wild creatures. His bold blood runs through the leaf. His green pulse stirs animal and human toward joyous, full living, coupling, and dance. There are many dances; shopping for food is a dance!

Assignment

Optional: Research a goddess and a god other than the ones I have suggested, choosing gods relevant to your present life. Then call on them for help. This can be an ongoing approach to them, as well.

Research well enough so that you know whom you are asking for help. Note the following well. There are aspects of the Gods that we may not be ready for. For instance, Cerridwen is sometimes a destroyer, so if you pray to Cerridwen for change, you may get a rough change. It's like choosing a therapist. Sometimes it is good to work with a very confrontational and challenging therapist; at other times that sort of approach is absolutely destructive and a problem in and of itself.

Don't let cautions about psychic work and spirituality scare you off from being a witch. Even a toaster comes with cautions; that toaster can kill if you use it in the bathtub, but who's gonna give up toast? You simply read your new toaster's cautionary pamphlet, then enjoy breakfast. Anything with power needs to be treated with cautions specific to that kind of power. The cautions of the psychic world, though, can be scarier; that realm is foreign to the modern mind-set, which views *anything* existing on the psychic plane, whether it be a machete or a butterfly, with fear and suspicion. Don't get morbidly fearful about invoking aspects or go to extremes doing research. Do what feels reasonable, trust that the Gods are kind and honor our mistakes, and know that we learn from our mistakes.

It is not necessary to invoke a specific aspect, however. All gods are simply aspects of the Great Mother who created all things, and of Her consort. If you invoke Her, that's all that is needed. She will come to you in whatever form you need Her. As with the Goddess, if you just invoke Her consort, our Father will come; you needn't decide which aspect to invite.

The Old Gods are not just metaphors. They are powerful beings. Do not invoke them lightly or as a way to show off. You never "mess around" with the Old Gods, or with the Faerie energy, for that matter. When I was in training, I was told, "Don't call on them as some sort of parlor game."

If this seems harsh, it is simply the harshness of the science/religion. The Gods are loving but will accept no nonsense. On the one hand, they want to be available to us in our everyday lives, instead of demanding the groveling and fear-ridden approach some religions' deities want. On the other hand, they want you to treat them and their power with respect. Honor them, and treat them carefully. If you treat them in a way that belittles them, they will not take kindly to it, and those who insult the Gods or who rudely underestimate their power can pay the price.

The same caution is needed for the Faerie energy and the Celtic altar. The Faerie energy and the Old Gods are at the heart of creation, and though Faerie power is a healthy, natural, and fruitful energy governed by loving Gods, it is also a wild energy that demands respect and care. It can heal or hurt! Faerie power will allow no foolishness. Treat it with the same thoughtfulness I want you to treat the Old Gods with, or the wild forces can turn on you and damage you immeasurably.

Again, this is not written to instill morbid fear in you. Do the best you can, and the Gods will not only welcome your honest mistakes and heartfelt scientific experiments, but forgive your human foolishness. These are not Gods who expect perfection; in fact, they know that we are, to use the cliché, only human, and so, being forgiving parents, they love, accept, and forgive us no matter what we do. When I warn you, for example, not to invoke lightly, that doesn't mean you can't experiment. Invoking a God because you are trying to figure out if God exists is a worthy attempt to learn about the cosmos. Another example: rudely underestimating the Gods' power isn't the same as not knowing any better. The latter doesn't insult them. They know that every person has a lot to learn about life.

You may also place objects on your altar that embody your goals and priorities. Here are a few ideas to help you come up with your own. Maybe you are studying anthropology because your heart's dream is to teach that subject. A picture of the briefcase you would like to own when you are a teacher might embody that goal. When you get your first job, you could even buy that briefcase, as a gift to yourself and as a simple ritual that is free of any trappings other than the purchase itself. If you are trying to heal from childhood abuses, perhaps a beautiful flowering plant or a picture of a dancing, laughing child will keep you inspired to do your healing work. If you want courage, you might put a picture of a lion on your altar.

Recovered alcoholics in Alcoholics Anonymous sometimes receive an AA "chip" (it's the size of a poker chip) that shows how long the alcoholic has been sober. An AA chip on the altar could remind AA members of AA's dictum to make sobriety their top priority. (Yes, there *are* sober witches. You are not alone.)

Another common altar object is the power piece: a rock from a sacred mountain, an amulet passed down in the family, a bell that when rung somehow calls in the wind to blow your blues away. Of course, you may prefer carrying your major power pieces on your person, or have good reason to keep them elsewhere. The cheering bell might be hung on the patio so that it swings in the breeze, its chime always warding off depression. The rock from the sacred mountain may be best used if carried in your pocket for confidence at a job interview. Even so, you might occasionally want to leave the object on your altar for a bit so that it automatically lends its power to all your altar visits.

It is important to have an offering plate of some kind on your altar. Food offerings are made both to express gratitude and because the Gods *do* need to be fed—literally! Offer them wine, bread, candies, or whatever other food and drink you intuit.

It needn't be more than a teaspoon each of food and beverage. This can be done when you pray for something, or at your meals, or at a time you plan each week, or at all these instances if you want. Then, at the first dark moon, either bury or burn the offering. You may also put it in the ocean or a river. Although it's not a good idea to toss sacred offerings in the trash, it is better to do that than to forsake making offerings for lack of proper disposal. Urban living and busy schedules sometimes limit our options.

If for whatever reason now is not the time to start making these offerings, don't worry. But, like us, the Gods need food. If you practice for many years and go deeply into the Craft, you should then make offerings at least every month or two.

Aside from, but not instead of, food offerings, the Gods enjoy flowers, incense, houseplants, and any other thing a person would like as a gift. Listen. Perhaps they will tell you what they want.

A third candle can be put on the altar, the Occasion Candle, the color of which indicates the nature of your magical goal. I will only introduce the Occasion Candle now. When you get to lesson 14, you can use or adapt the extensive candle material there for the Occasion Candle.

On a cloudy, cheerless winter day, you could burn a gold candle to create a happy, sunny energy in your environment. Candle magic need not be used *only* during ritual; it can also be used to bring positive forces into your daily life. In other words, you needn't do a ritual or even any ritual prep. Just light the gold candle and it will do its work. A gold candle is also good for prosperity rituals.

Green is a money color. You might try burning a green Occasion Candle when getting dressed for a job interview. Again, you can light the candle without any rigmarole, then dress for success. Green candles can also be used in money spells.

A pink candle can be lit when you pray for domestic peace, love, and harmony, and can also be lit whenever you are in your home, just to bring in that same energy. Pink brings in an energy similar to a hearth fire burning in the kitchen, bread baking in the coals of that fire—a warm, homey, loving feeling. An Occasion Candle needn't be on the altar. You might feel that warm glow better if the candle is in the kitchen while you cook.

Orange is good for any task that needs concentration. Try burning an orange candle on your altar or desk when you are studying for finals, balancing a checkbook, or writing a book.

A yellow candle works nicely during prayers for guidance, or when you need clarity. You might burn one either when making prayers for that clarity, or during the day while you just go ahead and live your life. It is also a good color to induce cheerfulness of spirit.

Purple can be burned for protection—without any ritual, or during a protection rite. Or when you want more power in your life. Gotta confront the boss today about his sexism? How about a purple candle while you eat breakfast, for power *and* protection?

Burn candles only when you are around. It is too easy to come home and find that your spell for a new apartment worked because your present home just burned down! In other words, don't be silly and leave a fire (candle) unattended.

No matter what you put on your altar, always feel free to decorate it. That's a way to make an offering, and besides, this is a *heathen* altar we're talking about.

Change your altar as often as you want. Just as one's needs change from time to time, so your altar might go from a garish and celebratory collection of fall harvest—fruits, nuts, fall leaves, silver bowls full of floating flowers, Florentine chalices with sacramental wine—so that you can give thanks for a fall harvest to, at another time, a simple contemplative altar of one white stone on a pile of black sand when you are particularly distracted by life's many trials. Or maybe you want a calming influence so that you are in touch with the God within and choose a different simple altar, consisting solely of a graceful bough of willow in an oriental vase, next to a statue of serene Buddha, all placed on a silk scarf.

It can be a meditation for me to build an altar. Simply searching for the right objects can tune me in to my inner cycles and the cycles of the natural world around me.

All that I say about altars is meant as a reality, *not* just as a metaphor. The altar is not just a symbol; it is a place you have relationship with. And it is a place that touches and empowers the part of us that is most intuitive and psychic, that same part of us that is closest to God.

You have endless personal choices as to how to make your altar. You needn't even have an altar. Many of the instructions in the "Making the Celtic Altar" section were optional. Read carefully: if an instruction was optional, I said something like "perhaps" or "a candle may be placed"; nonoptional instructions were often cued with a phrase like "It is . . ." or "One would . . ." When it's not as clear as that, use your common sense; a witch trusts straight-ahead, down-to-earth reasoning as much as her magic. In fact, practicality is *part* of her magic.

The Self as the Altar

Everything that I have said an altar is, is also true of your body. The knowledge that our body is an altar, and that we can use the body as such, is the most important altar information you can have.

Your body is: consecrated; the workbench; the focus. As a focus, your uniqueness is much. Your uniqueness is: holy; an offering; the workbench; the focus.

Your whole being—body, mind, spirit—is the altar. Your body and spirit are one and the same, so what is said here of the body is also being said of the spirit.

I don't mean you have to lie on a stone slab with a chalice balanced on your navel (not that there's anything wrong with that!), but you *do* need to treat your body as sacred, in ritual and in the mundane world. Have you brushed your teeth, eaten your veggies, gotten your Pap smear—you get the picture—today?

The world also is the altar, and so is the universe. Come to see each thing as an altar (it will only take a hundred years). There is power everywhere; it is a mystery.

Assignment

Your home is an altar. Before next week's visit, as an exercise, see your home as altar. What do you worship? What are you devoted to? This assignment need take only five minutes.

Before you continue reading, contemplate everything you have read so far in this section about the body. There is much to contemplate here, a lot of information in few words. Shamans are like good lovers: one short kiss can do more than a long bad session between the sheets.

Writing your thoughts about the material is a good way to do the contemplation. Often it is easier to focus your thoughts if you are writing. If you spend only five minutes in the contemplation, that's fine, even if only three words from the material have an impact on you, and the impact feels minimal. Remember, with any exercise it's the attempt that counts.

More About the Celtic Altar in Daily Life

A common theme in most shamanic traditions is the honoring of the planet as Mother. If you worship the earth as the Mother God—Gaia, as She was called by the Greeks—and profess the sacred nature of the earth, you recycle because it honors the planet as a God. I sometimes suggest the following: set up a lovely altar under which is placed a recycling bin. Don't consider this bin separate from the altar. It is *part* of the altar.

Shamanic religion is devotional, a two-way street. We not only pray at our altars for the Old Gods and Goddesses to give us help; we also give them ours. If we don't feed them and take good care of them, they don't have what they need to take care of us. Recycling embodies this principle. So does what has happened to Father Sky's ozone layer. Because we have not cared well for it, He cannot protect us from cancer-producing rays. The ancients made sacrifice so that their deities would be strong. This was neither stupid nor ignorant; those people knew their responsibility. A recycling bin embodies this same relevant and powerful sacrifice, and placing the bin under the altar reinforces this devotional obligation, without any invocations, prayers, or other trappings.

Any religion, whether earth based or not, needs to be a "living" religion, a part of daily life and always applicable to modern needs and dilemmas. The sacred and the profane are one and the same. One year, part of our class altar was a box for clothing donations for the homeless.

This introduction of ecology, coupled with what might have seemed to you like shamanic rambling, has further ramifications that will become apparent at different points in the rest of this section.

The shamanic altar is also, as I have said, each and every one of us, body and spirit. When we are attuned to our own inner nature, we take in God's grace and healing better than from any crystal or in any cathedral. When we listen to the sure, unique voice within us, we are more in touch with our spiritual objectives than when we are simply at a favorite beach spot or on a high mountain. Are you asking, "What does a sense of selfhood have to do with ecology?" This sense of selfhood is a part of the ecological aspect of Goddess Spirituality because when we find this special nature in ourselves, when we listen to our sure voice within, we discover that we ourselves are sacred, and that each of us is a living part of the earth, a moving, breathing part of the earth. Which means that we each deserve the care we are struggling to find for our planet. So I offer a simple ritual.

Assignment

1. Before next week's lesson, look at your specific commitments to, or concerns about, the planet, and then see if you can make the same specific commitments to, or address these same concerns in regard to, your *own* well-being. Here are some questions you might

ask yourself as part of the ritual: What do you pollute your body with? What sort of pesticides and additives go into your meals? Do you forget that you yourself are a nonrenewable resource; in other words, do you figure there's no reason why you can't take on one more political (community, artistic, business, familial) endeavor? (It makes me sad when I see ecological activists who always look burned out.) Do you struggle to promote farming methods that keep the soil rich, yet live a lifestyle that is devoid of emotional nourishment? These are just examples. Whatever you pledge to, or want for, the earth, you might need to pledge to yourself. You may have to do this slowly, over time.

2. Optional: Start to make and use an altar. You have enough homework this week that you might prefer to wait another week before doing this. However, most folks naturally crave and gravitate toward having an altar. If you want to start making one this week, consider delaying the see-your-home-as-an-altar assignment for a few weeks.

A Child Dancing in the Rain

Primordial Celebration of Power

Pre-ritual Purification

Before starting a ritual, one always does a pre-ritual cleansing on oneself. The goal is to be clean inside so that you're healthy and happy, and power just flows in you. This spiritual purity does not imply any uptight puritanical morality. When we are clean in this way, we are a clear channel of power and goodness, and we do ethical magic. And that's what Wicca is all about anyway—being spiritually whole, clean, healthy. Purification also means we can work with the wild forces of nature safely.

Reminder: If I give you your homework midlesson, read it then and there.

Assignment

RITUAL
Pre-ritual Cleansing

Tools and Ingredients

☾ Optional: tools that can facilitate the cleansing. Putting salt (preferably sea salt) in water, then washing yourself in the water as you pray for cleansing, is beneficial. Or you could burn sage, or frankincense with a bit of myrrh in it, and wave the smoke over yourself as you ask for purification.

Step 1. Ask yourself what inside you might keep you from being your best in a ritual. Are you carrying resentment, or a severe worry? Pray that it be removed. Do you fear you'll be punished for pursuing your own spiritual choices? Pray that the fear be removed. Is your head filled with what others might think about you? Ask that such thoughts be removed. Take stock of yourself, and when you see a block to good ritual work, pray about it.

One goal in the first part of this pre-ritual cleansing is to free yourself of anything that will keep you from being a clear channel of the Goddess's love and energy.

But that has nothing to do with cleansing away *ourselves;* we are reflections of the love of the Gods. Rather, it is a cleansing to wash away all that keeps us from being *fully* ourselves. So any fears you are having about being yourself at the time of the rite, any worries that are keeping you from focusing on the moment, are to be cleansed away by asking the Gods to take them.

You also want to pray to be cleansed of anything that will interfere with clear vision in a ritual. If you are carrying a worry or resentment or unhealthy fear or negative thought, you can't think straight.

These prayers needn't be fancy. Simply, and in your own words, ask the Goddess to remove the blocks you are seeing. She is very powerful; She will do quite well with a simple request. After all, She's God.

Step 2. Remove any internal blocks that are specific to the particular spell you are about to cast. If you are about to do a spell for prosperity, you might need to pray away any thoughts you have that you are unworthy of abundance. Or if you are doing a spell for self-esteem yet you believe that self-worth is built on feeling better than others instead of just feeling good in and of yourself, you would need to cleanse yourself of that belief. A formula: I am doing a spell to create X. What inside me blocks X's entry into my life? Once I know, I ask the Goddess to take it away.

None of this cleansing work is to denigrate very healthy "negative" emotions and reactions. In other words, you might want to refrain from washing away a *healthy* fear; the fear of walking alone in dangerous neighborhoods at night, for instance, is not unhealthy. It is a God-given fear meant to keep us safe. So it is with certain other human traits, including some anger. Anger is a healthy emotion. We need to be cleansed of it only when it is a problem rather than an asset.

Step 3. You might have to do nonritual cleansing. See if there is anything going on with you and the people in your life that needs to be cleansed in order for you to be a clear channel and to have true vision. Perhaps you owe amends to someone? Commit to making those amends. Or maybe you want to do a prosperity ritual, and that demands an apology to someone for financial stinginess. Once you know what needs to be done in this step, decide whether it needs doing before you start the ritual, or if your commitment to doing it is sufficient pre-ritual cleansing to go ahead with your rite.

Don't be a perfectionist about this or any of the work I give you. Though you should do your best at this cleansing, perfectionism is defeating, and is something itself to be washed away. Just get as clean as you can. It is a lifetime's work, so do your best, then trust the Gods.

Now you have an addition to The Magic Formula. Not only do you invoke and devoke, but you do a purification. Once you have used The Magic Formula for a session, whether that be our weekly meeting or a session in which you are doing your homework, you needn't apply any part of The Magic Formula to that session again, unless shown otherwise. When starting your weekly visit with me, forgo the cleansing until there is a rite to be done as part of the lesson. Any other time, you usually do the purification before the invocation.

I am emphatic about always using The Magic Formula only for now. Later, I will show instances when The Magic Formula is not needed. Later still, you will learn general guidelines whereby the formula needn't always be used. What good is magic if it is too cumbersome to apply wherever and whenever you want it? In the meantime, always using the formula helps you be safe and effective, and gets you in magical shape to do without it.

Primitive Spirituality, Poetry, and Power

This is a primitive spirituality—but not in the sense of unintelligent or ignorant. The first shamans of prehistoric times, so-called savages, were the first scientists and doctors. They were as sophisticated as we, or, as my anthropology teacher Kush said, they were just like people as you and I know people today.

These primitives—scientists, shamans—dealt directly with nature and its awesome power. They did this scientifically, studying physics not through objective means but through methodical personal interaction with nature. Unlike the typical scientist of today, they brought their passion to their research and interacted with the world around them, really experiencing it. They were not outside observers. This is part of what is meant by a primitive spirituality.

We humans are not outside of nature. We are a part of it, and that is part of the witch's magic. The deeper you get into Goddess Spirituality, the more you have a primitive exchange with the world around you, often dealing with nature and natural laws in their full potency, their rawness. That's what we are dealing with in witchcraft: the longer you train and the more you involve yourself with the Mysteries, the more you deal with the awesome dark natural forces of the entire universe, like a tornado or the energy of a star, and with the Goddess's comparable invisible psychic mysteries. Even when you first start to practice magic, you to a great extent tap into these very same things (Oowee, look out, world! One more new student has read these lines. The planet will never be the same), despite what I've written about the ever-increasing benefits of study.

The scientific observation of a mystic is not objective. It is not true that to understand something one must be uninvolved with it. Only by being fully involved, with your whole being, can you understand something. Do you get to know your neighbors better by having dinner with them or by watching them from a block away? Well, there *are* things you can observe better from afar, but the observation can still be viscerally, joyfully subjective, and involve an active participation.

Modern researchers in physics are finding that their observation of any phenomenon changes that phenomenon. In other words, there is no such thing as an outside observation. Witches are being scientific.

That subjective analysis is accurate does not mean that magic has no hard-and-fast laws. Magic is a sophisticated science. Just as no law of physics is violated by the fact that no two snowflakes are alike, so laws of magic manifest in endlessly unique and personal patterns without leaving the realm of fact.

Magic is true to the laws of physics. Physicists are still finding truths that have been known all along by witches. In fact, I wonder if behind the locked doors of some laboratory a group of doctorates haven't shed their white lab coats to don long black robes and stir a cauldron, mumbling, "Bubble, bubble, toil and trouble," to see if that will affect Einstein's theories of relativity. All kidding aside, *techno-pagans* make up a huge percentage of the witchcraft community. A lot of them come up to my San Francisco classes once a week from Silicon Valley. If you read a text on recent physics and find that the premise of it is in keeping with this book, you'll know why.

We are neither a religion nor a science in which everything is a metaphor for something else. The poetry, myth, prayer, and metaphor of this book are to a great extent to be taken literally.

Though the Gods *are* metaphors for scientific laws, they are also beings in their own right. The mysteries of a rose and its thorn are not only emblems but concrete *embodiments* of the Mysteries, and as such can be invoked as a force to use in magic.

The poetry of the Goddess is a precise poetry. The ancient Celtic society had a type of priest-poets who trained for many years as poets. Within their poetry, as within the poetry of this book, was the magical science. The subtle weave of the shamanic training, perhaps without your even knowing how it happens, develops *your* inner poet, the part of you that lives all of life as a creative process and views life through what my student Sara Reeder, when she is teaching her children to see the invisible realm, calls "Faerie eyes."

Sometimes magic can be spoken of in more obviously scientific terms. One still needs to understand all of Wicca in poetic terms. This book's poetry, myth, metaphor, and prayer are a concrete and precise expression of a science. There is much important magical science expressed in this book in that way, and I want you to understand it.

Good poetry and good science do not contradict each other. The more recent physics is as metaphysical as any invocation. Magic is often called "the Art." So should physics be, because the same truths shine brightly in both.

Therefore, when a magician calls on the forces of the Gods, it is a literal and enormous power being called upon. When we call on the wind, and the sun, and the ocean, those are literal powers being invoked. Think about it: a witch, in a *literal* and *real* sense, uses the power of the sun with all its fire and intensity, and the power of the moon with its ability to turn the tides of enormous oceans, and the power of the darkness that not only is between the particles of an atom but also is God Herself. We are given an enormous gift.

With all this power being tapped into with prayer and other magical practices, be careful! I repeat: *be careful!* Have a fear of this power, a respect for it. This is not a morbid, unhealthy fear, but a fear that *is* health. A terror that is also a pleasure.

The powers of nature, including magic, are at their heart

good. Dwelling in all things is the love of the Lord and Lady. Nevertheless, in another sense such power is neutral, neither good nor bad. It is simply power, like electricity. Natural powers can therefore do endless good or untold harm. There is an awesome potential for good or evil. So do not mess around with the material in this book; "don't use it for parlor games."

It was, partially, out of respect for this power's potential for unhappy events that I asked you to use this training as it is given. I want you to benefit from my experience; I was trained not only as a Master in my tradition, but also to teach.

The Celtic science of the magical Art is as precise as that of chemistry. No one in their right mind would walk into a chemistry lab and just start mixing without any prior knowledge. In the same vein, to mix and dabble in Faerie magic with neither knowledge nor guidance can be disastrous. It's one thing to go into the kitchen and mix cinnamon and flour as an experiment. There are simple magics that can be used just that carelessly, even in this book. But putting too much cinnamon into a spice cake is not the same thing as a lab explosion. Unskilled experiments in Faerie can cause raw nerves, ill mates, nightmares in your children, car accidents.

I state these magical cautions strongly, not only because they are important but also because our culture has such a hard time believing that magic is real that I sometimes have to shout to get it across that magic is not empty poetry but the poetry of physics, as real as a knife. You can do surgery with it to heal, but you can hurt yourself with it, too. If you tap into power, power will do something. If you tap in correctly, you are safe.

Assignment

A witch can have the same primeval exchange with the forces of nature as did the first shaman, thereby gaining sources of power and passion for use in magic.

When a storm gathers, feel the power gather. Feel the Mother's power in the thunder and in hard rain. Look into the expanse of the night sky, imagining it as endless, pulsing with Her dark creative force. Try to feel the power of moonlight. Try to get a *sense* of these things. In doing that, bring your whole self to it—your passion, intellect, imagination, cynicism, and inner poet. In imagining that you can sense the powers of which I speak, you then can begin to truly sense them. If you feel cynical—I am referring to a healthy cynicism, not a disrespectful, arrogant snobbery—it is a part of you and as such should come along to see the show. Your inner poet is the total of all these parts I have described, as well as the mystic, the risk taker who trusts the innate goodness of the earth, the fool, and the sensualist.

Don't forget to add the pre-ritual cleansing to The Magic Formula. Then, if only for a few minutes, explore a storm, or the night sky, or the ocean, or the moonlight, or the high wind on a hill, or whatever strong force you might choose or happen to meet. Do this twice over the next few weeks, choosing at least one thing to explore each time. After you do the closing ritual, check in to see if you need the grounding shown in steps 14 and 15 of the Becoming the Goddess ritual in lesson 2.

Rituals should leave you feeling pleasant and energized, but if you end up with more energy than feels good, send the excess up to God as a gift. Just make a ritual gesture of blowing upward. If that isn't sufficient, imagine the rest of the excess flowing into the earth; to do this, perhaps get down on all fours, your shins and forearms on the ground.

If you experience only a little, or even nothing at all, don't worry. Magic is a process, and what makes your effort successful is the effort itself. If you keep practicing magic and refining your skills, eventually you gain expertise. But like any other science, art, or skill, magic takes time and effort. The mere attempt to feel the power opens you up to feeling it eventually, and develops your inner poet.

A witch finds joy in these awesome powers. She glories in it, revels in it. Not in any way that trivializes it; that would be foolish and dangerous. But in respect, and with true pleasure, like a child dancing in the rain. And this pays homage to the awesome powers the Goddess surrounds us with.

So the goal is not to become morbidly afraid. Victor Anderson always says that anything worth having is dangerous. I would add that this power is part of our human heritage and a human need, and that it is far more dangerous to be powerless than it is to seek power.

Melektaus and His Fall from Heaven

Looking into His mother's mirror, the god Melektaus admired Himself for His great beauty. Taking the form of a great peacock, He shook His tail and filled all seven heavens with thunder. Then He cried "Ha!" and the sun rose in Paradise.

He told His mother, sister, wife, the most blessed

Queen of Heaven, what He had seen in the mirror, adding, "Behold how beautiful I am. Let us make those who can share in my beauty." She said to Him, "Do you wish to have slaves?" He said, "No, I wish those made in our image, male and female, to love me and rejoice in my beauty. And I may love them and rejoice in their beauty and freedom."

The Queen of Heaven answered, "Beloved Lord, Melektaus, my treasure, my self and other half, if you do this thing they will betray you, and your feet will be in hell and your plumage will be in heaven. And every pain in the heart of man will be a pain in the heart of God."

Melektaus insisted, "But I love them and wish to have them for my jewels." And thus humankind was created.

This is the true story of the fall, not brought about by sin and evil pride, but by love divine that is not quenched even by the fires of hell.

The story as I present it here was adapted from a Faerie Tradition myth told to me by Victor. If you have seen this story in print, please let me know, as I'm told there is a written source.

Assignment

A Ritual of Beauty and Plenty

Tools and Ingredients

☾ Amber resin or amber oil. If neither is available, a rose oil is good. Real rose oil is very pricey. An artificial rose oil will work fine. My experience has been that artificial scents work quite well for the spells in this book. If you are allergic to scents, skip this ingredient, or pretend you are using it.

☾ Clothing that is both comfortable and becoming

☾ A hairbrush

☾ A mirror

Step 1. Bathe, or if that's not possible, shower.

Step 2. Anoint yourself with the scent. If you want to, imagine you are anointing yourself as a priest, or use any other role that strikes your fancy.

Step 3. Dress.

Step 4. When your hair is dry, brush it vigorously, for it is your crowning jewel, whether you are a man or a woman. If you are bald, rub your head gently in a proud, enjoyable way.

Step 5. Look in the mirror, and proclaim, "Behold how beautiful I am."

Step 6. Don't think about the ritual. Let it go.

You will then have abundance. Make sure you *let* the abundance come to you, though, instead of forcing it or trying to force a person or situation to deliver the goods. When we draw the power of the Gods into our lives, and we open to the loving flow of abundance they provide, we can invoke their wrath should we betray their love through lack of ethics. This caution is, of course, not exclusive to this spell but is true for magic in general.

Sometimes, we try to force events in ways that, though ethical, are counterproductive. We might try *too* hard to please a new companion or a prospective boss, for instance. Do your best to refrain from this; however, be gentle with yourself if you are unable to break that habit yet. This is not to say you should refrain from doing the necessary legwork needed to bring good things to you. For instance, if you need a job, write the résumé, do the job interview.

Shamanic Safety

Shamanic safety is not covered properly by any one lesson. Instead it is a lifestyle and a training. All the parts of this training—such as the purification work, the respect for deity, The Magic Formula—add up to a sum that is safe. Then why, you ask, has this section been called "Shamanic Safety"?

Over the years, students have come to me with questions about psychic safety, or with other worries that just naturally arise. I try to draw on the experience I have gained in the years of that face-to-face work by addressing such concerns throughout the book. This section includes specific concerns students have had that weren't specifically relevant to any material we've covered so far, but that to me seemed relevant to your training at this point.

Don't use these rituals as a substitute for a counselor. If the problems in your life are psychiatric in nature, don't hide behind these spells to avoid getting help. There is no substitute for the care of a trained therapist or psychiatrist. (I often call the psychic readings I do for my clients "pastoral counseling, pagan style." My readings are transformative, spiritual counseling, and a means for my clients to move through the inner blocks that interfere with joyful living or the study of shamanism. But I am not a substitute for a therapist. So, though I am a *spiritual counselor*, to avoid confusion, I use the word *counselor* in the first sentence of this paragraph and in the next few paragraphs to refer only to therapists, psychiatrists, and the like.)

Everything has a spiritual, emotional, physical, and psychic aspect. On the one hand, spiritual illness can have emotional factors that need a professional counselor. On the other hand, if you have problems that need the care of a therapist, sometimes using the powerful tools for change in this book, and/or a psychic reader to deal with the spiritual and psychic aspects of your problems, in conjunction with a therapist, can provide a dynamic force for change.

Since these rituals work so well, sometimes a student is faced with emotional or psychic experiences that are puzzling and maybe even scary. At such times, follow-up help might be needed. And depending on the nature of the experience, one would seek either a therapist or a psychic consultant.

If you find that in using a spell you are confronted with troubling feelings or more emotions than you know what to do with, that could be great, because it might indicate a breakthrough. Just make sure you don't sit by yourself and let yourself get so overwhelmed that your efforts are counterproductive. Talking to a friend can be an excellent idea at such a time. At other times a therapist might be the only person who can give you the help you need to confront your unpleasant feelings and move past them. No shaman scorns the use of so-called nonspiritual tools. A shaman uses anything necessary to remain safe, powerful, and happy on the path. (Neon sign, billboard-sized letters, loud-speaker screaming: that last line speaks a primary shamanic truth.)

Another type of follow-up work might be done under the care of a psychic reader. If you are seeing confusing or threatening spirits, or are having dreams that worry you, don't be afraid to get help from a psychic reader. If you are experiencing unpleasant or evil psychic phenomena, and what you have learned so far isn't sufficient, go to a psychic. (See appendix 2 for information on how to get hold of me for that service.) Often your own tools are enough; a shaman, however, is not too proud to get help. It is only by getting help when we need it in our lives that we can truly call ourselves powerful.

I have a speech I give to clients and students when they think they have to be the American hero who stands on his own two feet, strong and square jawed, able to do it all himself. I tell them that the only reason the hero can fight off all the bad guys (cure cancer, climb the mountain, change all of society, or carry out any other act of valor) is because while he's in action, there's an entire film crew there with him, holding the camera, writing the script, doing his makeup, cueing him with his lines, and gluing his hat to his head so that it doesn't fall off when he's hanging upside down by one foot from the edge of a flying plane. In other words, the great American hero always has a team behind him, and that's why he succeeds.

Not only is it arrogant to go without help, it is unfair to yourself. If you want to make big changes in your life, you can't go it alone. You have to be willing to reach out for help sometimes. By doing so you can be embraced by the love of others who are also moving forward toward happy lives.

I am repeatedly asked, "I think I saw a spirit. Am I crazy?" (I always want to respond, "You're asking me? I'm the one who thinks she's a Faerie, remember?")

Many years ago I underwent a powerful rite. At the time, I had worked for years as a professional psychic consultant. I was already used to psychic phenomena—talking to spirits and the like—but only when I used special techniques to tune in to the psychic realms, in situations free from distractions. But the day after the rite, I was *waiting at a bus stop* and heard a gruff voice demand, "You, hey! Heal me!" *The words had come from a tree.*

"C'mon, I need help!" the tree insisted, its voice rough as tree bark.

Though amazed, I psychically healed the tree—helping it better cope with its sadness at its urban setting—only to then notice that the sidewalk was *singing to me.* It shaped the city's clamor, cacophony, car engines, and gusts of sooty air into a pulsing rhythm, an urban magic that celebrated life. It sang, "Dance to my beat, let your spirits be lifted by my music."

From then on I experienced psychic phenomena without cease, all day long. I was barraged by amazing phenomena. Everything one can see with the mundane eye revealed its magical aspect—wherever I was, whatever I did. Even when I was at a movie, or sitting in a doctor's waiting room, spirits came to me, to ask for help or to offer theirs. I felt wonderful, completely psychically attuned, with a secret world of beauty revealed to me. It lasted seven years. That is rare; it has happened to only two other people out of the thousands of witches I have met. In fact, I have met only a few witches who have even experienced this for a day.

Though deep down I knew that my new mode of perception had resulted from a powerful rite coupled with my unusual talent, I grew concerned. What if I was experiencing a psychiatric disorder? I went to a therapist who, though not versed in psychic matters, was open-minded and intelligent.

She reassured me that there was nothing wrong with me, adding that I would be fine as long as I didn't use my expanded consciousness as a drug, and *did* use it to serve others.

The point of this story is not that you should expect to hear trees talk and sidewalks sing all day. The daylong occurrence of psychic phenomena, resulting from my training in the family system of Faerie Tradition I spoke of in the first chapter, was dangerous even to me, who was suited to it. Most folks would neither be safe while experiencing it nor benefit from it, no matter how tantalizing it sounds. Take note: the Fey Folk can be alluring, but Rip Van Winkle lost all that was precious to him. Don't involve yourself in something just because it has a magical glimmer and casts an enticing glamour. Not all that the Fey Folk offer is for humans. A rare exception in surviving and profiting from this event, I paid dearly for those seven years. The remaining wounds are deep. Just call me Francesca Van Winkle.

My point is: if your psychic experiences make you doubt your sanity, you are foolish not to talk to someone qualified in psychology. A psychic may be useful—for example, in authenticating the psychic phenomena—but is not qualified to make a psychiatric diagnosis. A psychic is not a psychiatrist, and so is not qualified to tell whether someone is crazy or not. And authentic psychic perceptions can result from psychiatric disorders.

On the other hand, If you follow this path long enough and are diligent in your exercises, trust that you eventually will have unusual experiences. Even with great quantities of very specific training it is almost impossible to safely undergo an experience as extreme as the one I had, but witches might without harm see a spirit for a second or hear a tree talk for a few minutes. Maybe you will wake from a dream and that day it will come true. That is not a sign of insanity at all. At such times you might find it very reassuring to know that this not only is to be expected, but is a sign of progress and deeper psychic perceptions.

A more subtle and common ritual problem is being spaced out after a ritual. The act of bringing yourself back is called *grounding*, though there are other ways that the term *grounding* is used later in this book. Grounding in this sense of the word is important; you don't want to be so spaced out that you are unaware while driving, oblivious of your safety while walking in the city at night, or careless when cooking. Grounding after a rite also helps you automatically apply your spirituality to daily life instead of letting your head float up week by week like a balloon without a string until your feet are never on the ground. Up until now, I have grounded you after any ritual that might leave you feeling spaced out. Now I will teach you when and how to ground yourself.

RITUAL
Grounding

After a rite, or when our weekly visit ends, check in. Do you feel otherworldly? Is your mind fuzzy? Is there any way in which you don't feel fully on the mundane realm? Then you need grounding.

Even if you feel alert, you still might be spaced out without realizing it. This is a tricky one. You can feel alert, only to walk into a wall, so to speak, because you were alert to another realm but not alert to the mundane plane. One of the joys of The Third Road® is its subtle power; a lot can happen in a simple rite.

If you need grounding, you can use a method I have already taught you: stretching every part of your body. Don't be perfunctory; stretch each part of your body just a bit. Most likely, it will take only a few minutes. Then gently slap yourself from top to bottom. When you get to your face, use your fingertips to gently tap your face. Again, do not be perfunctory about it; do it all over yourself.

Instead or in addition, you might want to eat something. Not sugar.

And/or shoot the breeze with your study group or partner for a while until you are in a more "normal' state of mind. Often, discussing your experiences in the rite just done is excellent grounding.

Finally, you can come back to the mundane realm by paying extra attention to its obligations. Really focus on what is needed on that plane. This is the method to use if you are alert but elsewhere. It also works wonderfully for any spaciness. Ask yourself questions like: Is it so cold out that I will need a coat? Do I need to eat or have a glass of water? Then take care of those things. Also, be aware of the need to be careful if you are, for instance, cooking, or the need for street smarts if you are leaving the house at night. Pay extra attention to looking both ways before crossing streets at the first few crosswalks. Grounding keeps you physically safe.

Add grounding to The Magic Formula when you need to.

I talk so much about safety that I worry a reader will think Wicca too dangerous. When learning to drive a car, one is told a lot about how to do so safely. My cautions amount to the same thing. Cars are dangerous, and in fact kill many people a year. But folks don't quake with fear and debate whether or not to enter the car each time they pull out their car key. Cars are a useful, integral part of modern life. Your psychic ability is even more integral; it is a natural part of you. To ignore it is like ignoring the need to breathe.

I'll admit I got a little neurotic worrying about all this myself when I was first writing this book. For instance, I wondered why the Gods told me to include the prayer for healing through God's light, "A Prayer That You May Love Your Body and Be Cleansed in Spirit," so early on in the book (lesson 2), before my reader was to have much in the way of instruction. It effectively brings to light things in a person that he or she might have thoroughly buried— things that need to be cleansed. I worried that the reader wouldn't be able to handle it. And that I wouldn't be there in person to help him or her through it, as I do in my classes.

I worried further. The prayer deals with a white light. Like the similar brightness of sunlight, it can nurture or burn, so it must be used as instructed (psychic sunscreen?). Without the sexual healing one gets by using this whole book or something similar, prolonged usage of the light can give you a severe psychic burn, typical in the New Age movement: all light and no down-to-earth considerations. A healthy sexual pattern allows you to channel such a powerful light through you. This light is at the heart of creation. As such it needs to be treated with great care and reverence.

Talking to an elder in my tradition, I was told, "If they want to walk the path, they have to do the work. And don't worry so much; the Gods will look after them. Do you think you have to be right there in person for every person in the universe? You are not God. That job has already been filled."

Then I went for a walk on the beach. I like to listen to the ocean. It's a good friend, and gives excellent advice. It told me, "You are being overprotective of the reader. Wouldn't they be worse off if they kept their problems bottled up inside? Do people avoid going out into the sun just because it could burn them? These tools for growth that you are teaching them are part of life. Folks can't avoid life forever. This stuff is no more dangerous than getting out of bed in the morning. Life's just dangerous, period. You're giving people tools so that life will be safer and richer for them. And you're teaching folks how to use these tools safely. Fearing life too much can be a problem itself ."

So don't worry about driving your psychic car. It'll take you across town, across the universe, to all the best places. In fact, don't be neurotic about following my instructions. I can promise you, despite anything I tell you about how to work magic safely, that sometimes, maybe even constantly, you will forget my instructions, ignore them, make mistakes, skip doing your homework, and work in ways that will make you go, "Argh! Why can't I live up to my own expectations!?" The perfect achievement of any expected goal is an ideal. As such, it is useful only as a vision to work toward, not as a standard against which to measure yourself. Or as a friend of mine said, "Anything worth doing is worth doing poorly."

Trust the safety of the format, taught to you by a Master of the Art. (Cool title, huh? I wanna put it on the back of a baseball jacket.) There are many subtle safeguards built into the training. For instance, much of what you have learned has already helped you keep in touch with your inner God. This, and the rest of the training, helps you more and more gain an immunity to the less appetizing things in mundane life and in the psychic plane. My cautions are a preventive measure that keeps you from falling into the hands of an unscrupulous teacher who will rub his hands together, then maniacally scream, "Aha! You have no proper training? Now you are completely in my power." Demons shouldn't be much of a problem for you either, unless we're talking about the little adorable ones that wake us up at six o'clock Saturday morning. Wait! Those aren't demons. Those are our children.

Gifts of the Great Mother

Pleasure, Power, Purity, VCRs, and Anything Else We Need

A Magical Bath: For the Sheer Pagan Pleasure of It

It's a challenge to walk with the Old Ones. I've written a lot about growth and change in the past five lessons. However, a witch is a pagan: we exist to celebrate life.

The Goddess charges us, "All acts of love and pleasure are my rites." This is not a metaphor but is meant literally and specifically: any ethical act of pleasure—anything unethical cannot be called an act of love—is a rite unto itself. We are here to enjoy ourselves; that is our "meaning."

Our other meaning is helping others. If we enjoy ourselves we not only find joy in life but will be led, through the pleasure we pursue, to find a happy way to serve community and family.

Being happy and seeking pleasure are not selfish activities. They will not lead people to avoid work or to be irresponsible.

Rather, it is in finding work that we enjoy that we are motivated to serve others. For instance, what I love and find to be fun is teaching, and since it is fun for me I have enormously impacted many lives through my dedication. Students upon students have had major breakthroughs in their lives because of my work, some coming out of major periods of despair. Were I instead to try to take up medicine, another very worthy profession, I wouldn't be of service. I wouldn't find it to be fun; I am not fascinated by anatomy and the science of disease in the same way that I am fascinated by psychic anatomy and helping people change their lives spiritually. My lack of interest and enjoyment would cause me to render sloppy, unfeeling service, I would treat people with a resentful and therefore inhumane manner, and my lack of passion for the job would cause little dedication. Without dedication one cannot meet the demands of a vigorous occupation.

The fun and fascination I find in my work do not negate a real concern or deep caring for the students I am involved with. Only when caring and concern are coupled with a means to help that is self-fulfilling can we truly give to others. I am a serious, devoted teacher because that is fun for me.

So if we seek pleasure in all its myriad forms, we are doing what is best for all things. That which we most enjoy doing will be the very thing that will most benefit the community.

Assignment

This week, do something just for the pleasure of it. Don't do it because it is useful or meaningful, but *only* because you will find pleasure in it. The meaning and use will inherently be there, whether you see them or not.

I offer the following bath as a means of fulfilling the assignment, but if you don't like baths or can't find the ingredients, choose your own activity.

Blend the following herbs:

¾ oz. orange flowers

³⁄₁₆ oz. jasmine flowers

¼ oz. lemon peel

¼ oz. peppermint leaves

½ oz. orange peel

½ oz. aniseed

You'll have enough for two baths, three if you don't like to use very full tubs of water. Simmer half or a third of the blend for at least twenty minutes in a glass or porcelain pan. Strain the "tea" into your bath water. Then follow your teacher's profound spiritual example: I enjoy a good long soak in this incredibly scented and luxurious bath. Just the scent of it simmering on my stove is enough to lift my spir-its—mmm—not to mention the fact that it's good for my skin, which tends to get dry.

Further suggestions: Rent a video with no redeeming social or artistic value; watch sitcoms on TV; hike; watch a sunset; climb under the covers with your sweetie and do what comes naturally; climb under the covers by yourself with the same wicked intent.

The Mother Has All Powers and Forms Within

Having met a few of the aspects of the Goddess, let's explore the Goddess in deeper ways. As when meeting any woman, we get to know the Goddess better and better the longer we hang out with Her.

Though we legitimately invoke the Mother as Maiden/Mother/
Crone, this is only one of many ways in which She appears to us.
We see Her in Her threefold aspect because we live in nature.
Because we are capable of death, She appears as the Crone. But
She never truly dies, never degenerates.

If you get close to the moon, it no longer seems to be a sphere
of light but a rocky globe that shows nothing of full moon,
quarter moon, dark moon. The Goddess is like the moon. The
Goddess, in Her essence, in the heavens, is much more than the
three forms.

On the one hand, Maiden, Mother, and Crone are real aspects
of Her personality as Her consciousness impinges upon ours, and
these aspects can be invoked for their love, help, and guidance.
On the other hand, She is all the aspects shown in the lesson on
altars. On the third hand (the Goddess has a lot of hands), one of
the best ways to deal with the Goddess is to realize that the
Goddess contains all things within Herself, that She is everything—everything that was and ever will be. She can give you anything you need.

If you need a particular thing or energy from Her, She will
manifest in such a form as to give you that. Deal with Her experi-
entially: see Her, experience Her in all that is around you. And
when you invoke Her, unless you are specifically invoking an
aspect, be open to however She chooses to appear.

The key phrases are *experiential* and *framed within the context of
a specific time*. Just as you never step in the same river twice, so you
can never invoke quite the same Goddess twice. She is infinite in
the gifts and moments that She is and in the gifts and moments
that She gives. Try the following ritual right now.

RITUAL
Care from the Mother

Step 1. Think about what you are needing from the Mother. Is it comfort? Support? Advice? Love? Fun? A VCR?

Step 2. Invoke Her by asking Her in your own words to come. Let Her know what it is that you have chosen in step 1.

Step 3. Be open to however She manifests. Sit in quiet focus and experience that. Who knows what will happen? If you asked for advice, She might give it to you, or help you find it. If you wanted a VCR, She might tell you how to get one at an affordable price. (A friend of mine calls this the Shopping Goddess.)

Step 4. Thank Her for the gifts She has given you in this rite.

Use your discretion as to whether your request demands that you use The Magic Formula with the above rite. I could *almost* say that if in doubt, it never hurts to use the formula, but just as important as its use is our right and need to call on God whenever, and as quickly as, we need Her. Our Gods do not expect us to grovel and follow endless formulaic ceremonies in the hopes that they will accept our "unworthy" approach. Our Gods want to be part of our lives, giving us all the help we can use. If you need comfort, you needn't go through a lot of rigmarole. All you need to do is ask for it in the simple four-step ritual.

Your own best judgment as to whether to use The Magic Formula will be good enough, and using your judgment will teach you more and more about how to use it. Even your magical mistakes teach you.

A few examples about making this sort of decision: if the above rite is done to gain advice, time might be of the essence. On the other hand (we're back to all those hands the Goddess has), you might need to apply The Magic Formula so that you are focused well enough to hear Her advice, and hear it correctly. To use the request for comfort as another example: if you find it hard to receive comfort, a pre-ritual purification might help. On the umpteenth hand of the Goddess, sometimes we are so upset that we need comforting before we can even think of doing a pre-ritual format that we've just learned. And, on the closing hand (the one the Goddess uses to win at poker) . . . OK, I'll admit it, I actually have nothing else to add, but I couldn't resist the joke. Would you accept the excuse that I'm your teacher, and am trying to embody the lesson about doing something just for the fun of it? Back to the topic: you decide what's needed.

It's also up to you to decide if the following suggestion can help you with another aspect of this ritual. For the first several years of Craft work, you might not be able to just "feel" Her presence as my instructions imply. In that case, visualize, imagine Her as you need Her to be. Play it out in your imagination, in the present tense, seeing Her give you what you need.

This is an excellent use of visualization. Just because you are using your creative powers does not mean that She isn't really there. The Third Road is that of the poet. Visualization and imagination are keys to the invisible world, allowing you to better interface with it. Plus, it gives the Goddess a way to work with you. It is like pulling up a chair for Her to sit down in. Visualizing Her as you need Her to be in this rite is like sewing a garment for the Mother to dress in for a rite. God Herself will come to you.

This ritual is a good exercise in visualization skills. Through repeatedly using your powers of visualization, you come to perceive the invisible nature around you, more and more accurately. So, in fact, by imagining the Goddess in this rite, you are learning how to perceive Her more accurately the next time.

You already started developing visualization skills, by using your imagination in lesson 2 to be the Goddess, by imagining your impurities going into the earth in the first cleansing rite, and by trying to sense power in lesson 5.

Visualization is a magical skill that can take years to perfect. The deeper you move into the Art, the more you must develop that skill. While you are developing this and other Wiccan skills, it is crucial to be patient with yourself. Often I have had a student complain to me, "But I can't see anything on the psychic plane" or "I can only hold an image in my mind for two seconds" or "I can't concentrate. My mind keeps wandering." Each of these problems is to be expected; it is only through repeated meditations, exercises, and rituals that we learn to focus, see, and hold images firmly in our minds. The important thing is to just keep doing the work; that is all that counts. Because by doing so, and *only* by doing so, you can eventually get the skills you seek. Besides, whether you do the rite "correctly" or not in terms of being able to stay focused and the like is not important at first. As long as you do the best you can, and you do the work as instructed, without variation, you will gain spiritual benefits and inner growth, whether you see it happening or not.

Real Spirituality Is Humane and Practical

Real spirituality is humane and practical. Idealism is fine, but don't beat yourself up with it. Though spiritual ideals can be attained sometimes, a teacher who insists that you can achieve the ideal every moment of every day is unkind. Perfectionism is one of the biggest evils around. If you are suffering, it is not a sign that you are failing in your spirituality, nor that life is hopeless. No, no, no, no, no, you poor misguided shaman! All humans will always be very flawed. You will always have faults. Diminish them and even utilize them—even your perfectionism (which I said was evil only if you bullied others with it).

More Purification

Before you leave my hermit's dwelling, let's do a rite. As part of your ongoing purification work, use the simple Purification by Earth rite from lesson 3 on something inside yourself that is bothering you—for instance, a fear that is keeping you from doing what you want, or a resentment that keeps you from hanging out with your best friend, or an unhealthy belief that has been brought to the foreground of your consciousness as a result of this week's lesson. In other words, use the ritual on the same sort of thing described in that lesson.

A reminder to help you get used to doing it: end our visit with your devocations.

Finding Endless Sources of Power

Gaining More Power

In an earlier lesson I spoke of the awesome forces that surround us in the world we live in. As a part of nature, we have within ourselves these same primal and amazing powers. We are very primal beings. Magic is about drawing on that power from all things, including ourselves.

But first we need to keep that power in ourselves fed. Being primal beings, we drink in sunlight like a plant does. Yet sometimes I, an animal being, have starved myself by living too much in the city. I need high windy hills such as those the ancient shaman would climb. There the wind, the Winged Serpent, feeds me its power, grants me its many gifts, tends to my ailments, empowers me—not in some metaphorical and abstract spiritual way, but as the real wind, the real god Winged Serpent, feeding me in a very concrete spiritual way. This is the magic, the ancient forces.

Assignment

1. Go to beaches, high hills, forests, oceans, as much as you can. Drink in the wind. Lie against the Mother's breast and find rest and nurturance from Her. Imbibe the peace of the woods. Pull the moonlight into yourself even if it is just from your kitchen window. Breath in the fragrance of morning air from your roof. Use the elemental forces for spiritual nourishment; it is part of being a pagan. You can, of course, do this with or without using The Magic Formula.

I suggest you give yourself time to get about doing this homework; view this as a long-term assignment. You have plenty of assignments coming up aside from this one that will keep you busy over the next few weeks. Besides, it might take considerable time to change a habit of being city-bound, or to start drawing on what there is of nature that can be found in a city environment.

2. *For the advanced practitioner:* While doing step 1, you may also want to be a scientist: note what you observe. Remember that a shaman does research through personal subjective experience. The Magic Formula can deepen focus, sensitivity, and awareness of both the mundane and the psychic aspects of your visit with nature.

Recording your discoveries is valuable, but forget "creative writing." Just write down exactly what you saw, thought, felt, learned, or otherwise experienced or observed. That is the true poetry. Instead of worrying about being so-called creative, just put pen to paper, doing your best to express clearly and precisely your experience—even if you are going to express it only to yourself.

Never do an optional assignment, or any other assignment or guideline I give you, if it's too much for you. Overachieving witches don't have time for sex and chocolate. The point of a training is to enjoy life, not to use the training to make yourself unhappy.

Ritual Breathing of Power

All creation is made of power, a vital living power, an energy substance. Call it *manna*, call it *chi*; you hear about this force in culture after culture, by innumerable names.

This energy, because it is the matter out of which all things are made, is a basic tool in spellcrafting. The ancient Celtic shaman pulled it into herself both to feed herself and to do her spells. And for the sheer joy of union with the world.

In weeks to come you will learn to shape this vital energy according to your personal wishes by performing spells. Because a shaman shapes reality, she must learn to use this energy; it is the substance out of which that reality is made. Remember, if you can't use wooden boards and nails, you can't build a house of boards and nails.

A shaman also works for a healthy flow of this energy inside herself, much like a tai chi student performs exercises for the same thing. This is also similar to the work done by an acupuncturist. In Faerie Tradition we do many things to work toward this same healthy flow, this same clear channel of energy within ourselves. Part of how we do this is through our rigorous purification work, which clears us of the complexes, defeating emotions, unhealthy spiritual patterns, and negative beliefs that block this energy. Thus we become clear channels of this energy when doing our magic, not to mention being healthy and happy and a clear channel of goodness to other folks in our mundane lives.

This energy-matter is alive. Whether you are speaking of the basic substance of your blood or of a rock, it is the same matter, and it is alive, vital, cognizant, and sexual.

The nature of the universe is sexual. Every bird, every tree, every brook, every atom dancing its dance—each is a sexual, living, cognizant being.

Creation myths all over the world portray creation as coming from the act of sex. The etheric energy-matter out of which all things are made is a far cry from dry, lifeless molecules. We live in a much more exciting world than that.

This energy out of which all things are made is the basic life force itself, as vital as the act of sex. It, in fact, *is* the act of sex, yet we live in a culture that ignores this. What a tragedy! We are taught to ignore this living, vibrant nature that we could embrace in everything and every being we encounter. This awesome power goes untapped. Truly, we live in a death culture.

This is not a book about transcending life, but a book about vitality. Life as we know it, with its fun, good food, and sex, is sacred; it is not for transcending. This is a crucial part of the shaman's ethic.

On the other hand, this manna is no big deal (I agree with whoever it was that suggested swallowing two contradictions before breakfast), and for the exact same reason that it *is* such a big deal: manna is the substance of our everyday mundane lives. When we walk, we walk on it; when we sit on a chair, the chair is made of it; when we look at a tree, the tree is made of it. When we breathe the air, we breathe it in.

That all of reality at its most essential level is living, cognizant, and sexual has many implications. Take a moment to think about that by doing the following:

RITUAL
Energy Contemplation

Look around the room you are in. Everything in the room is made of manna, of an energy substance that is alive, vital, sexual. Just as everything in the room is made of molecules, so is it made of that invisible etheric energy-matter. Take a moment to look around you and contemplate; be aware that everything in the room is made of this energy substance, alive, cognizant, sexual.

Take as long as you need to write about that in your Book of Shadows, then do the following:

RITUAL
Breathing Exercise

The first section in this lesson, "Gaining More Power," showed how to acquire power in a natural, nonritual manner. A shaman also learns how to breathe in power ritually.

Step 1. Become aware of the tension in your body.

Step 2. Imagine this tension sinking into the ground beneath you.

Step 3. Note your breathing. Don't judge it, just note it. What is it like?

Step 4. Let your breathing become relaxed. Don't force it to become relaxed, let it. Let your belly relax, let your inner muscles and organs relax. If your belly relaxes, your breathing will happen of itself in a natural manner. You needn't make a breath happen, nor need you try to find a "proper" breath pattern. If you relax, a proper breath just happens: you inhale automatically, and you do it well. Nature abhors a vacuum, so a breath will happen of itself if you just get out of your own way. You needn't force it; *let* yourself breathe in a relaxed manner.

Continue our visit by doing the next exercise.

RITUAL
Ritual Breathing of Power

I have said that in order to be part of the dance of life you need to go up on hills and take in the power there, or go to beaches, or groves, or the like. However, this dance of life, of the substance of life itself, is always with us. Here is a ritual in which we can take in the substance of life itself, and consciously increase our participation in the dance of life.

When you do the following, always do the Breathing Exercise ritual first.

Step 1. Close your eyes and see the darkness that occurs naturally when your eyes are closed. It might be lighter when the room you are in has more light. Focus on that darkness, that "darkness of the mind's eye."

Step 2. Imagine that darkness is a screen onto which you will project images.

Step 3. Imagine that on that screen—it's a magical three-dimensional screen—you can see energy all around you, filling the room you are in.

Step 4. Imagine that this energy extends as far as your mind's eye can see.

Step 5. Imagine that, as far as you can see, reality is alive with this energy because the energy itself is alive.

Step 6. You might imagine it humming, singing for you. You might imagine it pink or gray.

Step 7. See in your mind's eye, still seeing the images of this ritual projected onto this dark screen, that this energy substance is glowing, vital with life.

Step 8. Imagine that somehow you can *sense* the basically sexual nature of this energy.

Step 9. As you breathe in, imagine this power, this energy-matter, filling your lungs.

Step 10. Breathe in power until it fills your entire body, three-dimensionally. As you do this, imagine that the power energizes you, that it wakes up your very cells.

Step 11. Feel powerful throughout your body. You might feel the energy singing throughout your being. It might relax you, or comfort you, or who knows what; it is alive and so could do many things.

Step 12. Bringing yourself home is sometimes very important after an exercise or ritual, so don't leave out this step and the ones that follow. Focus again on the darkness that is just there when one closes one's eyes.

Step 13. Feel the chair or floor you are sitting on.

Step 14. When you are ready, open your eyes. Stretch all over. Do not do this in a perfunctory manner; stretch every part of yourself, at least a bit.

Step 15. Lightly slap yourself all over. Again, do not be perfunctory about this; start with the soles of your feet and lightly tap everywhere. If you are working with a partner, do each other's backs. When you get to your face and head, let the gentle slapping turn into a gentle tapping of your fingertips all over your face and scalp.

Magic Is Poetry: Poetry Is Power

Magic, poetry. They're the same thing. Think about that, contemplate it, before reading further. Then write out what you find, even if it is just a paragraph about your confusion or inability to understand this statement.

There is a dream we need to bring to our waking minds. That is a primary goal of magic. This dream is not delusion, but speaks of real things. It is the dream—you could also call it the poetry—of magical truths, of the Goddess's mysteries. It is the actual magical life around us and in us.

Everyone has their own way of being a poet, whether you define poetry as actual words or the way you arrange flowers in a vase or the way you cook a meal. One of my poems is that I tell jokes when I teach so that my students' hard work doesn't become too burdensome and so that spirituality is fun.

I want you to trust that you have your own way of being a poet—ask one of your friends for help if you don't know what it is—and believe that your own personal poetry, your own dreams, have power and magic. The Goddess's invisible reality, Her psychic mysteries, the mysteries of nature can often be understood only through dreams, poetry, art. Again, define art as you will. Art is the way you hold a friend in need of comfort, or the way you motivate the folks you manage at work.

It may take a long time to trust this in yourself, but bit by bit you can. The training subtly supports this in you, and you might also consciously apply the tools you are learning. For instance, as a Catholic high school student, I got a low grade in English composition because my teacher, a nun, felt that a paper I had written was heretical. The premise of my essay was that humans were innately good. At age fifteen, in 1964, I was already passionate about spirituality, knee-deep in the Catholic Church's youth interfaith movement, and trying to understand why the church wouldn't let me be a priest. The spiritual ardor of my essay was condemned as rebelliousness. To make matters worse, I was later told by my college poetry teacher that I couldn't write. I came to understand that, in the 1960s, women's words were considered second-rate. Though by and large I knew better, some part of me believed both teachers. I used a purification ritual to wash away any remnants of the belief that it is heresy to passionately pursue truth, and to clear my professor's words out of my mind and soul. This has helped me trust that I have something to say as important as what anyone else has to say.

Bringing the Dream to his waking mind is part of how the ancient shaman brought his whole being not only to the Art but to daily life. After all, spirituality must be applied. Another way to put it is: for a shaman, life becomes magic. We live more fully if, for example, cooking a meal is considered a worthy poem, and if giving your crying two-year-old a hug is considered a worthy art.

Dreaming also brings our passion and the divine spark of the male God into everything we do. Magic without these things either doesn't work or works in wrong ways. This makes sense if you compare magic to sex and marriage. Sex is juicier when your whole heart and soul are in it, and a marriage is richer spiritually if its sexuality is nourished. However, when passion leaves the marriage only to be relegated to the shadows of extramarital affairs, something in the souls of the marital partners dries up, and deep wounds can occur.

Listen to your muse. She is the Goddess. If you listen to that aspect of Her, you will be able to perceive the Goddess's powers around you, you will develop power, and you will also bring your whole self to the Art and daily life. I had a student who wanted to use only logic. He didn't understand how poetry could develop psychic skills. I told him, "Poetry creates a magical universe. If you want psychic abilities, create a magical universe. In a magical world, all the powers of a magician exist in truth and in full power."

How do we learn to listen to Her, to the Goddess in Her aspect as muse, how do we find these dreams in our conscious mind? How to embrace our poetry?

Building your altar is one way. Another is the transformative experiences that the stories, myths, and lectures in this book can bring about. Also the exercises, and learning to pursue and trust your personal art. And the writing in your magical journal. (Not to mention having a lunatic for a teacher. I figure that my being a complete fool inspires folks to take the risk of trusting *their* own foolish dreams and visions. I guess the Gods know what they are doing when they made us; they created a method to my madness.)

More About a Magical Journal

Your magical journal needn't be made only by writing. The poetry of this journal might be a drawing, a stone found on the beach, or a piece of jewelry.

Assignment

Optional: In the next week, make an entry in your Book of Shadows about something you learned this week. This entry can be written, but it might happen that you find an *object* that embodies your newfound knowledge or experience. Perhaps you are walking along a beach and see a shell that reminds you of something I have written here. Maybe my phrase *bringing the dream to the waking mind* reminds you of a favorite knickknack.

You might put the object on your altar or in a place where you need inspiration. In the early 1960s, I was ridiculed for sporting long hair and blue jeans. I keep an old Levi's 501 poster on my office wall to remind me that my odd behavior has repeatedly been ahead of its time. That helps me stick to my guns when I come up with yet another theory or project that raises eyebrows. The poster is an odd journal entry about the eccentricity of my youth. (I confess: I'm still eccentric. But you probably noticed. In fact, I usually refer to my office as my *den,* as in a magician's den. I am so driven to teach and heal people that I have to avoid neglecting myself. A friend pointed out that working in a magician's den would remind me that spirituality means self-care. The magic of words is strong.)

You can put other people's writing in your magical journal. That's a great way to do this assignment. Perhaps a poem you run across embodies a principle I have shared in this visit. Maybe put that poem in your journal.

You can share these "entries" with your magical partner(s).

Continue, even if it is only once a year, bringing into your life an object and/or someone else's art that embodies what you learn.

And More About Power

We all know the cliché of the spiritually misshapen magician destroyed by his pursuit of power. Images of such practitioners abound in everything from science-fiction fantasies to anti-pagan propaganda. This is not surprising in a society that tells us that it is evil, or at best nonspiritual, to want power. Yet a real witch is diligent in the pursuit of power. If we are to negate the clichés and misgivings that easily come to mind, we need to further answer the question, What is power?

Real power is respecting your lover.

Real power is controlling your own life, not someone else's.

Real power means that if two people are in a room, they both are in control of the situation.

Real power is drinking in sunlight.

It is holy to strive for power. There is no virtue in being power-less.

Power ignored and suppressed becomes destructive. Either we use our power or it uses us. A witch uses her power.

The witch is a shape shifter, one who deals with all types of power by being a different person at different times. Power might be wearing a three-piece business suit. Or wearing a clown's hat at a business meeting.

Power is neither good nor bad. Like electricity, it is what you do with it that is good or bad.

Power is being rich with manna. Power is simply *being powerful*. Like a blue star. Or having a strong body that radiates manna. It is health, not dominance.

Do the following exercise about power, now. Put it in your magical notebook, because this will become an important document for you.

I have watched students write about similar assignments in class. If after a few minutes you are not done with a question, let yourself move on. I want you to be reasonable as to your expectations of what you can accomplish in one lesson's time. Fifteen minutes of writing time for the entire assignment is fine. You can always go back and write more later, whether that is in a week or a year. Questions like the ones you are about to answer always reveal new answers to you as you deepen your self-awareness.

With just a little writing about these questions, you can touch on deep parts of yourself. Be gentle with yourself. Take a break midway if you want.

Write answers to the following questions. Don't be surprised if the answers to one question overlap the answers to another. That's expected and is fine. The point is not to divide answers according to categories but to simply gather information. There are no wrong answers to these questions.

What do you think of when you hear the word *power*?

What negative things does this society say about power?

What negative things does this society say about power and women?

What negative things does this society say about power and men?

What are your personal problems about power? These might include problems you have about having it or wanting it, or internal blocks that keep you from pursuing it.

What are your powers, strengths?

What do you like about power?

Having done this assignment, you have given yourself a lot to think about. You can also see what you need to work on in yourself.

Don't try to change all of this at once. What you have written may be the goals of a lifetime, but that's okay. You have written your road map for change. When you are confused about your life, you can look at this writing and see if perhaps it shows what is blocking you, what you need to strive toward, and what your strong points are that can help you. We have to build on our strong points if we are to grow. To deny our strengths is false humility.

Reminder: get the support you need on your spiritual journey, because it is not easy to change. We need help and guidance from others in our pursuit of power and happiness. To try to go it alone can be too hard.

Assignment

Look through your answers for the inner "flaw" that most troubles you at the present time. Perhaps you are a woman who wrote that you are afraid that to be powerful means you will never be loved, and, because this misbegotten belief makes you push people away, you have gotten just too darn lonely. Or perhaps you are a man who wrote that to be powerful means to never show that you need help, and this belief is damaging your ability to work effectively as part of a team. Once you have chosen the inner attribute that is most troubling you at this time in your life, do the purification rite from lesson 3 on it.

The Process of Change

You have plenty of assignments, so don't use my following suggestion if it rushes the (often slow) process of change. The suggestion, however, is probably an important addition to the advanced practitioner's disciplines at this point. You can use the purification rite on an inner trait that disturbs your daily life. Magic is to *use* in order to *live a good life.*

Assignment

Do the Ritual Breathing of Power twice more this week. After this week, do it whenever you feel it might come in handy or you would simply enjoy doing it. Possibilities include using it as a substitute for your morning coffee (it's a much healthier pick-me-up), as a refresher during your work breaks, or whenever you want to feel more full of life.

Occasionally doing this exercise without The Magic Formula is fine. When you need it, and there's no time or willingness to do the setup and breakdown, on with the show.

Remember: Do your closing rite to end this week's lesson.

Being Whole

The Psychic Anatomy of the Three Souls

Every person consists of three souls, or selves. One is the "conscious" self. This, though, is not always the best way to describe it: the so-called conscious mind is oblivious of a lot of things. (Does *your* husband notice how he drops his dirty clothes on the floor?) Besides, the other two souls are quite aware. The conscious self is also called the "talking" self; it's the part of us that chats at parties.

Each person also has a Godself. It is actually a part of the person, the God within. The Faerie term for it is *Dian-y-glas*, which translates as "Blue God." Very hard to see psychically, it will appear to us in many guises—perhaps as a guardian angel, a spirit friend, or the Goddess or God. In actuality it is a blue sphere, above, and very close to, your head.

Why, if it is above our heads, is it called the God within? Because it is *within* us. We just don't usually perceive ourselves as having a portion of ourselves above our heads. Except for those guys who can't stand to take their hats off.

The Hawaiians call the Godself *Aumakua*, which means "parent" or "I am parent." Within ourselves we each have a loving parental deity who answers our prayers and takes care of us.

The existence of the Godself does not contradict the existence of a supreme deity, nor is praying to one or the other exclusive. A shaman prays to the Gods with her whole being; her Godself takes part in that process.

With a God within us, we need bow before no priest, nor any other authority. However, personal authority does not imply that we run no risk of self-illusion. You can inform *or* delude yourself, saying, "But this is what I am told by the voice inside myself."

The voice within is our surest guide, but it must be tempered; check out your inner guidance by talking with a friend or mentor you trust, someone who has common sense. Otherwise it is all too easy, even for the advanced practitioner, to cause harm to oneself and others by so-called spiritual and/or intuitive realizations that are actually delusions.

Nor does personal authority negate respect for elders, whether they be elders in your spiritual community or simply those who have lived longer than you. Adolescent rebellion, whether personal, political, or spiritual (I hate it when those three things are talked about as separate categories. Mea culpa!), is a reaction to someone else. Personal authority is not a reaction; it is a grown-up position and comes from an inner security with who you are. To disrespect elders is to disclaim the self-parenting—hence adulthood—implied in the term *Aumakua*. Rather, as the Craft expression states, "To respect your elders is to respect yourself."

There is also the unconscious, the part of us that is closest to nature and is intuitive. It communicates with the Gods and the

Godself. We do not speak from the conscious mind to the Gods, but from the conscious mind to the unconscious, which speaks to the God within and the Gods without. Obviously, *unconscious* is an inaccurate and misleading term. I prefer *inconscious* or *fetch*. I will explain the term *fetch* in a bit.

The average person has little communication between talking self and inconscious, so it might seem that the fetch *is* unconscious. Many people live whole lives with no conscious awareness of the depths of understanding within themselves. The fetch continues on in their lives, perceptive and offering guidance, yet unheard.

One of the most important goals of a witch is to integrate these three aspects. When the interaction of talking self and fetch is accomplished, the talking self becomes aware of the deep understandings of the fetch. This is part of bringing the dream into our conscious minds.

The so-called unconscious is wrongly seen not only as unaware, but as unintelligent, and dangerous. This stems from a fear of nature. Often nature is considered unworthy of trust. God-given instincts are viewed with suspicion, and a dark night in the woods scares the average civilized person far beyond any reasonable cause.

The forces of the natural world are surely dangerous. I am not going to stand under a tree in a thunderstorm proclaiming, "God created the lightening. I will trust Her." God also created common sense. Healthy fear and sensible cautiousness are fine.

But this culture fosters a morbid fear of nature. We are suspicious of the wildness, which is the dance of Gods, and of the instinctual drive for simple human companionship that in fact holds together the fiber of our social structure. Since the inconscious is our self that is closest to nature, society fears it as well.

In the same vein, the inconscious is seen as the repository of all that is evil in us. "Beware what evil lurks in the heart of man." Egad! The fetch falls in love with someone before the talking self is aware of it. The fetch is the part of ourselves that truly appreciates ballet or poetry because—note well, all ye who would master the art of making brooms carry buckets of water—the language of the inconscious is metaphor, art, and the literal use of language. This is important in your magic. How powerful would that scene with Mickey have been without all that music in the background? The disreputable fetch is also, as I said, the part of us that speaks directly to the God within and the Gods without.

Nature is sacred, and the fetch, being the part of us that is closest to nature, helps us embrace the sacred Goddess-given gifts of life, love, pleasure, and nature. The fetch is not to be likened to a debased creature but rather, as Victor would say, to a proud stallion!

Fetch once meant "to draw in," in the context of drawing in breath. To fetch a breath meant to breathe. The word *spirit* comes from the Latin word *spirare*, meaning "to breathe." If you break the word *inspiration* down into its parts, it is derived from the Latin for "to breathe in." In the ritual you are about to learn, you will experience the fetch's role in taking in the breath of life and divine inspiration.

The Hebrew term for the talking self, *Ruach*, relates our daily conscious mind to the Great Consciousness. Alternative religions are freeing us from organized religions' slavish worship of the logical mind to the exclusion of emotion and intuition. Don't go to the other extreme. Every part of us is sacred. Bringing the conscious and inconscious together is what makes a poet, a witch. Celts called the talking self "the fox." Being sharp and wily are good qualities for a witch.

A goal of this visit is to help you integrate these three souls. The things I have just written are true anatomy and not mere metaphor, but the distinctions I have made can be taken too literally. Unless you understand that each soul has the attributes of the other souls, you run the risk of further inner alienation, further lack of self-integration. Don't be too rigid in the tasks and attributes you understand each soul to have. Try the following ritual now.

The Ha Prayer

RITUAL
The Ha Prayer

It is important that the Godself take its full part in our day. To not have your Godself take its full part in your day is like a sighted person trying to read without his eyes or in the dark—absurd, and unnatural. The Ha prayer will cause you to utilize your whole being.

The Ha prayer also "makes the three souls straight." This means that the fetch and talking self are integrated.

Step 1. Say, "May all three souls be straight within me."

Step 2. Ask your inconscious to store the manna you are about to take in. One of the fetch's many functions is to create and store energy.

Step 3. Take in four breaths of manna.

Step 4. Breathe in energy, in these sets of four, until you have a good, strong charge, and are filled with Her power. While you do this, make prayer that your Godself take its full part in the day ahead: become as clear as you can as to what it means to have the Godself take its full part in your day, think about what you have learned about the Godself's part in our lives, and then ask for these things, upon which you have contemplated, to happen.

Also, make prayer that your three souls be straight within you, first by contemplating all you have learned about that in this lesson and other weeks' lessons, then by asking that it be so.

Step 5. In step 6, you will send to your Godself some of the manna you have taken in. This gives your God within the power with which to answer your prayer, and the energy to take Her full part in your day. If you were to send all the power you had breathed in, the rest of you would become drained. Your fetch knows the right amount to send and the right amount to keep in the parts of you other than the Godself. When you have a good strong charge of manna and your prayer is strong and clear, ask the fetch to divide the manna you are about to send.

Step 6. As you make a ritual gesture of blowing up (no, not as in exploding, but as in blowing a kiss), imagine some of the energy you have taken in going up to your Godself. Let the inconscious choose the right amount. Imagine that you see it going to a blue sphere above your head.

Step 7. One student felt guilty when she had sexual feelings at this point, and asked, "Isn't that wrong? After all, this is supposed to be spiritual." I answered that sex is at the heart of creation and creation is holy. Though there is no prescription as to what happens in this step of the rite, to be turned on is a sign of health—spiritual/physical health.

This is a special point in the ritual, for the God within you is giving you the love you need. This is truly self-love. Be open to whatever happens. Do not judge it. Our Godself knows exactly what we need, and that could take any form. Your Godself will shower down upon you whatever it is you need to be happy and healthy.

You might feel dizzy. The feeling will pass quickly.

Ha is the Hawaiian word for "to breathe." The word Hawaii breaks down into ha and wai, which means "breathe water"—water being a Hawaiian expression for manna—and the second letter i that ends the word is like an exclamation point: breathe manna! The Ha prayer was used not only by Celtic shamans, but by Hawaiians, who learned it from the Menehune, the Faerie Folk of their islands. In fact, the sound of ha is heard in the spiritual contexts of many cultures. James Brown often lets out a staccato, emphatic ha! in his songs, an echo of the gospel music that influenced his work. Ha is the sound of the exhaled breath of prayer sent up to God.

~~~~~~~

Assignment

Do this ritual every day upon awakening, using The Magic Formula only if you want. Just as it is natural to start your day by opening your eyes, so it is natural to do this as soon as your eyes open. Just as it is necessary to start our day by opening our eyes, so is it necessary to start our day with this rite.

The more you do this rite, the more your whole being will participate in your day. Otherwise it is like trying to walk on one leg: you are disabled. Although the impact of its daily use is enormous, if that is too much of a challenge, try to use it three mornings a week.

The Ha prayer is enormously important, its daily use a foundation of The Third Road®. One student, when she first did it, said she felt almost nothing. She later reported, "I still don't feel much. But when I do it, boy do I have a serene day!" Students feel the effect of the rite more and more.

Once you get used to this exercise it becomes simple, natural, easy, and done in a flash. After a while you can do it during your morning shower or while getting dressed for work. It becomes a natural part of your life.

Add this rite to the pre-ritual part of The Magic Formula. It is important that the Godself take its full part in any ritual, and that the three souls be straight before any ritual. This is like washing hands before dinner; it's natural and clean, similar to a raccoon's washing its food. And doing a pre-ritual Ha prayer is a necessary and powerful means to psychic safety in your rituals.

After your pre-ritual purification, do a Ha prayer. Your weekly lessons are an exception to this. Wait until you have come to a ritual you are going to do in that lesson, and then do the purification and Ha prayer.

The only change you make when you do this as pre-ritual work is that you add a prayer that your Godself take its full part in the rite ahead.

These two uses of the Ha prayer provide powerful protection, and this lesson on them is an important one.

Magic for the Home

By now you may have built your formal altar. Your home is a more important altar. If we keep an altar but neglect spiritual housekeeping, our formal altar, though a powerful tool for self-realization, can be lacking.

Spiritual Housecleaning

Just as your home needs dusting and vacuuming, so it needs psychic cleaning. Burning frankincense, sage, or sandalwood is good for this. To do a cleansing, burn the incense in each room of your home.

If you prefer, cleanse with salt water by sprinkling it about each room in your home. Some witches prefer sea salt to regular table salt. At times of crisis or when you have just moved into a new home, you might even wash the walls and floors with it. I prefer incense some days, salt water others.

As with day-to-day housework, your usual spiritual cleansings can just be a good, or quick, once-over in each room. (I wonder if you can sweep psychic disorder under the rug.) When you first move into a home, or in times of tragedy, it's a good idea to do a very thorough cleansing. As much as you are up for it, wave the smoke or sprinkle the water into every corner, closet, cupboard, drawer, and shelf. Get the cleanser high and low, into every nook and cranny. Don't be shy about using lots of the incense or salt water.

You might want to open windows and curtains to let fresh air and sunshine into your home on a regular basis. When you have need of a more thorough household purification, this is also a useful addition to the other cleansing procedures. God's light and beautiful fresh air drive out negative energies, and bring Her light and freshness into our home life.

Burning sage or washing walls with salt water may not be enough. Ordinary housecleaning can be part of spiritual purity. Perhaps you need to do that pile of dishes that is gathering mold!

I have a friend who won't do magic in a messy room, but I want, and need, to apply my magic and spirituality to whatever state my life is in. (One witch says to the other witch, "Why don't you do a spell to clean up this mess?" The other witch answers, "I already did. You should have seen this place before I did the spell.") My friend is too far to one end of the spectrum for me, but a reasonably clean and neat space might facilitate psychic clarity and spiritual purity. Besides, what is the point of doing so much training if we don't have a home we like to live in? The goal of pagan training is to live a life that is fulfilling in the physical realm.

Use your judgment as to whether or not to use The Magic Formula when psychically cleansing your home.

Assignment

Make a clean, neat home a goal, even if it is many years before you can achieve, or even take initial steps toward, this goal.

There are other steps that might be needed to cleanse your home of negative vibrations, like discussing with your roommate an unresolved tension, or ceasing to worry about work constantly when you are at home.

You may not yet be ready to do this sort of psychic cleansing. Perhaps you have not learned to apologize for a wrong done, or you don't know how to confront someone when you are treated poorly. Be patient with yourself. Very patient. However long it takes—and for some it is a *very* slow process—you *can* become cleaner in your dealings with folks. You might want to do a cleansing rite on the things inside yourself that cause you to act this way. Or it might feel like it is enough work for now to make a simple quick prayer, with no usual ritual format, that these attributes change.

On rare occasions a person might bring in a Catholic priest or a highly trained witch to do a spiritual cleaning of the home if the vibe is such that the practitioner can't handle it on his or her own; for resources, see appendix 2.

A spiritual cleansing of that magnitude is called an *exorcism*: a cleaning out of powerfully negative energy or of spirits who are causing disturbances through either maliciousness, misguided reasoning, or other causes. A person or home can be exorcised. I exorcised a home in which doors were often heard slamming at odd hours in the middle of the night. First I made sure it wasn't the husband sneaking out for a nip in the wee hours of the morning; there's a lot that can masquerade as troublesome spirits. Then I went into a trance and met the troublemaker: the spirit of a young single mother who had been living in the home when she died. She rattled around at night trying to get someone's attention so she could discover the fate of her child, who had been two years old when the mother died. The present owners of the home had bought it right after the mother's death, and so happened to know the child's whereabouts. I was able to reassure the spirit that all was well. After that, the homeowners were no longer awakened by anything more jarring than their alarm clock.

Lately, I've been doing lots of exorcisms for people. What an odd thing to say! I made that remark the other day to a friend and laughed. It's an odd life being a twentieth-century shaman. It's like the button I bought that reads: "I don't read science fiction, I live it."

Speaking of odd remarks and exorcisms: I had been hired to do an exorcism that would probably take all day. The house had been built on a spot rich with magical power. A witch had lived there in loving respect for the land's gifts. The grief that the site had felt upon the witch's death—yes, land can grieve—was so enormous that the new owners had never felt comfortable once they moved in. Having psychically perceived the cause in my initial interview with the couple, I knew it might take a full day to fix things. I needed to explain the situation to my clients, comfort and heal the land, and introduce the site to its new caretakers, two botanists who loved the site and who would honor it spiritually and ecologically.

I had also committed to bringing a baked chicken to a picnic the next day, and told a friend, "I just don't know when I'll have time to bake the chicken. The exorcism will take all day." My friend laughed, saying, "You know you've been hanging out with Francesca a long time when remarks like that no longer seem odd." I think being weird is lovely.

House Protection

RITUAL
Circle of Protection

To protect your home, say the following chant three to 48 million times. The repetition builds power and fervor. You may find the ritual stronger if you walk about the house as you chant. While you do this, you might enjoy sprinkling salt at all the openings: windows, doors, and fireplaces. Don't forget phones. And you techno-pagans, don't forget your modems. Salt is protective.

Goddess within and without,
make a circle all about.

Bring love in;
keep evil out.

As you repeat this, be clear in your intent: it is your home and all those within that you are protecting.

"Goddess within and without" refers both to the Great Mother and to the God within each of us. When we pray to Her we do not leave our whole being out. We also call on our internal deity, who is called Goddess whether for a man or for a woman. The *Aumakua* is feminine, though it is also both genders, because within the feminine both reside. Just as when we invoke the Great Goddess we are also calling upon Her son, brother, lover, and other half, because He is a part of Her.

It's important to not insulate yourself from good forces. Hence the "Bring love in." You want to be safe, not isolated.

You could turn this into a personal protection by focusing your intent on that instead of on your home. Perhaps you are in a store and an overworked, irritable clerk decides to vent pent-up emotions onto you. You could quickly throw up a protection circle around yourself. Or maybe you are going to confront an irate and impossible ex-wife. You might do the protection spell on yourself before you leave to see her. Once you have done this ritual a lot, you can put up a protection easily and quickly. You might even practice it the way a martial artist practices blocks, so defense is ready when needed.

This ritual can also protect you when you do magic. Although my instructions make you safe in your Craft work, there might be times to take extra precautions. Perhaps you want to do a ritual but your roommate is sulking and her ill temper seems to tangibly reach out and tap your shoulder. Adapt the protection circle by changing your intent; focus on the circle being one to protect you during the rite.

When you do the pre-ritual cleansing before any version of this rite, cleanse yourself of negative thoughts, fears, and other inner blocks about protection. For instance, do you believe that to "bring love in" you must bring in pain? Or perhaps you are fearful about a specific person. Do a cleansing of your morbid fears—as opposed to healthy fears—of that person, and of any other inner blocks concerning him or her that could interfere with your being a clear channel for the spell.

If you are in danger of physical harm, do the spell *and* call the police, not necessarily in that order. When immediate action is called for, you've no time for pre-ritual work.

As with the spiritual cleansing, you can do a larger or greater protection. When you do protections more often, it takes less energy per. If you do protections rarely, you might want to put more time and energy into them.

Using the protection ritual is a great way to apply magic to your mundane life, but it is only a suggestion. If use of the protection bubble is too overwhelming an addition to your life, as it likely would be if you are in your first years of Craft work, be patient with yourself. Though this sort of protection work is important, we can't change too much at once. Eventually you can add this option to your repertoire. My judgment call: for now, find safety through inner cleansings, self-integration, and other powerful safety factors instead of focusing on protection spells. The former seem by and large the excellent choice. Over time, you can more and more apply magic to every part of your day, but only when you are ready for each step of that process.

House Blessing

Like cleansing and protection, your more frequent blessings needn't be big. At certain times, like when you first move into a home, you make an extra-special effort. You can bless your home by doing any or all of the following, none of which necessitates using The Magic Formula, unless you choose to add it. Faerie magic is simple. That's what makes it so effective.

Bless your food. If you say grace over your meals, good spirits will be drawn to your abode. This needn't be a fancy prayer. A simple, heartfelt "Thank you, Mother, for this food" will do wonderfully, and the Mother will be grateful for your gratitude.

Fill your home with people you love. A gathering of friends joining in love and festivities blesses a home.

Put cut flowers in your home, and/or green plants.

Burn sandalwood incense.

Make love. Whenever we make love, we bless ourselves, the earth, the Gods, and the place we are in. Always make it ethical sex, for sex is sacred. When I say *sex,* I mean the real thing: sweaty, fun, loving, natural sex. Don't be pseudospiritual about it; just have a good, fun, sexy time.

Use the following house-blessing/offering potpourri, which draws love, peace, sunny energy, abundance, good spirits, healing, and the Lord and Lady into our homes. (It also makes a good house-warming present.) Combine:

$^1/_8$ oz. orrisroot powder

$^1/_8$ oz. lavender

$^1/_8$ oz. cedar chips

1 oz. wheat berries or bulgur wheat

27 drops sandalwood oil

Put the full amount that you've blended into a shell or attractive bowl. Even a jar will do. Place the container in your kitchen or another central location in your home. After three months, ritually dispose of the blend by burying it, and, if you choose, refill the container with a fresh mixture.

Part of blessing your home is making offerings to the Gods that dwell within. Every locale, whether a forest grove, stream, or house, has Gods that dwell within, what Hawaiians call the Akua Kini, the Little Gods. When we make offerings to those gods, our homes are blessed by them and we also live in loving harmony with them.

You can use the potpourri or another offering when you first move into a home, but offerings to the House Gods should not stop there. Regular offerings to the Little Gods are a pagan tradition. A witch who wants blessing in her home makes regular food and drink offerings to the House Gods, as well as the food offerings made to the Lord and Lady, mentioned earlier. It need be no more than a teaspoon each of any food and beverage from your meals, but it is important, both to gain blessings from the Little Gods and to live well with them. Put these offerings on the kitchen altar, or wherever imagination, intuition, and/or convenience dictates.

You can also use your imagination and intuition in choosing offerings. I like to offer my favorite foods, the way one shares something one likes with a friend. I love eating frozen cherries, cold and hard, straight from the freezer. My house spirits seem to like them too.

Occasionally putting a few tablespoons of whiskey in a dish is also greatly appreciated by the *Akua Kini*. If you do not like alcohol in your home, use a glass of orange juice. Leave the liquid out overnight, then dilute it and pour it on the ground. This whiskey or orange-juice offering is also a good practice when doing a major spiritual housecleaning. It makes the cleansing work better.

As you make these offerings, do so in awareness. Empty ritual is just that: in some ways it is empty. Fill the ritual with intent and emotions. Think about what you are doing. And enjoy it. The spirit world is a great place to hang out in. Take pleasure in it and have fun.

There are many things to do when first traveling The Third Road. You don't want to take on too much. If you cannot make the offerings with cognition and depth, at least try to make offerings, even if you do so mindlessly. (At last, my chance to make you my mindless follower. Please? No? Drat, I'll never get a cult going if you insist on having rights.) The Gods will appreciate the effort, I assure you. They'll get to eat!

If you cannot do regular feedings of the Little Gods, see if you can occasionally leave them an offering. Every full moon? If you can't do even that much, don't worry. Eventually you will feed the Gods.

There are several reasons for doing a house cleansing before doing the protection spell. First of all, it protects you from further psychic filth. But also it's not a great idea to "protect" the negative energy in your home. Generally, the formula for spiritual housekeeping is to cleanse, then protect, then bless. This is not a hard-and-fast formula. It's best to just do it however you can get it done. It can also be foolish to delay bringing blessings into your home until it is cleansed. The blessings of flowers, sex, and good company might give you what you need to get the cleansing done, and in and of itself might drive away some bad vibes.

Learning about household magic and the reasoning behind it is important at this point in your studies, but you've been given plenty of other work to do that might keep you too busy for a while to actually do this household magic. Add this material to your repertoire now if you can, or start five years from now if that is as fast as it can happen. Add it in bits and pieces if you want, like the way you furnish a home over time. (Furnishing on the spirit plane? Psychic decorating? Spiritual homemaking? Great ideas to play with.)

Adopting any religion as a way of life is a process. You cannot do it all at once. I kick off this book with a ritual, only to, in later pages, write that rituals should never be done without a pre-ritual purification and a Ha prayer. This is not a contradiction but an embodiment of an important spiritual principle: you can do only so much at once. I made a judgment call. Please do the same; never beat yourself up by trying to grow too fast, or by trying to take on too many ritual practices at once. Bit by bit you will adopt all the practices needed.

It took me years to make these household practices a regular part of my life. For a long time I did them sporadically, though I was very disciplined about my other exercises and rituals. Some students have needed a long time to use these household rituals at all. There must be a good reason for that, so feel OK about how you proceed.

I started mostly with house protections, to the best of my memory. I have such a fascination with the psychic realm that the huge amount of magic I did very early on drew lots of power to me, and I wanted to make sure I was safe in it.

Cleansing, protecting, and blessing your home are three enormous steps you can take in changing your life. It *can* be dangerous to neglect these practices, but you do what you can, and trust the Gods to pick up the slack.

That last sentence might confuse you, since it is hard to realistically convey the dangers of the magical realms in the first place. So many people see witchcraft as spooky, a topic in the same genre as horror tales. Others, trying to show magic in a better light, have swung to the other extreme. They paint an idyllic view of psychic matters, as if the only things one might encounter are cute little gnomes, or propose that absolute trust will keep you from all and any harmful forces that might arise in the etheric realm. In a bit I'll do my best to debunk the latter premise.

A more accurate and useful view: magic is no more dangerous than the rest of life. It is dangerous to drive a car, but most adults do it, and many take infants along for the ride. Magic is just as dangerous as driving a car, but I do it because it is just as useful as driving a car. If someone had a gun to my head, I would try to trust my God, but positive thinking is not going to stop a bullet from piercing my flesh. And though I can find a gun to my head in the mundane life, and something just as harsh might happen to me in the psychic realm, I am neither going to lock myself in my home peering out of a shuttered window all day, nor deny myself the big wide world of magic.

We can only try our best, and no matter how hard we try and plan, there will be plenty of errors and "falling short" of our goals. Massive quantities of errors and falling short are simply a sign that we are living; it is only people who try nothing who seldom fail. And theirs is the largest failure of all.

The Process of Change

If you repeatedly lose concentration during a rite when you open your eyes to read the instructions, you might want to tape the ritual. If you do, read the text slowly, and make long pauses after each step in which to follow the instructions.

Don't forget to ground after rites when you need that.

For the Advanced Practitioner

I suggest you use the household spells that are given here, unless the allowances given above to less advanced students are useful to you.

The more advanced my work gets, the more important it becomes to do my household magic. To live a life of ritual that is not applied but divorced from practical use distances me from myself and my real goals. The more you do magic, the greater the consequences of such divisions can be. Also, as my Art (the art of making magic) delves deeper, I become more sensitive to psychic intrusions and so have more need of the precautions.

I cleanse my home and altar room on a regular basis. As a master practitioner, I sometimes find the simple practice of keeping a psychically clean work space vital and necessary to my magical workings, so I often do this cleansing right before I do a spell.

I don't set up a protection circle each time I do a rite. I use one only when circumstances in a ritual might merit it. However, my home is always protected, hence so are my rites. Rather than suggesting that you use the above protection whenever you do a rite, which would be a silly waste of your time and power, I suggest you use the protection rite on your home to create permanent protection, keeping your home, and hence all your in-house rites, always shielded.

To do this, use the spell as it is given. Then, occasionally, use your intuition or a divination form to see if the spell needs renewal. If it does, renew the spell.

Pride and Sex Are Holy

Changing Your Beliefs About What Is Sacred

A Witch Seeks Pride

"Pride goeth before a fall." "Oh, don't be so upset; your pride is just hurt." "My, aren't you full of pride!" "Don't be so proud!" These are the sort of things we hear about pride. Yet a witch seeks pride. The following provides a more witchy perspective on pride.

Honor your accomplishments. Take pride in them.

Acknowledge the value of what you give to the community, and to your friends and family. Take pride in it.

Know your worth. Believe that you have worth.

Strive for self-esteem.

Believe that you have worth just because you exist.

God's children of the animal kingdom have dignity, pride.

You needn't *do* anything to be a worthwhile addition to a roomful of people. Know how valuable your mere presence is to those around you.

Instill pride in yourself, just as you would wish to give that sort of self-respect to your child.

When someone says, "My, aren't you proud?" say, "Thank you."

A witch takes pride in the things she does and who she is.

Pride is having a balanced view of yourself; true humility is seeing both your faults and your good traits. Seeing only your faults, or speaking only of them but never of the wonderful things you are and do, is false humility, spiritual arrogance.

Having delivered my liturgy on pride, I will admit it: yes, I am an evil temptress; I don't believe that pride is one of the seven deadly sins, nor that I will go to hell for loving myself. Bad shaman! Actually, I do believe that false pride is deadly, but that's for a later lesson. In the meantime, the above "liturgy" displays both an ethic and goals that embody that ethic. It may take you a long time to live that ethic. Think of it as something to embrace over time. Or over a lifetime. My bias is that no one ever totally achieves what is stated in my liturgy; life is a process of ever-deepening change. I do my best to move toward the ethic and goals stated above, and try to take pride in what changes I make.

Next, while you're still in my hermit's magical dwelling, write answers to the following questions in your Book of Shadows. It will become an important document. It is fine if the answers to one question overlap the answers to another.

Don't feel rushed, but don't spend too long on a question

either. It is usually better to answer each question a bit than to answer only a few perfectly. Be reasonable about your expectations of what you can accomplish in one short writing session. This is just one step in your deepening awareness of pride. You can always write more later.

What do you think of when you hear the word *pride?*

Are there ways it is hard for you to have pride as a woman, or as a man if you are male? Hermaphrodites—this is not a joke, folks—answer the question in your own terms.

Name just one way in which you feel disenfranchised. For instance, are you lesbian, Native American, or a person with a physical disability? If you have chosen something, write down how it affects your pride.

What do you take pride in?

Do you fear that pride goeth before a fall? If so, were you punished as a child for talking pride in yourself?

Are you punished, put down, or made fun of when you take pride in something?

What unhealthy beliefs do you hold about pride?

Having answered these questions, you likely know more about who you are and what you need to work on in yourself. You have a road map for change. Don't try to drive to the end of that road all at once. (Look, Martha, that woman is driving her car way too fast. And she isn't going anywhere.) What you have written may indicate the goals of a lifetime.

When you are confused about your life, this writing might

show you relevant blocks, what you need to strive toward, and what your strong points are that can help you. We have to build on our strong points if we are to grow. Again, to deny what strengths we have is false humility.

As the next part of this week's visit, do a ritual. Look through your answers for the inner "flaw" in yourself that most troubles you right now. Perhaps you have just achieved a major goal, such as graduating from college or finishing a year's commitment to be in a support group for incest survivors, and instead of being proud of yourself you are besieged by an inner voice telling you that you should have done better, that all your work was for nothing. Do a cleansing rite, washing that voice out. Or maybe you can't write a résumé because you feel that no one would be impressed by what you have done. Wash that belief away. In other words, do a purification ritual on something related to a lack of healthy pride. Don't forget to add the Ha prayer to your pre-ritual work.

Sex

Sex is morally good and holy.

All matter is alive, joyous, sexual.

Sex is the act of creation.

We deserve pleasure.

The Gods created us so that we could enjoy our lives. We are here *for* pleasure. It is our "meaning."

Sex is energy.

Sex is powerful healing.

Sex can wound deeply. For instance, callous nonmonogamy.

Sex brings us close to God.

Sex is at the heart of the Mysteries.

Because sex has so much power, we must always be moral in our sexual behavior. Never use the Wiccan view of sex as an excuse for moral lapses. Sex is one of the most sacred things there is; treat it as such.

Everything I've just said about sex is meant literally, and I mean real sex: messy, satisfying, rollin' 'n' tumblin' sex! To think I mean otherwise is to desecrate sex.

Don't think you can be spiritual and avoid sex. It is at the heart of every breath and atom of air you breathe. It is the essence of the spirit.

Do you disagree with something I've said about sex in this book? Good. I want students who can think for themselves.

A friend of mine who is deeply spiritual and celibate disagreed with me about sex being the essence of spirit. I answered, "I express sexuality even when dancing, doing a math problem, or brushing my teeth. I don't mean that I always dance in an overtly sexual way, or that I'm having sexual fantasies while performing dental hygiene. On a subtle level, I enjoy the innate sexiness of anything I do. Sexuality is part of everything." When I described it that way, she agreed with my premise. Phrases and words about sex have a very personal meaning for each person who hears them. Not to mention the fact that (who was it who said?) the exact opposite of any spiritual truth is also true. Once again, The Third Road® provides an alternative to the either/or roads. Psychic physics thrives on contradiction. (Aha! That's how Francesca can all on one page say she is talking about literal sex, and really mean it, then say she's talking about brushing her teeth.) This is a basic premise of The Third Road, utilized throughout this text, though often not pointed out as such. We will address it more explicitly in a later chapter.

My discussion with my friend shows only one of the ways celibacy could be seen as being in harmony with this premise. If you have disagreements with me, I invite you to a spiritual challenge. (I'm not slapping you in the face with my glove, and asking you to name your choice of weapons: wands or candles. I'm talking about a challenge in which one competes with oneself to improve one's life.) Get creative about ways in which my words can translate into ideas that give you the power *you* seek. If that doesn't work, I support you to think as you will.

Write down answers to the following questions. Follow the instructions I gave before your pride writing in this lesson, which are summed up in the following: don't feel that what you write has to be a complete or perfectly organized assessment of your sexuality. Write at a comfortable pace, trying to answer each question at least a bit. Don't expect too much of yourself; a little goes a long way. Write more later if you want.

What negative things or untruths were you told about sex when you were growing up?

Growing up, what negative things or untruths were you told about men and sex?

Growing up, what negative things or untruths were you told about women's sexuality?

What in this society might keep a person from a happy sex life?

What inside yourself gets in the way of a happy sex life? See those problems as locks on the door to the divine.

What would you like your sex life to be like?

What one thing can you do to improve your sex life?

Having finished your writing, read on. The last two questions were not abstract or theoretical. Paganism is not a mere metaphor, it is about how we *live*, and about honoring the material world as sacred. That includes our body and sex drives. Do not make the sexual issue an abstract one, a metaphor for something else. Victor told me a Japanese saying: "Sex is not a doorway leading to something else, it is not a symbol of something yet more divine, but a pathway leading toward the infinite horizon. We begin any path by being what we are. We do not grow into something else but into what we are."

Having done this assignment, you likely know more about who you are and what you need to work on in yourself. Don't scramble for your car now and start driving nowhere fast. Sexual blocks can be the hardest to change, because they are at the heart of things. Be patient and persistent. All aboard! The psychic-mobile is leaving now! You can have a great trip, but it will be a slow and long one. Along the way, you can lose the baggage you've been carrying about sexuality, though it will only be bit by bit. Eventually, however, you'll be carrying a whole new bag of tricks.

If you think it would help you during the rest of this training, refer back to your writing, using it as your sexual road map for change, and perhaps as a diagnostic chart when you are trying to find out what inside yourself is giving you problems with your sex life. You might find a clue in the writing you have just done. If you choose to follow the path of the shaman after you have finished this book, continue to use this writing, now and again, for as long as you find that it helps you along the way.

Assignment

Look at your sex writing. Pick one thing inside yourself that is interfering with your sex life, and cleanse yourself of it. Perhaps you are a recovered alcoholic, and without a drink you are afraid to ask your mate for what you want in bed. Cleanse that fear away. Or maybe you suspect you are gay, and are afraid to talk to anyone about it. Cleanse that fear away. Or maybe you want to ask a special person out on a date but feel you are not sexually desirable. Cleanse yourself of that belief. The following cleansing ritual is an alternative to the one you have already learned.

RITUAL
Purification by Water

Tools and Ingredients

☾ A bathtub or other body of water into which you can fully submerge. If none is available, use a sink or basin.

☾ Optional: Basil, steeped the way you would steep a cup of tea. Use about as much basil as you would if you were brewing a cup of tea. Basil—yup, the stuff you cook with—is a purifier.

Before the ritual, strain the basil tea into the water in the bath or basin.

Step 1. Before or after your pre-ritual work, climb into the tub.

Step 2. Spend one to two minutes taking deep breaths. Nothing fancy, just deep, natural breathes, as if you had just woken up and were taking in the first breath of the day. Focus on nothing but these breaths.

Step 3. Choose one thing inside yourself that needs to be cleansed away. Perhaps you are a woman who is ashamed of your intense sexual desire for a man you have just started dating because you believe that women shouldn't have strong sexual feelings. Or perhaps you're ashamed of sexual feelings you have for a member of the same sex because you have been taught that homosexual desire is bad. In both instances, you could cleanse the shame and the negative belief that accompanies the shame. Or maybe you resent having sexual needs at all, because you were never taught to take joy in such feelings and so when you have sexual feelings you are uncomfortable. In that case you might cleanse the resentment. I give sexual impurities as examples because the assignment is to do a sexual cleansing, but this ritual is great for removing any type of internal block.

Step 4. If you are using a sink or basin, now is the time to put your hands in the water. Imagine the impurity draining into the water.

Step 5. Pray that this impurity be transformed into pure life force, then returned to you as whatever positive attribute(s) the Gods think should take its place.

Step 6. Make a deeply pitched *ah* that resonates throughout your being. Sustain that *ah* for as long as you can. Make it with a whole breath. Continue to make *ahs* as you imagine yourself filled with a glowing energy. Imagine that this life force is alive, vital, sexual—an energy of love that perhaps is pulsing in you.

Step 7. Having made your prayer that the impurities be transformed and returned to you as positive traits, imagine that this has in fact happened. While continuing to make these *ahs*, imagine yourself to be a new you. For instance, if you cleansed yourself of shame about your desire for someone, you might now see yourself as comfortable and happy about your sexual desire.

When I do this rite, and don't know what the new behavior or feeling should be, I stay open to whatever good feelings or ideas the Gods give me, and go with that. Just do your best.

When you imagine or visualize yourself to be this new you, see yourself that way *now*, see it as happening in the present tense.

Saying Thank You to the Gods

The Gods treat us well all day long, not just when we are in ritual. You might express your gratitude to them for this. Giving thanks can be developed as a practice done regularly, or just when it feels right—for instance, when a particular spell bears fruit.

I give thanks if for no other reason than the pleasure of doing it. The deities are real, so saying "thank you" is a natural part of my relationship with them, in the same way a child says "thank you" to his mother for a cookie, perhaps giving the mother a happy hug.

I put flowers and food on my altar, or anywhere else the Gods might enjoy them. Burning a candle in Her praise, when I have been given a special blessing, is also nice.

Gratitude can also be expressed in actions. "Goddess, I will perform in a benefit as a way to say thanks for this beautiful new guitar." If you want to see your new lover, but he's out of town, you could offer the Gods your solitude in thanks for the new relationship.

Simple, easy, and to the point, an unadorned thank-you always makes a God happy.

The Process of Change

If you are having trouble with ritual techniques, that is to be expected. So is useless worrying about such trouble. (Well, worrying isn't entirely useless. As a hobby, it can fill hour after hour. It's also a fabulous way to avoid changing the things in oneself that keep one from being happy.) In time, the exercises will become second nature, but it takes time to perfect your skills. Just do the best you can. Be patient and persistent. You will become quite adept at any technique you repeat over and over. By simply *doing* the exercises in this book, however "well" or "poorly," you are building skills and improving your life.

The Third Road is deeply transformative. If you need more support than I can offer on the written page, get any and all the help you need, whether from a friend, psychic, pastoral counselor, therapist, house pet, Twelve Step group, houseplant, or anything else you come up with.

If it will help: I, here and now, before all the powers of creation and all the readers of this book, give you permission to get any and all the help and support you can in order to improve your life. (Sometimes folks don't feel something is OK to do until someone tells them so, and I am hoping my permission does that for some of you.) Don't try to do it the hard way by going it alone. That can be too much to handle and even self-defeating.

Many of my students have done longtime committed work with me while simultaneously committed to a therapist and/or a Twelve Step group and/or a variety of other supports and tools for growth. Get the support and tools necessary to be a happy, free person. Look through the listing in appendix 2, "Supplementary Magical Resources," for relevant services.

Don't Be Lonely

Getting in Touch with Yourself, the Earth, and the Old Gods

We Are a Part of the Earth

After your pre-ritual work, do the following rite as the next part of our visit. Read through it once so you know what to do your pre-ritual cleansing on.

I use plural pronouns in this rite, like *we* and *us*, because you are never really alone while you do this ritual. Within some steps of the ritual there are several ministeps. I have placed ellipses (. . .) between such inner steps, letting you know that you should use what you have been given before moving on.

RITUAL
Grounding no. 2

Part 1

Step 1. Sit on the floor. If that is not a comfortable option, stand. If neither of these is comfortable, do what seems best for you.

Step 2. Rock back and forth, feeling how solid the ground is beneath us, how solidly we are held by it . . . Use your imagination to feel how solid the ground is beneath us, how solidly we are held by it.

Step 3. Stretch your arms and body up, feeling the wonderful lush energy of the sky and air. If you do not feel this lushness, imagine you do.

Step 4. Reach out into this lushness of sky and air not only with your body but as far as your mind can imagine, and use your imagination to feel what's out there . . . Drink that in from as far as your mind can imagine, and imagine you are being filled with power, joy, and love from these upper realms.

Step 5. Use your imagination to do the remaining steps of the grounding. Start by feeling that part of yourself that reaches down into the earth, that part of you that reaches down into the topsoil . . . Feel that part of you that *is* the topsoil. Imagine this . . . Feel the power of the topsoil filling you.

Step 6. Feel that part of yourself that reaches down deeper into the earth, seeking the dark coolness of the Mother's safety, feel that part of you that *is* a bit deeper part of the earth. Imagine this . . . Feel the power of this part of the earth filling you.

Step 7. Feel that part of yourself that reaches down deeper into the earth, burrowing past rocks and underground caverns, underground rivers. Feel that part of you that *is* this deeper part of the earth, these rocks and underground caverns, underground rivers. Imagine this . . . Feel the power of these things filing you.

Step 8. Feel that part of yourself that reaches down even deeper into the earth, where it is safe, dark, and rich with fertility, power, and love. Feel that part of you that is this part of Mother Earth, where it is safe, dark, and rich with fertility, power, and love. Imagine this . . . Feel the energy there filling you.

Step 9. Feel that part of yourself that reaches to the deepest core of the earth where there is a core of molten fire. Feel that part of you that *is* this fiery core of the Mother planet . . . Feel that fire filling you.

Part 2

Step 1. Stand up. If that is not a comfortable option, sit. If neither of these is comfortable, do what seems best for you.

Step 2. Use your imagination for the rest of the ritual. Tell yourself that we are of the earth . . . Feel your muscles, feel the earth that they are made of. Move a bit—or a lot, if you wish—to help yourself feel this. We are moving parts of the earth, we are of the earth. I want you to experience that we are of the earth. As you move, really *feel* your muscles, feel the earth that they are made of.

Step 3. As you continue to move, try to feel (imagine) in your own body the rhythms and movements of the earth's body, of the ground beneath us.

Step 4. Take deep breaths, and as you do it feel (imagine) the earth breathe. We are a breathing part of the earth. We are a moving part of the earth like a river or stream.

Step 5. We are a moving part of the earth like the fish and trees. We are a moving part of the earth. Take a moment to explore that truth with your mind, body, and imagination. You may find your movements to be small and contemplative or large, bursting into outright dancing. There is no right or wrong in this. Do whatever feels correct—explore!

Step 6. We are a dancing part of the earth like a falling leaf. We are a dancing part of the earth. Take a moment to explore that truth with your mind, body, and imagination. You might find that your dance is quite slow and imperceptible, like that of an old oak tree. Or small and fast like the giggles of a brook. But you are a dancing part of the earth like a falling leaf. What is your dance today? Enjoy.

Step 7. The earth gets to dance when we dance. This is a truth, not a metaphor: the earth gets to dance when we dance. Take a minute, or take a *very* long time if it suits you, to explore this truth: we are a living, thinking, moving, breathing, dancing part of the earth, and the earth gets to dance when we dance. Whether your dance is balletlike or funky, or just a gentle shuffling that most people would not consider a dance, when we dance the earth gets to dance.

Assignment

1. Do this ritual once more this week, then once a week for the next three weeks, using both parts of the rite.

2. If you choose to continue with the Faerie path after you have

completed this training, use the ritual occasionally. Feel out how often you need it, whether that is once a week or once every few months. Do both parts of it or just the first part. See which feels better, but occasionally add part 2, even if it is only once in a blue moon.

Grounding no. 2 is not interchangeable with the grounding ritual in the fifth week's lesson.

The Magic Formula, in Outline, with Additional Instructions

1. Pre-ritual cleansing
2. The Breathing Exercise from lesson 7, if you need or want extra focusing
3. Ha prayer
4. Grounding no. 2, part 1 or all of it. Add Grounding no. 2 to The Magical Formula when you want to feel more "real," in tune and grounded. When Grounding no. 2 is done as a rite in and of itself, you would of course do it *after* all the pre-ritual work.
5. Blessing the Path
   a. God invocations, either formally as in lesson 1 or less formally as in lesson 4.
   b. Anointing of the forehead with water and dirt. This anointing can be done either with or without its accompanying prayer. Or use any other variation I have taught you. Do what seems suitable. If Grounding no. 2 is used you needn't do the anointing, unless you so desire. Do whatever seems suitable.
6. The main body, whether that is a ritual or an event such as your weekly lesson with me. If the main body is a purifica-

tion rite, and you have used the breathing exercise as step 2 of The Magic Formula, you may eliminate the first step of the purification rites you have learned, which is taking deep breaths for one or two minutes.

7. The closing
   a. Grounding, if needed
   b. Blessing the Path, part 2. This consists of devocations, as given in the first or fourth week's lesson, and a, as of now optional, closing prayer. The closing prayer can be the one given in the first week's lesson or one in your own words, but its purpose is to carry into your daily life the work you have done. For instance, at the end of a week's lesson you might pray:

> *Dear Gods,*
> *during this week ahead,*
> *help me use all the things that I have learned in this lesson*
> *so that I and those around me are happier and stronger.*
> *So mote it be.*

Or at the end of a ritual you might pray:

> *Lord and Lady,*
> *help me to live the rite that I have just done.*
> *So mote it be.*

The point is that a ritual or lesson is useless if we don't *live* it in our daily life, so we ask the Gods for help in this.

Self-Acceptance

Many of us have been taught to condemn ourselves for having Goddess-given human wants and needs. This can happen in subtle and insidious ways. We often judge ourselves harshly, deeming our perfectly healthy traits as wrong. I teach classes that start at 7 P.M. and end at 10, often ending with a ritual. One night, I was about to lead that ritual. I felt very tired but thought to myself, "Francesca, get your energy up so that you can offer a high-energy event for these people. You should do a good job." I realized I was being unkind to myself, condemning the healthy response I was having to what had been a particularly challenging, tiring session. The work had probably tired my students as well. Not to mention the fact that most of my students work nine-to-five jobs and the class was on a work night. I decided that what they and I needed was not rousing magic but quiet, peaceful ritual suitable to a tired bunch of witches.

My fatigue was a healthy signal telling me of my needs, and helping me better serve the needs of my students. In other words, I acknowledged that fatigue is the healthy response to its being 9:30 P.M.

Have you too often expected yourself to rise above the real and simple human fact of fatigue? Have you ended up ill because you became run-down doing too much for your mate? Have you ever gone overboard doing too much for your child until you were exhausted beyond reason and then snapped at your child, making you, your child, and anyone else in the vicinity miserable? Do you beat yourself up because you get tired?

There are other healthy thoughts, feelings, and actions about which some of us become ashamed. Would you berate yourself, or pat yourself on the back, if you said "Go away" to an intrusive, rude man who approached you on the street?

Would you feel guilty for refusing a reasonable request for help? Each of us has limited energy and simply can't say yes to everything that needs being done in this world, and still stay sane and healthy.

Do you thank the Goddess that you can become angry if treated poorly? The Gods gave us anger to let us know that something is wrong in the way we are being treated. Being submissive is not a sign of spirituality.

Would you feel childish if you were bored and distracted when something was not worthy of your interest or at least not what *you* should spend your time listening to?

Do you celebrate or denigrate intense sexual feelings?

Often the things in ourselves that we judge as wrong or try to transcend are powerful messages. God gives us loneliness to let us know when we need company. Yet how often have you been guilt-tripped for needing companionship? She gives us restlessness to drive us toward our truest life goals so that we can be happy and useful. I want you to be your own unique and special self, not only without shame, but in celebration of that self.

Before you go on with the lesson, do the following rite. You have already done most of your pre-ritual work. All you should theoretically need to do is any pre-ritual cleansing relevant to this particular exercise, but this exercise does not need that.

RITUAL
Spell for Self-Acceptance

Step 1. Close your eyes. Do not do the things that you might associate with starting a meditation and with getting into a spiritual frame of mind, such as relaxing your body, quieting your breathing, or clearing and stilling your mind. Instead, become aware of the tensions in your body and the worries of your mind. Really focus all your powers of concentration on them.

Step 2. Keeping this strong focus on those parts of yourself, pray to those parts of yourself, saying:

> I greet the Goddess.
> Thank you. I am in your service.
> Let us be in joy, for all things eat of one another.

Step 3. Listen to those tensions and worries. I am not implying that you should cling to a neckache. You should surely try to relieve yourself of it. But perhaps that neckache is trying to tell you something. Go through your entire being and, focusing on one place or aspect at a time, listen to what messages the tensions in body and soul might be giving you.

Step 4. Tell yourself:

> We are all dancing,
> in patterns that make
> oceans move,
> mountains fall and rise again,
> and love bloom in all hearts.
> The heart of the earth is blooming now.

Step 5. Sit for five minutes. This five minutes is not to trance or to deepen your focus. Rather, it is for you to absorb and perhaps contemplate what you just did. It is like the period of rest after a chiropractic adjustment. If you jump up off the table right after the adjustment, you might cramp or end up much worse than when you started. A similar need exists in this spell. This ritual affects us deeply, moving much energy, perhaps without seeming to. A five-minute rest makes it a safe psychic adjustment. If you go into a trance, you won't have the chance to absorb and take in what has *already* happened, and might not gain the considerable though sometimes subtle power of this rite.

Step 6. Make the vocal sound of two very short *oms*.

Step 7. Do something very grounding and mundane, like washing dishes, gardening, watering plants, or paying bills. Five minutes might be enough.

Assignment

Do the rite again this week, then once a week for the following two weeks. After that you might use it whenever you feel the need for more self-acceptance. This also helps keep you integrated when you are experiencing rapid growth in your psychic development. As we travel more deeply into the realm of psychic mystery, we need to simultaneously become more integrated as a person. So, for instance, you might use this rite if you suddenly could see spirits, or if such awareness suddenly improved in great measure, though often rapid surges of growth are not so spectacular. In such times you might use this ritual three times in a week or only once. You might do it once a week for a few weeks, or maybe even several times a week for several weeks. Feel out what you need.

Another excellent use of this spell is to perform it before having sex. Your partner needn't do it with you, in fact needn't even know you've done it. As long as you are respectful, loving, and considerate of your partner's sexual needs, your spiritual practices are your own business, and can only greaten the pleasure of your partner.

This spell not only helps you love yourself for who you are right now, but has other rewards that I will leave for you to discover over time.

Honor the sacredness of being human. Though some religions tell us that to be human is synonymous with being sinful and innately evil, Wicca tells us that to be human is to be divine.

Talking with God

The Goddess is a friend and a part of my life. All day long I talk to my Mother, and I don't always do some hocus-pocus production just so I can say something to Her. Celts didn't genuflect and tap their heels together three times, chanting, "There's no place like home," before being worthy of an audience with God. She's always there for me, always ready to listen, quick to answer. The same goes for the Lord. He is my Father, whom I need not fear. You don't need The Magic Formula just to talk to them as you go about your daily life.

I hope you don't think that because The Magic Formula is usually necessary, the Gods are distant, or unapproachable without a ritual context. They are our loving parents, and we can talk to them and listen to them whenever we want. They want to be *with* us, *in* the world, *in* our lives. When we call on them, they will walk with us all day long.

On-the-Spot Purification Work

Sometimes during the course of the day I find myself doing, thinking, or feeling something that I need to change right then and there. Perhaps I am irritated with my daughter or fear I am about to lose my temper with my boyfriend. Or maybe I need to quickly muster the courage to walk away from someone who is being rude or abusive. Perhaps a self-defeating belief is getting the better of me when I have only thirty more minutes to meet a deadline. It would be absurd to forgo a prayer that I be cleansed and changed simply because it's not possible to use The Magic Formula that should usually be used for a purification rite.

At such times, you can simply ask the Mother to cleanse you. This needn't be any more complex than: "Lady, please cleanse me of this fear." If you do not know what you need to be cleansed of, tell Her that; just say in your own words, "Mother, I don't know what inside me is blocking me this minute, but would you cleanse me of it?" If you prefer, just quickly get in touch with the block—the impetuous anger, overwhelming shame, or other hampering attribute—and send it down to the earth. This rite might take no more than fifteen seconds.

This approach is also great if it's one of those days when you might benefit from continually asking, "Mom, give me a hand here, would ya?" Though there are exceptions, it would usually be exhausting and discouraging to use The Magic Formula over and over in one day. Our Gods want to help you all day long. As I said before, use your common sense and discretion when listening to my dictates.

On-the-spot cleansings are excellent during a crisis. If it feels helpful, you can later do a more extensive purification.

More About Goddess Aspects

The Goddess has children who are gods. They are referred to as Her aspects, in the sense that everything in creation is an aspect of Her. This is different from an aspect of Her personality like the Crone. Her children are entities in their own right. The God also has both types of aspects: His children, and aspects of His personality.

Over time, one's sense of which type of aspect is meant becomes good enough for practical usage.

The Ethics and Laws of Wicca

Psychic Physics

The word *law* might scare some folks off. Many of us turned to alternative religions because we didn't want to be dominated by unfair societal and religious laws. And rightfully so. When presenting a lecture to about a hundred witches at a conference, I was asked, "If one of your students is starting something that might hurt them, like a bad relationship, how do you get them to stop?" To the knowing laughter of my pagan audience, I responded, "When has any witch done what *anyone* tells them to do?" That's one of our strengths.

There is another kind of law—the law of nature. If you let go of the glass you are holding, it will drop. If you drop it often enough, there's a good chance it will break.

Spellcrafting is a natural thing, governed by the *psychic* laws of nature. Though it is an option to believe that the glass will fall or that it will not fall, finally it is not a matter of opinion. Even if you chant, "Presto, mitchakaboola, abbadazoola." So it is with magic. If you do certain things, the laws of psychic physics will cause certain other things to happen. No matter what you believe or chant.

The ethics of magic are inextricably interwoven with the laws of nature, which are one and the same as the laws of physics. Sound ethics are not just theory that popped into someone's head. A student of mine insisted that there was nothing wrong with sleeping with his best friend's wife: "After all, we are all grown up, and we all love each other." Although those are convincing words—sound rhetoric disguises a multitude of sins—he learned that the reason some people call sleeping with another man's wife immoral is because the laws of *human* nature are such that someone gets hurt physically or emotionally.

Magical ethics are the same: the physics of humankind and of the spirit world are such that if you do harm there are natural consequences. A loving Goddess created the universe, and so, down to its last molecule, creation is at heart moral. In the long run, it refuses to be betrayed. For instance, our neglect of our planet's health may be our own demise. It is impossible, and a false dichotomy, to put ethics and psychic physics into two separate sections.

Laws and ethics of spellcrafting are to be found throughout this book. Shamanic lessons are usually given within a context. There has been no context in which to teach the following:

If you wouldn't do something in "real life," don't do it in a spell. When you are doing magic you are not exempt from your simple common sense. Never suspend the use of your plain old common sense when using magic, regarding ethical or any other considerations.

Magic is not a metaphorical system constructed to help us

understand ourselves and the world better. Magic is as real as a knife. As such it can cut deep. Use it accordingly.

It is wrong to force our will on someone, magically or otherwise. Oddly enough, people who would never think of forcing another human being to do something that wasn't motivated by that person's own volition forget to have the same respect when it comes to magic. This is a perfect example of suspending common sense. It's as if magic were a realm where common courtesies and thoughtfulness that usually go without saying do not apply. Silly shamans. Again, try to think of magic as real so that you approach it with the same down-to-earth approach you would take with any mundane situation.

It is wrong to force your will on someone even if you think it's for their own good. You might think it would be better for your best friend Louise if she weren't involved with the fellow she's been seeing. Yet you need to realize that Louise is a grown woman and deserves the chance to live her own life, even if that means falling on her face. It is not a sound idea to interfere magically with this relationship. Imagine what would happen if you did so nonmagically. *Ouch!* Once again, magic is as real as a knife.

You might apply your magic to yourself—for instance, by invoking the Goddess and asking what She wants you to do on the mundane plane to help your friend. The Goddess might suggest you confront your friend instead of hiding behind a spell. It is wonderful to be able to confront a friend that you feel is blind to self-destructive behavior, and in doing so you still leave your friend the power to do as he or she deems best.

Anything you do magically, or mundanely, comes back to you three-fold. If you give out good, then that's what you get in return. If you give out bad, then that is what you get. This law can be quite specific. You may get returned to you the exact thing you sent out.

An important aside: by and large, I do not teach how to apply the spells in this book on someone other than yourself. Though there is nothing wrong with that per se, the theories, skills, and ethics of that type of spell are different from what you are learning about doing spells on oneself. I generally cannot address the additional application in a way that shows you how to do spells on your friends safely and effectively, and still leave room for more crucial material—a judgment call on my part as to what is crucial.

From here on, I *will* show you a few safe and powerful rites that you can use for others. In my judgment call, I chose what seemed crucial and safe for most folks, while in early training, to use on something other than themselves; I made this decision happily, knowing that an individual will not get everything he or she needs from one book, and can fill in the gap by pursuing shelves of magical books or talking to a friendly witch. See the listing of resources in appendix 2.

Over and over, students come to me feeling they just *have* to cast a spell on someone to help them. A great deal of the time, that is not a necessity. Too often people do not respect a loved one's right to his own decisions. Or his right to learn from his own mistakes. Another common flaw is applying magic to others as a way to avoid facing one's own problems and shortcomings. I don't need to tell you that spells with these often unconscious motives don't turn out well.

Often, however, a friend or other loved one has a problem about which we have a legitimate motive for putting our hand in magically. In the lesson on using herbs, candles, and incense, you will learn ways to help and influence folks magically without controlling them or in any way casting a spell on them. Once you've gotten thought that lesson, and you feel at any time you *have* to cast a spell on a person, thumb through that section for a possible alternative. Helping out magically always means not meddling more than you have the energy for and the right to.

There are additional alternatives. What do you do if you want to cast a spell on your friend Bill, who is ill with a cold? If a friend needs help, one of the best things to do is to pray for guidance as to how you can serve him without doing a spell on him. After your prayer, sit silently and see if anything comes to mind. Or if you know how, read your tarot cards with that question in mind. Or walk by the beach listening to what the waves answer; they speak with the voice of the Mother.

Maybe the Gods will say, "Make him some chicken soup." By going about it like this, you are accountable for the results of your action. Bill is not awakened in the middle of the night by a spirit who is attracted by your guilt over his illness. The worst that can happen is that Bill won't like your soup.

Or you might be given guidance to confront Bill about the fact he is always getting sick because he doesn't take good care of his health. Confronting a friend is hard, but it is surely more ethical than taking his life into your hands with a spell you don't really know how to work. Also, I choose friends who will call me on my negative behavior. It's a necessity to sound living.

Once I've taught you how to do a few spells on people and things, continue to use two principles: when doing spells for others, more can be less; it is very easy and dangerous to fall into the habit of doing too much magic for others.

If you now ask, "But isn't it my duty to protect my loved ones?" my answer is "Yes, yes, yes it is. It is a witch's privilege to take care of those he loves. Whether that means doing protection spells on an ongoing basis or in an emergency is up to you. Not everyone wants to take on such responsibilities. Maybe they need to focus more on themselves before they can really help someone else. But if you are ready and wanting to undertake the very sensible practice of protecting your children and loved ones from harm, the instructions are below. If you do not live alone, you may have already protected your loved ones simply by magically protecting your home. Oops! Not a problem. Just one of those things. You put psychic locks on your doors, and the entire household benefited from it. Now you will learn to do it better.

RITUAL
Protecting Others

Use the Circle of Protection ritual in lesson 8, adding the following instructions. In your pre-ritual purification, cleanse yourself of any urge to control another person's fate. Although parents of young children need to do this cleansing, they also have permission from God to be a bit more controlling. "You have to go to bed now" is a controlling yet loving thing to say to an overtired, hence tearful, five-year-old. Parents of wee ones have to take life-and-death responsibility for their children; the child can't. In a—Goddess forbid—airplane emergency, I would force an air mask onto the face of a frightened and uncooperative child. But there's a limit to that.

Do this cleansing, even if you don't think you need it. There's almost always something that remains unseen until we look for it, and I don't want your unconscious mind shaping the spell in an ineffective or unsafe way.

If you think that is too much effort to go to just to take care of folks, then perhaps the motivation to protect them is not a good one.

To use this spell on adults, get their permission. If they are afraid of witchcraft, substitute phrases like *psychic protection* and *visualization for safety.* I am not suggesting you be deceptive—just careful, creative, and minimal in your choice of words.

The magic of The Third Road® is powerful and effective. Don't use it indiscriminately, or you'll drain yourself and have to go to a Twelve Step meeting for codependents. Even on the more mundane plane, children aside, people usually only need a modicum of protection from others.

A *strong, passionate will is part of a shaman's ethics.* Using this book develops such a will. *Will* is a fancy word for *want.* A witch needs to acknowledge how important her own unique desires are. This is not a religion of self-deprivation or self-abnegation. It is a religion in which the self is developed fully and honored. To deny yourself the things you want is to deny the Gods and the planet what they need as well, for as we treat ourselves, so are we in a real and scientific way treating the world around us.

We must not only know what it is we want, but allow the natural awesome strengths of such desires—passion—to flow through us, motivating us toward our dreams. For instance, if you are lucky enough to know that you want to be an actress but you tell yourself, "Well, that is a silly thing to want," then you never *will* be an actress. But if you instead feed and strengthen your desire for the stage, that will help you overcome your inner and outer obstacles. The following exercises can be used, alone or together, in any order, when there is a goal you want to achieve.

SPIRITUAL PRACTICES
Make a Wish, Then Desire It Strongly

1. Honor your desire for a specific goal as God given and sacred. Use your own words to tell yourself this. Create an altar dedicated to the holiness of your own wishes. Or thumb through this book looking for ways to use your new skills to honor a desire.

2. Cleanse away the fears inside you that keep you from following your own star. These fears come in two categories: your fears of following *any* dream; and those fears specific to one dream you want to work toward right now or soon. Leftover anxiety from an overly critical parent might make you hesitate to try *anything* because you fear attack, while the idea of specifically becoming a singer might be blocked because you were told that scientific pursuits were respectable but art was silly.

3. Tell yourself that you have the abilities to do what you want. If you don't have those abilities, cast a spell to gain them. You can invoke the Goddess and imagine Her giving you those skills, or use "The Spell Itself," which you will soon learn.

4. Remember, you can pray for help to free your desires and to achieve your goals.

Your desires can become like a powerful ocean wave on which you ride toward your dreams. Magic surfing! Better than surfing the World Wide Web—and I *love* the World Wide Web. It might take time; part of the shaman's discipline is to develop such force of will. Without such an inner force it is easy to fall by the wayside.

Assignment

1. Use one or all of the above steps at least once in the next month to fuel a specific goal. It can be a large or a small objective. Continue to use the steps when needed, and also if you continue with your shamanic training after using this book—including teaching yourself. You will strengthen yourself in a way that is not only important to you as a person but necessary to you as a shaman.

2. Make the following prayer once a week for the next four weeks. As with all other tools I give you, you can then use it as needed.

PRAYER
Grant Me Will

Most Holy Mother,
Who created this beautiful universe
out of Her desire for Dian-y-glas,
help me to know what I want.
Make my desire strong enough
to create a universe worthy of Your passion.
Help me to find my own strong will,
that I may create a world to my liking
and so honor your gift of creation.
So mote it be.

You might be surprised that I include strong will as a topic in a section on ethics. It is an important part of the Faerie ethic to develop a strong will. It is godly to fight for what you want in life, and our passionate will is a reflection of the will of the Gods. With this in mind you will not misunderstand and be led astray by the next topic.

Misuse of will is unethical. Unless we know what we truly desire, truly want, truly will, our hopefully well-honed will can backfire on us and the people in our lives. As an important part of a witch's training, the subject of finding this true will has been touched upon in many areas of this book. In this further exploration, I will touch on two aspects of the misuse of will.

It is amazingly easy to be deluded about what we really want. Any person can be driven by what feels like a strong will or God-given passion but is instead an unhealthy fear, low self-esteem, obsession, or the like. At such times we try to force events to come about as we think is best. We push and push and push, all the while frustrated and unhappy because we don't seem to be getting anywhere. (Silly shamans! When will you be perfect?) Even if we achieve our goals, we are miserable. When we act this way we are being driven by our wounds, pushed by our inner weakness.

Let's say a woman thought she *had* to get a job in a prestigious law firm to make her life happy and worthwhile. Let us add to this fiction that the woman is motivated toward the law firm not by her heart's desire but by a deep-seated and unconscious belief that she is not a worthwhile person. She sees the law firm as proof of her worth. Until she acknowledges the true nature of her drive, she never finds a job that will make her happy. And she works miserably at the law firm.

I know a man who did lot of volunteer ecological work while he earned his living as a truck driver. He was always exhausted, but he seemed dedicated, telling friends that the freely given work would help him establish a name in ecological circles so that he could work in that field. He became so run-down that he had serious health problems. He finally admitted that he had been fooling himself. Actually, he had volunteered because he was afraid to risk rejection and failure should he try a new job. He accepted his true will to be a natural-means farmer, and successfully faced the fear and challenges of starting a new career.

A third example further explores the dimensions of such self-delusion. I had a student who was a professional actress. She used sheer determination to get through the terror of auditions, exhausting performance schedules, and the deprivation of the artist's life. A fine use of will per se. She felt it was worth it because she "knew" that someday acting would make her happy—until she realized that her parents had always insisted that if she wanted to be happy she needed to be creative. She ritually cleansed away her belief that her idea of happiness had to be the same as that of her parents, who were active in community theater.

She dug up the lawn in her backyard and found her own kind of creativity in gardening. She found happiness in dirty hands, budding leaves, and providing her friends with gorgeous bouquets.

Your true will is in harmony with the Greater Will. When that is the case there is nothing wrong with intense driving desire or striving hard toward your goal. This kind of healthy passion is not the same thing as competing with God!

When necessary—once a year or twenty times a day—remind yourself that material goods, companionship, sex, and trips to

Hawaii will not make you happy if your pursuit of them is motivated by unhealthy drives. Also remind yourself that you will be happy only if you seek what you truly desire.

When you have a spell in mind, it sometimes helps to cleanse your desire. For instance, soon you will learn The Spell Itself, which can be used in innumerable ways. Let's say you decide to follow the path of the Shopping Goddess and use the spell to get new clothes, but you don't feel quite right about it. Ask yourself if you need to purify yourself of anything that might be masquerading as an honest desire to dress up, such as low self-esteem, poor body image, compulsive spending, a belief that you are unattractive, or the shaky status of your relationship. Once you have done the cleansing, you will be better able to know whether or not you really want those clothes. Strong will and good magical technique without the balance of clear-headed intent are dangerous; many men, and women, use strong wills to live a workaholic lifestyle and work themselves to the graves. (That's something you can do a ritual to change!) The consequences can be just as severe in magic.

Another means to this clear-sightedness is—you guessed it—endless purification. I mean the cleansing rites that seem unrelated to the issue of false will but that you would do regardless, because they are needed to clear blocks in another area of your life such as sex, health, or money. This sort of rigorous purification, done on a regular basis, helps you become clearer and clearer about everything in your life, including your true motives. Then you are better able to see whether a given spell is motivated by a desire for, say, self-fulfillment and fun, or if you are deluded by morbid fear, obsessions, and the like. This ongoing cleansing work is not a substitute for the pre-ritual cleansing mentioned in the previous paragraph. The two are both part of the same thing.

A good tool for knowing your true will is *divination*, the magical skill of both learning facts about the present, past, and future, and gaining spiritual guidance—all through something more than the five senses and logic. This can be done through an interpretation of signs given by numerous forms, such as tarot cards, the I Ching, and ocean waves.

Divination can also be practiced through psychic skills. *Scrying* means gazing into crystal, water, or flame until you *see* what you seek to learn. Clairvoyance is seeing things in your mind's eye that prove to be true. Finally, there is what some folks call a plain old hunch!

When you learn The Spell Itself, you will find suggestions on how to use divination. In the meantime, or if the forms of divination don't work, talk to a sensible friend. Or get a psychic reading. Or pray for guidance. Or ask a tree. The last three are also forms of divination.

If you continue to develop yourself as a shaman after you have finished with this book, be vigorous in your clarification of passion. Knowing your true will and avoiding misuse of will is essential to the Craft, as it is in any religion. It must be a goal that you are willing to work hard toward. Otherwise you will fall prey to an unhealthy, twisted will.

Mistaking addiction, fear, and the likes for passionate will is only one way desire is misapplied. A second misuse of will is lack of pliability. I used to give shamanic counseling—an upscale term for psychic readings—to Kate, who wanted to be a professional musician. My client was a fine blues artist, worked hard, was well connected in the field, and was willing to make sacrifices to achieve her goals. Yet no matter how hard she worked, she rarely got a decent job. It seemed like an absurd comedy. She would show up for an audition only to find the job had just been taken.

She got a one-night blues gig, and her car, with all her band's equipment, broke down on the way to the job. She got a nine-to-five job as a lady's companion (which paid her bills) to work closer to where her band practiced. A week later that rehearsal studio closed down. She couldn't figure out what was going wrong.

At her first appointment with me, she told me everything I've just told you. I asked her what she wanted to do at this point, and she responded, "Give up! I'm disappointed and exhausted."

I suggested that she do just that. I use shamanic counseling to help clients from all religious denominations. Kate is Jewish, but my suggestion that she do what a shaman would do in her situation was in keeping with her religion: I asked her to pray: "Okay, God, I give up! I'm too tired to go on anymore! I need to lie back and not force the flow. You show me what you want and I'll go along with it."

Shortly after her exhausted prayer in my office, her employer decided to tour Europe and asked Kate to accompany her. Kate hated traveling but felt too tired and discouraged to look for another job.

She showed up for a second appointment, in which I suggested she pray: "OK, God, this is not what I want, but I trust you. If this is the only thing you'll give me, I will give it a try and see where it takes me."

Her decisions to be willing and flexible were by no means easy. Such choices seldom are, at least not when you are first learning the art of pliability.

A few month's later, I got a postcard from her that read: "God played a wonderful trick on me! I'm in England where I heard some old ballads that I loved more than anything I had ever heard! Now I am driven and ecstatic, collecting English traditional tunes while I accompany my employer about England. Everywhere I go musicians appear as if by magic (!) offering me songs."

Upon her return to the United States doors opened miraculously. Mrs. Albey, the woman she had traveled through Europe with, impressed by Kate's diligent gathering of folk music, introduced her to a producer. Unlike what happened with her previous attempt in the business, one thing led to another with relative ease. She quickly became a popular and well-paid musician.

Without all her initial disappointments she never would have found the musical genre that made her happiest, nor would she have found a patron in Mrs. Albey.

Instead of allowing ourselves to be driven by what only appear to be our truest desires, we have to be flexible. Rigidity can keep us from our fullest happiness. Sometimes there might be a great deal more at stake. One can so ignore the will of the Gods, and therefore one's own true will, as to push and push and push until one has pushed oneself into total destruction. We can will ourselves into destruction, thinking we are doing what we really want. We need only to look at the prevalence of heart attacks caused by workaholism.

When I realize I am forcing the flow, or swimming against it, I might ask the Mother for serenity, so that I can say, "OK, Gods, I am willing to trust you. It seems that you might have something better in mind for me than what I think I want. I guess I will try to believe that all this craziness in my life is for some reason that I don't understand, and that it will all turn out for the best. So you lead; I'll follow."

A witch knows the immense value of this sort of flexibility, so she pursues it as much as she pursues the development of a strong will. Take note, grasshopper: such flexibility can be a *very hard thing to achieve.* It can take everything you have in you to not force an issue. You are not alone. Most witches find this a difficult part of training.

Wicca is a *discipline*. It can take rigorous attempts and rites, done over and over, to achieve this goal. By applying the relevant magical tools in this book, including the tools I've already given to avoid misuse of will, you will achieve pliancy and through it a relaxed, happy life. The will of the universe is the will of the Gods; if we are flexible, we can coast along, on the motion of the universe, toward the things that will make us happiest.

Pliability also means that when you've done the best spell possible and it doesn't work, you ask yourself whether to try again or whether the Mother has given you an exercise in acceptance and flexibility, a chance to sharpen your skills. If you decide it's the latter, remember: the Goddess has chosen to give you your very own private lesson!

Having presented two ways in which will can be misused, I want to add that it is not always easy to know the difference between true will and false desires. Or to know when to fight like a God for what you want and when to go along with what you trust God intends for you. When I first started on a spiritual path I almost never knew what I really wanted! For one thing, passion and instinctual drives can sometimes seem like addiction, and vice versa. Though now I am clear a great deal of the time, sometimes I still get very confused. Don't get discouraged, grasshopper. Even when you can walk on the rice paper without tearing it, and turn lead into gold—yes, I am splicing lines from TV's Kung Fu with an alchemical proverb until they produce nonsense, but you get the idea—you will continue to be confused by false desires. Perhaps the adept gets most confused of all, for it is a challenge that never stops. Be extremely patient with yourself.

Shamanic training hones us until we achieve a healthy balance and blending of strong will and flexibility. We clarify our minds and beings so that we know the difference between passion and a drive toward self-destruction. Steadily pursue the Craft and you will improve. More and more you will find yourself in tune with the will of the Gods, able to find the more appropriate path at any given moment.

A last note: magic practiced with the wrong use of will backfires. For one thing, you might regret it if the Mother lets you have your way. And I don't know a witch who hasn't had to learn that lesson the hard way!

Whatever you cast is first and foremost cast on yourself. You can't get away with malicious intent in a spell, because any spell you do, whether it is on yourself or on someone else, becomes you. In the process of casting a spell you always become the spell itself.

Power is not unconscious. Power doesn't like to be abused. If you use it to bad purpose, it will turn on you sooner or later. Your lack of integrity will come back to you. Power is a part of us, so doing wrong is like abusing your own power.

On the other hand, all power is in our Lady's service, and it wants to walk with you in that capacity. To be a part of the holy weaving of all things that the Mother created is a joy past imagining. In any spell, become one with the power by having integrity.

Don't limit yourself to the ethical considerations in this book. This book is a Wiccan primer. No spiritual teacher would try to completely explore ethics in a single book. A book provides a starting place, from which you can jump off and develop your own sense of right and wrong.

In Wicca, no one dictates to you what is right or wrong. No *shamanic* priest says, "Only I hear God, so you must do as God tells *me* to tell *you.*" Freedom from a religion or priest telling us how to run our lives demands all the more responsibility on our part.

If no one tells us what to do, we have to do the hard work of thinking things out. As witches, we are each listening for God, each exploring our own moral goals and beliefs, and committing to what we trust is the truth. So, having read this book, don't stop there. Since no pagan priest will tell a witch what to do, you are responsible for the consequences of your action, including your magical acts, so you *yourself* need to consider what is right. Constantly be willing to face up to your own moral ideals and dilemmas. The Gods ask that of us.

We also have to know that any wrong action can be justified by proper or glib rhetoric. We cannot avoid being misled by clever or misapplied maxims without, yup, endless purification, and rites to strengthen ourselves, so that a balanced psyche is navigating the rough shoals of both spiritual rhetoric and finding our own unique sense of morals. The mind alone cannot make moral decisions unless guided by a pure heart.

The concept of self-defined morality might seem a contradiction of my earlier statement that ethics is a science bound by scientific laws. The natural current of power that runs through me is as different from the one that runs through you as the food needs of a tree are different from the food needs of a cat. The same laws of physics operate for both cat and tree, but don't expect their diet, or morality, to be the same. If a cat is doing what the Gods intend, it will act like a cat, not a tree. So it is with magical ethics.

A Celtic shaman would channel his power in his own unique pattern, just as one witch might find lifelong marriage powerful because it is a commitment to finding full power with a loved one while another witch might need a divorce to spare her children the abuse of an alcoholic father. The scientific laws of ethics express themselves uniquely in each of us. And, just as some trees grow dark and dry in winter months yet stay quite healthy, your ethics might change as the seasons of your life turn—all for the better.

Personal authority necessitates dialogue with others to better understand what our Mother is telling us. Otherwise it's too easy for us to be self-deluded, wrongly thinking it is Her voice we are hearing. The need for personal truth also demands respect for spiritual elders; to do less is to court psychic disaster. Our Wiccan elders are our link to power; it is through your spiritual parents that your power flows to you from your ancestor the earth.

If you are working with a partner or group, perhaps stop reading to share your thoughts and feelings about the ethics and laws of Wicca. This might feel awkward or silly. Remember: sometimes folks have nothing to say, but their listening is a contribution.

If you are working alone, perhaps write down your reactions. If you get nowhere, don't worry. Your effort will pan out, if not now, then later. Just do your best—even if that is staring at a blank page in your Book of Shadows for three minutes—and trust the results to the Gods.

The Heart of Darkness

A deep truth from the ancient Celtic culture is that the universe, including the Gods, ourselves, and an honorable moral system, is at heart dark. It is time to further explore the issues of darkness and polarities. Familiar elements from earlier lessons can now be presented better, in light of another vital part of the Faerie Faith: the heart of darkness.

The Celtic worldview is at heart dark: in the center of the universe is a dark heart. It is loving and beats with the pulse of the

Mother's rhythm. With a dark heart of love beating at the center of life itself, the Celt was not afraid of life's darker aspects, such as anger, enormous sexual appetite, intense desires for personal fulfillment, and the drive to survive. As a matter of fact, it was more than a lack of fear: a Celt understood darkness to be a *basis* of sound, virtuous, practical morality.

So a shaman does not see passion as something to fear or equate with violence. In the trailer for the movie version of Anne Rice's *Interview with the Vampire,* the voice-over said the film had passion, while the video portion showed Tom Cruise smashing a mirror in a destructive rage. Another absurd view of passion is also shown in film: passion is equated with obsessive sexual destructiveness. The bad woman stabs the nice man who scorns her. Oh, I forgot a crucial element: he deserves it because he really enjoyed sex for once in his life when he made love to her.

I reverently honor passion as a gift that God gives me, through which I am strongly impelled toward acts of self-love and community service, and which I enjoy for its own sake because passion makes life worth living.

Anger, in this culture, is often, at best, viewed as a necessary evil: "Oh, hang in, and eventually you will stop getting so angry." A shaman learns to see anger as a glory. There is an Indian goddess, Kali, who gets very angry. You don't want to cross her! When a grave injustice has been done, she gets quite mad about it.

As does any healthy person. Anger can be a wondrous driving force. Unless we are blinded by it, it guides us to right action and change in the world. Without healthy anger, we might be wimpy doormats who could not fight for our rights and for the rights of our children.

If you have ever seen a mother's dark anger when her children are threatened, you know what I am writing about. She is like a fury tending her young. And so she should be. The Goddess gave her the responsibility to take care of her children, and the anger sometimes to have the chutzpah to do so.

Yet over and over children, women, and men are told to tame that wild dark energy in themselves, that it is bad, to be ashamed of it, as if it were the cause of evil. In the name of such pseudo-morality we are taught to be doormats, wimps. Many people need serious healing from this abusive conditioning.

I do not write *doormats* or *wimps* to shame or denigrate those who do not know how to fight for what they want, or who have been crushed in the name of spirituality or mental health. For many years I was deeply ashamed of my passion and strength, until I was too crippled emotionally and spiritually to earn my living or live a life that offered me self-respect. I learned that if you are overcome by cultural abuse, it does not help to call yourself names, see yourself as lacking some special trait, or see everything as your own fault: "If only I would try harder this wouldn't have happened to me."

It is important not to shame yourself in any way. The fact is that we are talking about *injuries*, done to spirit, mind, and body, and what will heal such injuries is loving-kindness and compassion. Additionally, not everyone has the same opportunity to heal themselves. Pardon the clichés, but a black mother of three with no income may have less chance of attending self-help groups than a middle-class white single man.

I say *doormats* and *wimps* to make a forceful statement: much of what parades as guidance to spiritual and psychological health is a means to injure, maim, and cripple us in spirit and lifestyle, to turn us into wimpy doormats, milquetoast martyrs. Anger is seen as a sign of imbalance; witness, for instance, the revictimization of oppressed people who have a right to be angry because they are being treated poorly. "Don't get so upset, you take everything so seriously!"—when someone says that to you, the real message just might be "Could you lie down? I need to wipe my shoes off!"

People die from such injuries, out of an inability to fight for what they need. Recognizing all this, we can embrace its shamanic counterpoint: we each have the right and responsibility to do whatever is in our power, physically, spiritually, and politically, to heal ourselves from the wrongs done us. A shaman is a warrior.

I do not want to imply that we have a right to be thoughtless of others. For instance, healthy anger does not justify an outburst of rage or abuse. That, again, would be a false polarity: the dedicated political activist who passionately fights for human rights doesn't get to be thoughtless and abusive in the process. Such behavior is a *reaction* to an injustice. When you react, either by acting in a like manner, or by going to the opposite extreme, or through fearful immobility, you embody the same principle against which you rebel, for you are polarized.

As the Mother is dark hearted, so is the Lord. Just as we do not lessen the female by seeing her as a balancing complement to the male, we do not do the opposite. It is not the way of the Faerie shaman to see our God and Goddess as a balance to each other, God light and Goddess dark, God fierce and the Goddess nurturing, God aggressive and Goddess receptive. They are beings in their own right, who are in love.

Nor do I disparage a God of light, a dark Goddess, a fierce God, a nurturing Goddess. I worship the light and dark aspects of our male God with great and equal reverence. I find tremendous solace in our Mother. But I also find our God to be nurturing, and our Goddess to be bright! Both Gods have within them all potentials and personalities! They are endless in their possibilities.

Many Wiccan traditions worship a Goddess who is the embodiment of the "feminine" principles, and venerate a God who is the embodiment of the "male" principles. I support with a deep commitment the right to worship as one chooses, and to love and be loved by the Gods one has found by virtue of searching one's own heart and mind. Yet a novice who had not read these last few paragraphs could easily assume that Faerie shamans worship as do other pagans, and thus miss a vital gift of the Faerie Craft.

Rigid categorizing helps us lose sight of reality instead of taking a good look at things. Looking at what is really going on is vital to walking the Faerie path—and to happiness in plain old daily living. So, in embracing the dark gifts of life, I do not make less of the light. That again would be a reaction, a swing to the other extreme. Where would we be without the sun? And the brightness of my daughter's smile is just as important to me as her dark heart, for her sunny smile reflects her happiness. The light is also godly and moral in our understanding. Light and dark are each something unto themselves.

We, as reflections of the Gods, can know we are like them: "Male and female exist as something unto themselves, not to balance each other. They are two manifestations of the same thing. It is an illusion that they need to be brought together and balanced. They are each the expression of the same force, a complete force." (So said my teacher, Victor Anderson.)

If you are a forceful, dynamic woman, don't cast spells to instead be a gentle balance to masculinity. Be yourself. Any strength is feminine if a woman has it.

On the other hand, if you are a woman in love with a man who has a strong personality that you enjoy taking shelter in, do it. Do not allow notions of so-called balanced self-development to lead you from your true needs. The point is to be who you are—fierce, mellow, or both; competitive, easygoing, or both. Don't try to be an "idea" that has nothing to do with how people really are.

If you are a man looking for a woman with a fierce mother-dragon protectiveness, don't be embarrassed or think you should be just the same for her. Be the same only if you *are* the same. Otherwise, seek a woman's protectiveness.

I am not saying that any man or woman can avoid taking responsibility for his or her own life, but we need to know who we really are, and that includes knowing our true needs, so that we can do the best possible job of responsible living. If and when your being an unprotective type gets in your way, then you might need to change that. And magic is a great way to do it.

My examples about men and women in love portray principles that hold true for lesbian and gay couples, platonic relationships, office politics, and group dynamics. In the same way this society tell us that men have to be one way and women another, it also demands that if one person is a leader then the rest must be followers, as opposed to mutual leading. Or that if one person is enormously creative, the members of her family must be the support for that creativity to the exclusion of finding their own creative outlets. If someone has power of any kind, it is supposedly at the expense of the other folks who are present, rather than there being the possibility of a mutually empowering situation. The Gods are beings in their own right, not merely in relationship to one another. We, as their children, have the right to be who we are, and the need to strive toward that.

If you fall into conventional categories, I support you. I seek to destroy only the prison of convention, not its better aspect. For instance, leadership is an important service, providing organization, motivation, creative ideas about direction, and inspiring example. If you are a natural leader, be one! If you need a lot of leading, get it! As for my example of artists thoughtless of their families' needs, we all need any support possible for our creativity. I suggest only that you not give this support at the expense of your own goals. Once again, be who you are, love yourself for it, love others for their oddities, and realize you are a gift to the universe for being yourself!

I opened this section, "The Heart of Darkness," by saying that not only are the Gods and ourselves and our morals dark, but so is the universe itself. If our magic is constantly used to achieve balance, we are going against the laws of nature. Note the word *constantly*: though not the norm that it is usually considered to be by the Western mind, balance, being a part of the whole, does occasionally occur in nature, and is embraced by the Faerie shaman when actual or relevant as a goal.

I am not suggesting you put aside your common sense. When I am working hard (which is always—I've been too busy to check, but I think I've got a new roommate, and she's been here for about a month), I need to balance that with rest and recreation. And because I work constantly with people's pain, I need to balance that with a lighter perspective so that I don't become bitter and hateful toward the people who caused that pain. And because I am passionately committed to using my powers as a witch to help others (just call me Glinda the good witch), I need to balance that enthusiasm with laughter and quiet walks on the beach so I don't drive myself or others to distraction in trying to achieve my goals. Important aside: laughter is a perfect complement to almost any spiritual task, including fish or red meat.

Notice a cypress by the ocean: it achieves stability by leaning far away from the water. It is hardly balanced. Instead, it is *integrated,* and *in harmony* with itself and with all of nature. It is like the three souls after a Ha prayer. Integration, harmony, and whatever leaning I need to do in order to survive are ideal magical goals, not balance. Be like nature.

If you are lobbying for your rights in a job situation, you might need to integrate your anger with the grace and courtesy of a diplomat. Some see that as balance, but usually implicit in that belief is the notion that the anger in that situation must be squelched a bit, or be no more powerful than the courtesy. That is not always the case. No! Bad shaman! OK, this is not a shame-based religion. Sorry about that. Anyway, we need every bit of life force the Gods give us. It is a holy gift, not to be squandered.

The best fighter has grace and courtesy. A diplomat is a fighter for good relations between countries. And it is the full power of the diplomat's dark-spirited fighter's heart that harmonizes with and impels courtesy and grace, like a martial artist who moves as liquidly and as lethally as a venomous snake.

The Goddess wants us to love hard and fight hard. You can't do that and work toward a constant balance all the time. Nature doesn't attempt that, so why should you? Balance can make you a milquetoast pseudospiritual martyr. The path of the shaman is a warrior's path.

Yin/yang is a Chinese concept within natural philosophy. It is often misunderstood by the Western mind to mean a simple mechanical balance of light and dark, male and female, negative and positive, and so forth. Although the Chinese do work toward a balance, it is conceived as an ideal, not as a true goal—to truly achieve such a balance is seen by the Chinese as death!—and their definition of balance is different from ours. Chinese philosophy describes the whole world as two parts dynamically interlinked within the same whole. Within each part is the other, and the parts are considered not as polar opposites but as two aspects of the same thing. In your mundane and magical life, work toward your true goals and you will embody the heart of darkness.

Do the following rite now.

RITUAL
Dark Healing

This ritual helps you experience darkness as a loving force, then draws upon it to heal wounds that keep you from using your internal darkness—healthy passion, male aggressiveness, motivating competitiveness—to improve your life.

Step 1. Choose one way in which you have been shamed or made to feel guilty about your darkness. Perhaps you have a passion to paint and have been told that would be an irresponsible career choice. One needn't choose between passion and integrity. Or maybe you are embarrassed by your vehemence because you are a Hispanic person in a predominantly white workplace where fellow workers look at you funny when you become vehement about company policies that are unfair to the Hispanic community. Or maybe you are dark of color and have been told you are ugly. Pick only one such thing that you would like to heal from.

Step 2. Find any guilt and shame you have about your darkness that is associated with this incident.

Step 3. Close your eyes and make yourself comfortable.

Step 4. Focus on the darkness that you see when your eyes are closed.

Step 5. Imagine that darkness to be a night sky . . . then imagine you are surrounded on all sides with that sky, and that it extends as far as you can imagine.

Step 6. Sense this dark universe pulsing with the love of the Goddess's heart. Imagine all the parts of what I just said: not just a heart or Her heart, but the love of Her heart.

Step 7. Imagine that that loving pulse is a wave sweeping over you and through you, and that it fills you with her blessings.

Step 8. Holding this image as well as you can, focus on the guilt and/or shame that, in the first two steps of this rite, you chose to be healed of. Really get in touch with the guilt and/or shame, and any other connected injuries, so that you can show it to the Mother for healing. You might want to feel the wound as a tangible energy substance throughout your being.

Step 9. Imagine you feel the pulse of the Goddess's love continue to flow through you, and that it washes away your pain, guilt, shame, and other associated hurts.

Step 10. Now that the wound is cleansed, you can heal the injury. Imagine you feel the Goddess's love gently moving through your entire being. Visualize it soothing and healing you.

Step 11. Visualize this pulsing love continuing to flow through you as it fills you with Her blessings and makes you feel whole, happy, and proud of who you are.

Step 12. Focus on the darkness that you just naturally see when your eyes are closed.

Step 13. Open your eyes and stretch every part of your body. You needn't take more than a few minutes in all, but do stretch each part of your body just a bit. Then gently tap yourself from top to bottom with your palms. When you get to your face and head, use your fingertips.

Step 14. This ritual can make you very spacey. If you are going outside when you finish this lesson, make sure you are in touch with reality. In other words, if it's nighttime keep your street smarts about you; if you are driving, make sure you are not spaced out. If you are staying inside, make sure you are alert when doing things like cutting up vegetables for dinner. You might want to eat something after our visit to help you be less spaced out.

Most of the examples I used of following your dark morality—such as following your passion to paint—can be misunderstood, as can any moral tenet. So see each thing for what it is and do not get stuck in or hide behind models, thereby deluding yourself into immoral choices. Divorcing your unemployed wife and forgoing your financial commitment to your child, saying "I have to take care of myself by following my passion to paint," is callous selfishness. Decide what is moral according to what is really going on in your life.

Assignment

Read at least parts of this chapter again this week. The Craft is just what the word says: a craft. As such, it demands study. Reading something once is not always enough. Having gone through this week's lesson once, you know *of* it. Now I want you to *know* it. While one never knows any magical material until one uses it, sometimes the first step is studying.

For the Advanced Practitioner

This optional assignment is excellent for students at any level. To more fully explore how our society's concepts of darkness and polarity affect us, write out answers to the following questions.

1. What are examples of racist, sexist, man-hating, and just plain nonsensical uses of the terms *dark* and *darkness*? A clue: the greater proportion of the ways the words are used is pejorative. If you get stuck on this assignment, just start using sentences with these words in them. You will quickly have answered the question.

2. What polarities do you trust in? In what ways do they help you? Are there any ways you are trapped by these beliefs?

3. How has balance been a necessary spiritual and emotional goal for you?

4. How, on the other hand, have maxims about balance been a means by which you were told not to be your best self, and not to live in freedom and integrity?

The Process of Change

Students might find themselves wavering about finishing a fifteen-week training. It is a normal, understandable response to feel overwhelmed when we are about to finish a project. If you have ever gotten a college degree, or finished the last rehearsals for a performance, or even put the finishing touches on a meal, you have experienced those last-nine-yards jitters. At such a time you might think, "There is no way I can do all the work involved to finish this project" or "I don't want to do this anyway." Well, the fact is, maybe you *don't* want to do this anyway. But I strongly suggest you wait until you have accomplished the work before you decide whether that is true. Just hang in a few more weeks, and *then* decide if you should have finished.

When I was wrapping up my college degree—which took twenty years, by the way—I called a friend in tears. I was going crazy trying to finish my thesis on time. I wailed, "I didn't go back to school for the degree in the first place, and now I am going nuts trying to get it! I only returned to school to get reinvolved in the community!" Let me go a bit further back in time:

Developing the curriculum for The Third Road has been a life's work, and, hermit though I love to be, I felt isolated in the first years. Although many people do research and development, they were not fellowship for me. In earlier years, I had received most of my college credits in the arts, in nonacademic classes. And now, in the same vein, mine was not a science of the laboratory or library; picture the fairy-tale cliché of the lone wizard, sequestered for years in his stark high tower, bent over his own odd scribbling that records the effects of the bizarre chants he has created, as he tries to figure out how to get rid of the pesky little spirit that his latest spell—which he made up himself; it was supposed to improve one's musical talent—called up, and how to polish that spell so that the next time it only creates better musicians and no unwanted guests appear. That's kind of how I went about it, but without as dramatic a dwelling. No wonder I felt isolated. If you are tracking my chronology, this was during the many years I was in constant trance.

So, in 1987, I went to college mostly for camaraderie, however unlike mine any college's idea of scholarship would be. The Gods were looking out for me: under the care of a loving and eccentric professor, I continued creating The Third Road unhampered by academic parameters. I have nothing against academia, but there are some things you just can't create according to academic expectations. My work is one of them. Then the college said it would let my odd labors be my thesis! My Gods have a sense of humor. A lot of the rest of my credits were gained through other nonacademic projects, such as writing ritual music.

My friend convinced me to finish my degree, so I applied my magic to it: I prayed to the Goddess, asking that She help me finish. I also searched for any underlying fears, doubts, or resentments that could keep me from completing things. And I am very proud of the certificate on my wall, partially because I was willing to go a zillion years, and then the last nine yards, to get it. It also gave me confidence in my own odd ways.

If you have blocks that might keep you from finishing your training, you can cleanse yourself of them. Examples of things that might need to be cleared away include a fear of success, a belief that successful people lose the love of those around them, and anger that no one is going to finish the job for you. You might also want to ask a friend for some encouragement. Taking these measures can avoid a wild-goose change, which is a common way to defeat oneself at the last minute. This is not the time to ask, "Should I become a nun?" or to tell yourself, "Maybe I should break up with George!"—no matter now restless you feel.

Healthy Spirituality Means Striving for the Good Things in Life

Casting Spells for the Good Things in Life

By doing psychic readings, I often help clients through a crisis. Afterward, there's often a moment in which my client starts to squirm, and asks in an embarrassed, apologetic voice, "Do you see anything about maybe me finding a lover? And how about my family? Will they stay healthy? And will I have enough money this next year?"

I am sad to see how ashamed clients get because they are concerned about their mundane affairs. They've been taught that we're not supposed to care about ourselves or our material affairs. We are raised to think that it's bad to want nice things for ourselves. And as spiritual seekers, we're supposedly meant to completely transcend such concerns.

Yet it is in the arenas of love, money, family, work, and sex that we really learn how to be spiritual. Spirituality in a void is useless. Although selfless sacrifice is a vital part of any spiritual path, and we will explore it in depth in a later lesson, it is only one part of right living. To walk The Third Road® means combining apparent opposites: the ancient Celts knew that another focal point of spirituality is gaining a warm bed, a good meal, and loving companionship, sexuality included. Applying spirituality to our mundane affairs doesn't mean that we should be pseudospiritual martyrs, making sacrifices that leave us miserable and no good to anyone including ourselves.

The Mother gave us life so that we could honor Her beautiful gift by living to the fullest. This is the true goal of spiritual journeying—to be fully human. Only then can we fully tap into our enormous ability to love and give to others.

I'm not endorsing heartless living, or irresponsible sexuality. I work hard to be giving and courteous, I'm devoted to my loved ones, and I hope I am responsible as to how my sexuality affects others. But if I were tied up by guilt so that I allowed myself no earthly joys, I would have no reason to live. I might end up in a permanent drunken stupor instead of living a useful life as a spiritual, loving person. (Besides, I hate alcohol. I'm not morally against it. It's fine if you like it. But I can't see those pretty pink elephants when I drink. I see spirits only if I stay stone-cold sober.)

All this is to say that magic is about being human. And casting spells for the good things in life is part of that—spells for money, a nice home, a new car, and so on. Celtic magic is live magic, magic that you can apply to your daily life.

Otherwise magic has no point. Yes, it's fun to do rituals and it feels good—in a way that is enough of a reason to practice magic—but if we're not using it to live well and to love well, hey, maybe it's no better than going to mass on Sunday, then sinning all week long. Don't think that it is "unspiritual" to cast a spell to bring you goodies; you'll miss a spiritual concept of *enormous importance*: we are worthy of all the good things in life we want. Any other way of looking at it can be unhealthy self-deprecation, pseudospirituality, and spiritual arrogance. Summary, class: it's important and spiritual to use your magic to bring good things into your life.

If you disagree with some of my premises, so do I. I will argue the flip side in another chapter, so I hope you take my comments in stride.

During the rest of this week's visit, you will learn a basic all-purpose rite called The Spell Itself that can be used to gain life's goodies, as well as relevant techniques and knowledge.

Visualization Techniques

Without its having been pointed out, a good number of exercises to develop visualization skills have already been given in this book. Now you get to deepen your ability. The farther you walk on the road to Faerie, the more you deepen both this skill and the richness of its rewards.

In The Spell Itself, a witch shapes reality through visualization: as you see it, so it becomes! Thought is a form of energy, and energy is the same thing as matter. So thought, or concept, becomes energy becomes manifestation!

Here are some keys to successful visualization:

Plan your visualization carefully before actually starting the spell.

Below you will learn what needs to be considered in this planning.

Use any of your five senses that are relevant, not just the visual. For instance, were you to do a spell for a steak, you would not only see the steak but also smell it, taste it, and feel its juices on your tongue as you eat. (I enjoy it when vegetarians squirm at this example.)

Use your feelings of emotions. Imagine you are feeling happy and content because of the steak or tofu you are eating; imagine the pleasure it gives you.

Feelings are power, energy! Think of the impact a gospel choir has, as opposed to the effect of a bone-dry sermon: the choir uplifts, empowers, whereas mere talking may do no more than bore. Feelings energize magic.

Another reason you use your feelings is that emotions are part of being spiritually whole; they are not contrary to being Godlike, they are an echo of God! If I feel love for you, it is the love of the Goddess I am feeling. This is another reason the gospel music feeds you, maybe even changes you for the better. The joy in music reflects God's joy.

This use of emotions in a spell is another ramification of magic's being an art that requires the practitioner to bring her whole being to the rite.

Finally, you use your emotions in your visualization because they greatly further precision and accuracy in spellcrafting.

Be precise in your visualization. I had two friends who did a spell for the perfect apartment. They visualized the right rent, the right number of rooms, two bathrooms, a landlord who allowed children, convenient public transportation, and so on; they had a list a mile long. But they left one thing out: location. They found the perfect apartment, but it was in a nasty part of town, by train tracks that carried noisy freight trains past them continually.

I had another friend who never had any dates. So she did a spell in which she imagined herself surrounded by gorgeous men. That was way too vague; she was also looking for work at that time, and ended up finding a job as a receptionist in a health spa. She was surrounded by gorgeous men all right, but none of them were for *her!*

Be as absolutely specific as you can, and visualize every detail you can think of that might be relevant. However, this need for precision can be misleading. It is easy to believe from this that the Godself is a god of mathematics. But the Godself is a part of you. And it is loving, not exacting. Precision is important because you are developing skills in a science, but don't be neurotic and take that too far; put together the best spell you can, and your Godself will do its best with that. Trust the God within you.

See the things you desire as happening NOW. So if you are doing a spell for a steak, imagine that you see, taste, feel, experience it right here and now.

Leave others out of your visualization (with the obvious exceptions—like doing a protection spell on your wife, should you use your imagination in that spell). This might seem extreme, but visualizations are not mere images, they actually shape reality. To move someone about in a visualization is to move them about as if they were a pawn on a chessboard. We have no right to treat a person that way, even if we cherish them and are concerned about their welfare.

You also keep others out of your visualizations because, as stated earlier, there are specific skills needed (skills that you have not yet learned) when doing a spell on someone other than yourself.

It might seem quite difficult to avoid putting another person into your visualization. Yet it is much harder to deal with the consequences of having done so! Again, don't be neurotic; if, after dialoguing with a friend or elder, you see no way around it, it might be fine in that particular case. For instance, if you want to talk to your boss with confidence, there is nothing wrong with building a picture of that.

Visualize the results you want to achieve, not the means. A new client came to me for a reading, hoping to find a solution to his depression. He had already done a spell in which he visualized a great deal of money coming to him, because he felt that having the money would improve his attitude. But when the spell proved successful, and the money actually manifested, it was a disruptive influence on his relationship with his wife. They argued about the best way to spend it, and his spiritual well-being was in worse shape than it had been in the first place. In other words, the spell backfired.

The Goddess told him, through me, that he was turning to money because he had forgotten that happiness can come only from within. The Goddess revealed that his unconscious guilt over having cheated on his wife—yes, I psychically knew that without his telling me, that's what psychic readers are for—had dug a hole in his self-respect until he felt that life and he himself were worthwhile only with cash in hand.

I taught him a cleansing ritual to wash away such a negative belief. (When doing the money spell he had neglected a pre-ritual purification, since he had never heard of one. Had he done one, he might have realized then that he was misled in doing a money spell.) I also suggested that making things right with his wife was a necessary purification before attempting a spell on his depression and, in fact, might of itself cure his low feelings. And it did to a great extent, after which he cast a spell focusing on the results—

freedom from depression—not the means, trusting the Gods to know the correct means: he visualized himself having serenity, wholeness, and self-worth. The spell bore fruit in the form of a realization: he didn't want to be like his own father, for whom he lacked respect. Instead, he wanted to cut back on his sixty-hour-a-week job to spend more time with his young children.

Below, I will tell you two exceptions to this rule. There are other exceptions as well, but it is still an excellent rule of thumb. When at all possible, use it.

The example given above is one of changing your emotional state. However, the rule holds true for spells to affect your external life. For instance, if you want a car, picture yourself the happy owner of a car, as opposed to suddenly having the money to purchase one.

When doing a spell, always add, "I pray this spell be for the highest good of all." In other words, during the visualization you pray that your wishes cause harm to no one—an obvious exception to the above rule since it deals with how your wish is attained. There are many variations upon this theme in folk tales and science fiction. One such variation is the man who is madly in love with a rich woman and so prays for money because he wants to marry her. His prayer is sadly answered, for the woman dies, and though she leaves him all her money, his life is totally impoverished by this tragic event.

Always close the door on your spell. This is the other exception to choosing the ends over the means. (I have Cora Anderson to thank for the phrase *closing the door*.) I can best convey what this rule means by summing up what might happen when one creates a visualization.

Let's say I want a new job. Over the course of an hour or the course of a month I would work out a visualization. With a smaller spell, or if you are a quicker thinker, this planning may take only minutes. Reviewing the visualization techniques listed here to decide the best possible visualization for the goal I want, I might plan an image of myself as happy, working a job I enjoy, with coworkers and a boss I get along with, in a work environment with sunlight and good ventilation, at a salary I desire, for the number of hours per week I desire, with potential for advancement, and so on until I have a detailed, precise visualization of my ideal goal.

Then I would plan how to "close the door" by imagining every possible booby trap that might be inherent in my goal. In other words, I would try to think of all the things that could go wrong in my life both while I was trying to get the job and once I had gotten it.

My troubleshooting might result in the following list of things I wouldn't want to happen: losing my present job, thereby having to endure poverty while looking for another; unnecessary anxiety while looking for work; and the new, wonderful job lasting only a few weeks.

Then, when I actually use the visualization in my spell, I would imagine such mishaps being avoided. In other words, I "close the door" on those possible problems. This can be done by imagining a door closing on them, or however else you wish to imagine your list of possible pitfalls left out of the weaving of your goal. Always close the door on your spell.

Do not let my precise instructions about visualization make you morbidly fearful about doing spells, or run from doing what you desire. Cautions are a part of any science, and care must be taken with any power one wields, whether it is political, physical, or magical. And remember, no matter how hard you try to do *any-*

thing in this life, your best efforts are far from perfect. Victor once told me, "The Gods take no perfect sacrifice." Just be as vigorous as you, personally, can be in your application of these lessons, and trust that the Gods will look after the results.

Choosing Your Magical Goal

What is it you need in your life? Abundance? Self-love? A new apartment? A wonderful new dress? A sturdy suitcase for a trip you're planning? A new bedspread? Peace of mind? A VCR? Here are some guidelines for deciding.

Sometimes the best idea is to choose a small goal, a smaller step in your life, over a large one. It might take less energy to pull off a small spell. Also, growth happens at a speed that's often slower that we think correct; don't try to make changes you're not ready for yet. You can always do more later. Having taken this training, you have a lifetime of tricks up your sleeve!

Simplicity is at the heart of the Faerie Faith. Often it is the best policy to choose a very simple goal. There is a purity to the simple spell that brings peace and power, and opens up possibilities. And avoids psychic mishaps. Again, you can always do more spells later. You're a witch! (If you want to call yourself one.)

It is also a good idea to choose a goal that's more likely. A spell to find a job is more likely to succeed than one to find a million dollars on the street, because the former is a more likely event, more part of the flow. However, don't let this notion limit you; miracles happen every day. If miracles happen as often as that, then miracles must be a very likely thing. Which means you can make magic for some pretty "unlikely" things and they just might happen. (Does this paragraph seem one big contradiction? Why am I not bothered by that?)

When choosing a goal for something important like a new place to live, you might want to carefully evolve your goal over a long period of time. I might take two to four weeks to write a list of everything I want in an apartment, because I want it to be the right place for me. This "simmering" of a goal can be a lovely process, because in it we get to dream about exactly what we want. *Mmm!* That dreaming might add power to the spell when you finally do it.

Sometimes it is hard to decide what you want or need. Perhaps you don't know whether to take a big step, a small step, a simple step, a side step. Or perhaps you are a hairdresser wondering if you want to work at a different salon. Try divination for spiritual guidance.

You can divine what the intent of your spell should be through a variety of approaches, such as scrying, reading tarot cards, or any meditation form from which you receive guidance or which gets the cobwebs out of your head so that you can think and intuit clearly. Divination also includes walking on the beach and listening to the waves until your head is clear, or the beach or the waves speak to you. Or pray for guidance, and then be open to however the guidance comes. Or use your own form of divination—whatever way it is you use to pick information out of what seems thin air. The prayer "Grant Me Will" might also help you decide.

Back to the hairdresser example. Through divination, you may be told, "Nope, no spell for a new job yet. You only broke up with your boyfriend last week. Until you get over him, you've too many inner blocks for a job spell to work. Do a healing spell before any career magic. Besides, you're so upset about the breakup, you're not up to a job hunt yet. You will be overwhelmed by making too many changes all at once in your life. You should also take a class to polish your job skills so that you can work in a more upscale salon."

Once you are more secure in your new single life and in your job skills, you can do a spell to find the perfect salon. Obviously, from my example, knowing what one wants is not only about choosing a goal. Even when you have chosen a goal, you also have to know whether it should be an immediate priority or if there is other magic you need to do first.

Once you have chosen your goal, plan its visualization.

The Spell Itself

The Spell Itself, central to Celtic shamanism, and one of the most powerful bits of magic that exists, will come easily to you now, after having made twelve visits with a shaman. It is basically none other than the Ha prayer that is done every morning and before every rite. Though The Spell Itself will have some differences, you will recognize, and be quite used to doing, much of what The Spell Itself requires.

RITUAL
The Spell Itself

Make sure you use The Magic Formula.

Step 1. Ask the fetch to store the manna that you are about to take in.

Step 2. Breath in power just as you have been doing in the Ha prayer, taking it in sets of four. If needed, use your powers of visualization to do so, perhaps visualizing that manna is all around you and that you draw it in with every breath you take.

Step 3. As you are taking in this energy, visualize the goal you have decided upon—owning a VCR, having a healthy body, taking a vacation in Paris, or whatever else you have chosen. As you do this, pray that what you visualize comes to pass.

Step 4. Continue with this until you are filled with power, your visualization is strong and true, and your prayer is made.

Step 5. Ask the fetch to divide the manna.

Step 6. See your Godself as a blue sphere above you. Making the ritual gesture of blowing upward, imagine (visualize) that some of the energy you have taken in flows up to your Godself.

Step 7. Be open to whatever gift your Godself sends you. You might receive reassurance that your wish will be fulfilled, or courage to strive for what you want, or guidance about practical steps you can take to reach your magical goal. Who knows what wonderful thing you might receive at that moment!

Step 8. Live the spell.

A woman moved into a new home in a rural area. She was taught by her new neighbor, a very old and wise witch who lived next door, a spell to make the flames go out should her new home catch fire. Then the old woman handed her young new neighbor the phone number of the local fire department. The young woman said, "But doesn't the spell work?" and was told, "Yes, but not without the fire department helping."

Whatever you have made magic to create, follow up your spell by creating it in the more "mundane" sense as well. If it was a spell for a new job, you might write your résumé. If it was a spell to love yourself better, you might discuss with your therapist what's blocking your self-love, or ask a few friends about ways they are nice to themselves. If it was a spell for peace of mind, you might go for a peaceful walk on the beach instead of pursuing your usual hectic pace.

Now, in addition to all the spells you have already learned, you have an almost all-purpose basic spell through which you can pursue almost anything you need. What bounty the Gods give us!

Assignment

1. Before you apply what you have learned, give this chapter a quick scan, and spend a few minutes on any sections that jump out at you.

2. Choose a wonderful goal for a spell. Think of an inner trait you would like to have or some wonderfully mundane thing you would want. A new armoire? Excellent. A pair of fourteen-karat-gold hoop earrings? Yum! The courage to attend medical school? Great! Then, go for it—cast The Spell Itself! A reminder: do not use The Spell Itself on people other than yourself. Don't push yourself; if it takes a month or two to do the assignment, that's fine.

Do not make the goal one of purification. Though The Spell Itself can be used that way, for the sake of this assignment don't do it. Save that for any other time. Endless purification, unless it is coupled with empowerment, becomes a tearing down. If you bleach a dirty piece of fabric to cleanse it, that is grand. But there comes a time to stop bleaching or the fabric weakens and eventually will rip and fray.

So it is with ourselves: if the only focus you have in your magic is on cleansing, you are falling prey to the belief that you just can't ever be good enough, as if you were innately bad. Your endless cleansings tear away at yourself. There comes a time to stop bleaching, and dye the cloth and make a garment out of it.

My metaphor of the bleached cloth is not perfect. Shamanism is an endless series of cleansings. But we do not believe in innate evil, or that we have to be perfect. The work simply needs to get done. It's kind of like taking a shower after work. And we are not as likely to fall into false beliefs about our endless purification if there is also empowerment going on.

Part of empowerment is casting spells for positive attributes. If you lack courage, cast a spell for it. If you want peace of mind, cast a spell for it. Use The Spell Itself for whatever you truly desire to be!

Empowerment is also casting spells for the good things in life. Otherwise we get caught in a pseudospiritual mode, thinking that spirituality is something other than embracing the gifts the Goddess has given us. We are here to enjoy our lives—and I mean that in the most mundane way it can be taken. Cora once said that magic is what the farmers use to make the crops grow. The goal of spiritual living includes a good meal, a warm bed, and a loving partner in that bed. And without these good things in life we might become hollow and bitter burnouts—the Goddess gifts us Her grace and sustenance through the love of other people and through mundane pleasures. I wish you luck with your spell!

The Process of Change

When a student asks me, "Why do you think I've had a lot of bad luck lately?" there are a million reasons I could give. Answers can range from "Don't blame luck because no one wants to be around you lately, you lost your job, and you're not having any fun. You have been really impatient, judgmental, and uncooperative with everyone" to "The spirits in your new apartment are not very nice."

Even if you don't know the reason for your problems, doing a psychic housecleaning, protection, and/or blessing can solve them or greatly improve your situation.

Another solution is The Spell Itself. During step 3—in which you breathe in manna—instead of doing a visualization, ask to be shown the source of your bad turn of fortune. When your Godself showers back to you its gifts, you might be given guidance about your poor luck. Or you might receive direction later, through any number of sources—an intuition, a comment from a therapist, a TV show you are watching.

Sometimes events occur in our lives that we do not realize are connected to our magic. You gain a higher caliber of friends. Or your daughter has nightmares. Your husband becomes more attentive. A serious accident happens. Or a serious illness mysteriously disappears. If you are puzzled by a bad turn of events in your life, analyze your magical and spiritual practices to see if there is a relation—perhaps by leafing through this book—or use The Spell Itself for guidance about a possible relation.

Bad luck aside, The Spell Itself can be used to obtain guidance about any life situation. Instead of praying for insight about luck, ask for guidance about any situation. For instance, you are dating a new guy and can't decide if you want to keep seeing him. Use The Spell Itself. While you are breathing in manna, ask for guidance about whether to continue seeing him. Right after you send the manna to your Godself, your Godself might say that you need to date the fellow a few more times before deciding. Or several days after you have done the rite, a friend might point out that this guy is a true peach and you're just afraid of commitment.

A Cup of Love

The Love Spell

If you would like, forgo using The Magic Formula to open the rest of our lessons. Once you have used it over and over, it is not needed as consistently. In the next lesson I will explain why, when I explain when and how The Magic Formula is needed.

It is the next step in your training to read this lesson, whether you intend to cast the love spell right after our visit or never. You will gain basic shamanic knowledge.

Love and sex are at the heart of creation. They are at the center of life, and are the pulse of the Mother's deep caring for us. Love and sex are the binding of the atom, the gravity of the earth, the force that created all things and that continues to create the universe every day. The mysteries of sex are at the heart of Celtic shamanism, and love is the greatest power of all.

These are not metaphors—love really is what makes the world

go round. Truly an immense driving force. It can be the most joyous healing magic or the deadliest, most misguided use of power. To ensure that your love spells produce the former and not the latter, this lesson will contain numerous cautions and special considerations about love spells, and I will teach a special love spell instead of suggesting you use The Spell Itself.

There isn't much that impacts a person more than romance, for good or for bad. The care that goes into your mundane dealings with matters of the heart must go into spells. All the confusions and complexities of romance, all the potentials for disaster, are just as operable on a psychic level as they are in your regular life.

The fact that love is the heart of all matter also makes a love spell the happiest, most natural, and most sacred spell. I said in an earlier lesson that a witch revels in power—dances in the rainstorm, so to speak. So have *makahu*—a healthy fear/respect for power—follow the instructions as given, and dance in the rain!

There is an additional reason for my cautions and considerations.

Though all sex and love touches the heart of the mysteries, I am going to teach you a specially potent spell. Applying all your lessons to a powerful love rite not only is a fun, sexy, juicy way to use a lot of what you've learned, but also seems a fitting way to really drive home to you that a witch's spirituality is down-to-earth.

This spell will deal with all the ins and outs and details of romance, until bit by bit you will have built a song of love that sweeps across the universe, sings to the stars, and carries back to you the magic of true love. Having done this training, you are ready for a love spell like this one.

The following spell is not done with a specific person in mind.

If Jane is the person you want and Jane is the right one for you, and you do this spell, which asks God Herself to choose the right person for you, Jane will come a-knocking. But if you do the spell on Jane, you might push Jane away for good.

This love spell is fine to do if you are involved. It will improve your relationship. In fact, your sweetie and you can both do it.

Don't adapt this spell any more than you would the others I have given you. Jane running away and the subsequent heartbreak are mild compared with what could possibly go wrong. A healthy fear of and respect for power might be doubly important with a love spell.

The goal of this spell is to create true love and romance in its full implications, including a powerful and sexually fulfilling relationship. As a matter of fact, the oil used in the spell acts like a psychic perfume that says, "Mmm, I want some good sex!" The red bag or cloth in the spell helps you be in touch with that pulsing sexual beat that is in all of creation.

Ritual: The Cup of Love—A Love Spell

This spell can also be a powerful healing in the area of sex and love, and offers deeper insights into this very important part of living and paganism.

The Cup of Love consists of three separate rites, each done at least a week apart. This lets the power simmer on the psychic burner, making the spell work correctly and powerfully.

Since romance seems to cloud the mind and heart, it might be easy to forget that love magic needs all the considerations that other spells do. Be aware of your usual spellcrafting considerations—such as knowing what your true will is, and being aware of ethics. In the same vein, the ethical issues I will touch on in regard to love spells are useful when doing other spells given in this book.

FIRST RITE
The Cleansing of the Vessel

Part 1: Questions to Ask Yourself

Cupid lets loose an arrow, and lo, it's a comedy of errors. The usually polite man blurts out horrific, embarrassing suggestions. The usually assertive businesswoman acts like a shy, nervous schoolgirl. The enormous power of sex doesn't always help.

Sometimes, there is no comedy. The caring, sensitive kindergarten teacher becomes jealous and cruel. And the most moral person lets ethics fly out the window because she can't stop herself, or just doesn't know better. Instead of becoming a vessel of love, one can become a chalice of insecurity and discord, or even hate. This first rite makes you a fit vessel, one that can hold love. Love will flow easily and fully into you from a beloved, and you will be a channel of that same love for another person. You may also become more respectful of your needs and those of another person, and more fully enjoy a mate.

Answer the following questions to discover what stands in the way of your being filled with love and the joy of sex. Having done similar work earlier, you are ready to go deeper. Don't be put off by so many questions: only some will be relevant. Read them all, for your education as a witch.

After answering the questions, you will do a purification ritual to make you a clean cup, ready to be filled with love. It might help to write down your answers so that they are right there in front of you when you do the cleansing. Take as long as you need to answer these questions, whether that is an hour or a month.

Do you consider yourself unworthy of love? If so, why? Remember that we are all lovable.

Do you think that having someone in your life means that you won't have to be responsible for your own life? If so, you will be praying not for a mate but for a keeper.

What beliefs, fears, and behaviors have kept you from fulfilling experiences with someone in the past?

Do you believe it is wrong to strongly want sexual fulfillment? I love sweets, but sugar makes me very ill, so I never eat it. Wanting sweets is not a sign of being a bad person; it is perfectly reasonable to want the stuff, it tastes great! I simply can't act on that desire. In the same vein, I can have healthy sexual desire for a man, but if he's inappropriate—in my case, someone other than my boyfriend, with whom I have a monogamous relationship—it's not a good idea to act on that desire.

Pseudo-attraction can also happen. There is an amethyst used in this spell, which gives you freedom from desperately seeking love because you don't love yourself. Or from mistaking a drive to self-destruction for the God-given healthy and powerful drive for companionship. Many people know that one—choosing a fickle and cruel person to fixate on because deep down you are being driven to the abuse that person can offer. There are many variations on pseudo-desire.

Upon learning this, my student Janet promptly announced that she would leave the amethyst out because she wanted a relationship that was powerful. And I answered, "Of course you do!

And powerful love and powerful sex are not gained by compulsion. Compulsion is not the same as healthy lust and the compelling urge for romance."

On the flip side of the same coin, healthy, hearty lust might be mistaken for compulsion because nature, in its demand that we do our best to be happy, can really push us sometimes! But real passion comes from self-respect, randiness, and a need to give. A compulsion, though easily mistaken for the force of true love, is driven by an emptiness that no one but you yourself can fill, and is fueled by low self-esteem, lack of self-nurturance, and addiction.

An important aside: when I use the word *lust*, a friend of mine comments, "Ugh!" Lust for most folks implies sexuality without moral restraint, resulting in destructive irresponsibility. That's not really sex, though. It's cruelty and hate. Fulfilling sex that is *truly* unbridled can be achieved only through compassion and ethics. And that is what I mean by lust, so that I always remember that a pure and kind heart makes for the best time between the sheets—or on the floor—and that sexual freedom is not the same thing as irresponsibility.

What manipulative thoughts need you be cleansed of? You might be puzzled at this question, saying, "Why should Francesca ask this? I am a nice person."

You may be the nicest person in the world, but I was taught, and have found it to be true, that one must always examine oneself about this issue before casting a love spell. Romance is one of the most dangerous arenas of life in which to manipulate someone. Search yourself and you will almost certainly find at least a bit of desire to force the issue onto someone. It's only natural.

A Hawaiian saying goes, "If you can make love, you can make hate." Romance is just as tricky in the magical realm as it is on the mundane. Luckily, the ethical use of magic can help us better navigate the rocky shores of our love life, and even prevent damaging behavior.

Magically forcing someone to want you is somewhat akin to psychic rape: no one can make another person really want someone. It is an injury that will rebound threefold, even were you to think, "Well, once they have slept with me, they will like it." That's what a rapist or child molester says.

Very nice people who have never done any magic have come to me in great grief over harm they have done in their love life. The subtleties of human relationships make it easy to seriously hurt others with the best of intentions. It is only logical that the same grief can be caused magically, yet it is easy to forget that the same drive and subtleties come into play when you cast a spell; you yourself are the primary magical tool, so all these things affect your magic. Free from coercion and manipulation, your relationship can be like the wind: powerful in its freedom.

Do you feel you need romance no matter what it costs you? In an extreme version of this, a person might be so afraid of being single that he can't say no to unprotected sex and risks AIDS. In less extreme cases, people settle for mediocre relationships because they are afraid to risk waiting for the right person to come along.

Review the writing you did about sex in our ninth visit. It might give you clues as to what else needs to be cleansed.

Search your soul, asking yourself any other questions that might reveal your blocks to romance, for only you can really know.

Special Questions for Heterosexual Women

All the special-interest questions should be read by everyone, as part of your lesson in witchcraft and because questions appear there that can be adapted, or used as is, by folks not in the special-interest group.

Do you think love means you have to give up your own career or needs?

Do you fear that because you are a strong woman, or a tall woman, or a successful career woman (fill in the blank), you are doomed to loneliness?

Do you have unfair expectations of a man? For instance do you expect a man to know what you want in bed without being told? Do you think it is written in stone that a man has to pay your way whether or not he is better off than you financially? Unrealistic expectations block the real gifts a man might offer you.

Do you blame men for all your problems? It is kind of silly to want a man of your own if you think men are no good.

Sexism kills women, spiritually and physically, and should in no way be made light of. Women are subject to every kind of brutality, at a statistical rate that can be called nothing other than warfare. But maleness is not the criminal; the male is an aspect of the divine Mother, a sacred, loving reflection of Her own sacredness and love. The criminal is patriarchy: an injured maleness, a twisted parody of male divinity.

I am in no way suggesting that a woman adopt a Pollyanna attitude or pretend false forgiveness. If you have been deeply injured by men, you can be open and loving to them only when you have healed your injuries. Don't fake love. It gives you indigestion. Admit, and perhaps even embrace, your anger, your fear, and, if need be, your hate. It is only once we have faced and validated those things in ourselves, and gotten power from them, that we can find the love in ourselves.

It is perfectly reasonable to be angry at sexist men. Anger is a gift the Mother has given you. It is even perfectly reasonable to find yourself angry at all men. Let's face it, that's a very human reaction in a sexist society. But such justifiable anger does not mean that it is also justifiable to target all men for one's anger.

And one has to *do* something about that anger if one wants to be a loving companion. You have learned lots of magic; this might be a chance to thumb through this book looking for a ritual that is just right. If extensive work is needed, you might consider therapy, or ongoing guidance from a shaman. See the listing of resources in appendix 2.

Men, you might need to cleanse yourself of any unhealthy blame you place on every last man for all the problems of the world. If you are to let love in, you need to see yourself as worthy of it. And if you are gay, some of that blame and anger will fall on your beloved.

Special Considerations for Men, Gay or Straight

Do you think it's wrong to be passionate? Men are told: "You can follow your passion and do what you want, or you can be a responsible loving partner. You have to choose." That's nonsense. Love is not a trap. A man needn't give up his freedom in exchange for the yoke of responsibility.

Self-love and passion for life fill a man with the drive and kindness needed to be responsible to those he loves. It is far easier to work at something if we have passion for it.

Do you think you are not tall enough, strong enough, successful enough (fill in the blank) to win love? Men are told that their worth is measured by the amount of money they earn, the car they drive, the size of their penis, and other criteria that have little to do with masculinity, desirability, and immanent value. God is in you, right here and right now, and you are worthy by that standard, not by some standard set in TV advertisements and romance novels.

What sexist views do you hold? This is relevant to gay men. Gay partnering can fall into sexist patterns. After all, your mom and dad were your role models.

Are you saying, "Gee, I'm not sexist. What is she talking about? I'm a nice guy!" Sexism is subtle, and has been drummed into every man alive today, built into men's modes of survival, communication, giving and receiving love, sexuality, and spirituality. You might be the sweetest guy in the world, but in an ancient shamanic culture anyone who had been through what you have been through would have received years of healing rites to free him of these chains that bind not only women but you yourself.

After a lifetime of brainwashing, all men and women who are conscious and caring will be working on their own sexism—and racism and classism and . . . —until the day they die.

To have a relationship that is sexy and has dignity, look at yourself and sexism, whether you feel you need to or not. If you are to draw on the power of this rite safely and effectively, this is a must—even if you are one of those guys who were on the vanguard of the feminist movement in the late 1960s. Victor used to tell me, "Just because you took a shower on Thursday doesn't mean you don't need one today!"

When doing ritual, there are certain aspects of your life that must be examined to see if they need cleansing, whether you feel the need or not. For example, in a love spell or a spell to protect others, one must examine oneself for a tendency toward manipulation. Search yourself. If you find nothing, great! If you do, once cleansed, you will flow with a fully potent power that a very lucky person will recognize and desire.

Just to get you started, here are a few questions about sexism.

Do you respect assertiveness from your mate only when you want it, as opposed to its just being a part of daily living?

Do you expect all of your nurturance to come from women? A man needs and deserves nurturance from himself, women, and other men. Any other expectation makes the love spell that a straight man sends out into the universe a request not for love but for a baby-sitter. And when a gay man can allow only women to nurture him, he can accept no nurturance from his relationship.

If your head is filled with what a partner should and shouldn't be, you might not be able to recognize it when the Goddess sends you someone, and thus miss a love with gifts that far surpass any notion you may have come up with.

Gay men, do you think you are the only gay man who wants to settle down into a real relationship? Do you know how many times I have heard that?

Special Considerations for Lesbians and Gay Men

Do you have shame, anger, or fear about your emotional and sexual desires for the same sex?

Do you fear rejection from family, friends, and associates because of your sexual preference? This is a valid fear. I am afraid to jump out of a fifth-story window. I will not do a purification ritual about it. Homophobia is real, and each person with homosexual desires must choose for himself or herself whether or not to act on those desires. But if you have chosen to act on them, yet cannot do so because of fears of societal rejection, you might have to cleanse yourself of such fears.

Do you believe that a commitment between same-sex partners just can't last?

Women, do you feel inadequate because you cannot make love to a woman in the same way a man can? Don't. A man can't make love to a woman in the same way you can. Men, adapt this question. And the next.

Are you in any way running from men by being lesbian? I am in no way suggesting that lesbianism per se is a reaction to men. Women love each other for the sake of loving each other—period. It has nothing to do with men. Nevertheless, sometimes the cliché is true: a heterosexual woman runs from her fears and disappointments into the arms of a woman whom she will not really appreciate or be kind to. Or a sincere lesbian drive becomes muddied by running from problems with men. If this latter case is yours, you will be better able to love another woman when you are cleansed of such patterns, because you will then love her for herself.

Do you expect the problems that go on in any relationship to somehow disappear because you do not have to deal with the opposite sex? (Who made up that term *opposite sex*? Not the sort of sweet nothings I want mumbled in my ear. "Darling, my opposite sex longs for yours." And what is opposite sex anyway?) Any partner in an intimate relationship is human: faulty, imperfect, and subject to typical shortcomings. To expect otherwise is unfair.

Perhaps ask your own questions, looking for what needs to be cleansed. If you need to, pray for clarity.

Use the cleansing rite below after answering all the questions, or use the rite several times, each time applying it to a batch of questions. Use The Magic Formula.

FIRST RITE
The Cleansing of the Vessel

Part 2: The Actual Cleansing

This part of the Cleansing of the Vessel is simple and effective. It and the other rites of this love spell are an opportunity to apply the tools gained in your weeks of learning magical skills. For instance, your visualization skills will be used in this rite, and even strengthened further.

Optional Tools and Ingredients

☾ A white candle

☾ Frankincense

Step 1. Optional: place the white candle before you and light the frankincense.

Step 2. Contemplate for a moment your deep desire for happy fulfilling romance ... Dwell on your own personal wonderful vision of what love means. For me it includes quiet companionship, giggling, relaxed contentment, excitement, fun, the satisfaction of a good time in bed, and someone who stands by me when I'm down ... Affirm that you deserve your ideal, that it is your right as a child of the Old Gods.

Step 3. Imagine that the Goddess is with you. Picture Her as you will, but imagine She is as kind as you could ever possibly imagine—kind as only a God could be kind. Imagine Her filled with maternal love for you, without harsh judgment or blame, and imagine that She wants to heal you with Her love.

Step 4. Focus on the problems made apparent by answering the questions. Really get in touch with the fears, angers, and other blocks that you have listed . . . Trying to stay in touch with them, become aware of how they are stopping you from romance, of the pain they cause you and those around you.

Step 5. Keeping all that in mind to the best of your ability, say the following prayer with as much feeling as you can muster. It's easier to muster feeling if you stay focused on the pain your blocks cause you, on your hopes of and right to a happy, fulfilling romance, and on our loving Mother.

> *Kindest Mother:*
> *I show you these wounds*
> *that I have suffered.*
> *Though I did not cause these wounds,*
> *in my pain I have hurt myself further*
> *and perhaps hurt others.*
> *I am ready now to be cleansed of all these things*
> *that pain and bind me.*
> *Cleanse and heal me*
> *so that I am a vessel not of pain*
> *but of love.*
> *Cleanse and heal me*
> *so that I can be filled*
> *with the passionate caring*
> *that you feel for Dian-y-glas.*

Cleanse and heal me
so that I can drink in such love
as You and my God feel for each other,
a love that echoes all of creation.
And now guide me,
showing me a new way,
a path of love and healthy lust.
[Now light the candle, if you're using one.]
So mote it be.

This prayer is to a loving, kind Mother; don't say it to beat yourself up. Any self-defeating thought or action, even any hurt you have caused another, results from some injury done to you in the first place, either as a child or later in life. Original sin is not part of Goddess Spirituality; the Gods didn't create any junk.

If you are acting in ways that hurt you or others, abuse and harsh judgment won't heal you of that behavior. Bitterness, lack of caring, and hate are the wounds we suffer from the unfortunate circumstances and tragedies of our lives. They need love to heal them. When you pray, She will look upon you with kindness and will love you into health again.

Earlier in this book I wrote of the need to sometimes clean things up with other people if you are to be truly clean spiritually. After the above cleansing, look at your answers again to see if there is someone you have hurt because of your own problems.

Again, don't beat yourself up; everyone makes mistakes. They are a sign of being alive! Thorough self-examination is not the same thing as browbeating oneself.

And you *can* make it up to any person you hurt. You needn't do so right now, but at least plan to do so sometime in the near future, after the three steps of the spell have been done.

Alcoholics Anonymous follows some very good practices, relevant to this part of the spell. (No, AA is not a coven of witches, but it provides a good spiritual path, and most spiritual paths have much to offer each other.)

AA suggests that sometimes it takes time to become willing to make amends. If you find yourself unwilling, pray for that willingness. AA also suggests making reparations to people, "except," to use their words, "when to do so would injure them or others." If a person has said, "Never talk to me again," perhaps it is not a good idea to approach that person with an apology. But you could resolve to change your behavior in the spirit of amends. To borrow an example that AA uses: if you have been unfaithful, a full disclosure of everyone's names might not be a very loving way to heal the damage. AA also points out that unfair damage to yourself isn't a good idea, either. The point is, use your common sense and cleanse things between you and the person harmed to the best of your ability.

Amends might not be possible for a long time; the person in question might be out of the country for the next two years. It is the spirit of things that counts. Resolve to be willing when the time is right.

You needn't be perfect in this external purification. If you are not willing or able to do some of it, don't worry. Romance is not reserved for perfect people. If you have an overwhelming pile of amends, the tiniest start might be enough.

When following my instructions anywhere in this book, keep in mind that we will always be far from perfect beings. The best you can do is the best you can do. Period. The thoroughness of this love spell might mislead one into thinking, "Well, I guess I'm not ready for love." We needn't be perfect to gain the love of the Gods. All we have to be is ourselves. With all our frailties and faults, we can still do a spell to gain a loving relationship with another human being. And a loving relationship might heal us of the wounds from our painful past and encourage us to make recompense for past behavior.

The acceptance of oneself as just another human being, with all the faults that go along with that, is an important step for a shaman. A shaman is not trying to be a saint. Our Gods do not demand that of us. A shaman seeks the love of the Gods. A shaman seeks to develop all his Goddess-given talents, magical and mundane. A shaman seeks to do everything in his power to serve the human, animal, and mineral community. The Mother of us all welcomes the errors of our sincere efforts. To avoid life because you think you are not good enough injures you and those who might have gained from you. Keep all this in mind as you tread the Road to Faerie.

A final note on this cleansing rite: though the entire love spell with its three parts can generally be finished in three weeks, sometimes it takes longer. A friend of mine was lonely and wanted to do a love spell, but a psychic told her, "No, you need to do some other spells first."

She spent two months doing ritual purifications because she had much inside her that would keep a lover at bay and those very same things were strong enough to override any love spell she cast.

If there is any doubt in your mind as to whether this is a time for such a spell, you might seek spiritual guidance. If you are guided to do longer purification work, simply do The Cleansing of the Vessel over as long a period of time as needed. Perhaps ask the questions, doing the follow-up cleansing, twice a week for a month. However, spending one week on The Cleansing of the

Vessel is an in-depth preparation that will give the love spell tremendous power!

SECOND RITE
The Filling of the Vessel

Tools and Ingredients

☾ A piece of paper

☾ A rose quartz crystal. It can be no more than a tiny rough piece of the stone, sold for as little as twenty-five cents in metaphysical and occult shops. See the listing of resources in appendix 2. You can also find inexpensive rose quartz beads at bead shops.

☾ A small red bag or red cloth that you can make into a bundle

☾ Jasmine oil or cinnamon oil

People are drawn to a person who fills himself or herself with love. Having done the previous rite, you are a clean chalice, more fit to be a vessel of love. The next step is to fill the vessel yourself. You mustn't expect someone else to fill it for you. You must fill it yourself so that you have love to share, so that you can give and be given to.

The Magic Formula needn't be used in this second rite unless the need becomes apparent.

Step 1. Write your own name enough times to fill the piece of paper.

Step 2. Wrap the rose quartz in the paper.

Step 3. Place the paper-wrapped quartz in the bag, or into the cloth by making a bundle out of the cloth.

Step 4. Anoint the bag or bundle with the oil.

Step 5. Carry this bag on you for at least a week.

Step 5. Every day, anoint the bag with the oil.

Step 6. This bundle represents self-love and sets up a very high spiritual vibration. It is part of filling the vessel yourself.

During the week you carry the bag, perhaps after your morning Ha prayer, ask yourself if there is anything lacking in you or in your life that you mistakenly believe a lover will make up for. It could be an internal or external attribute, like money, self-esteem, security, happiness, job satisfaction. We ourselves must fill the cup with these things; we can't expect someone else to do it for us.

It is not always on a conscious level that we are misled. Many's the time a woman has come to me for shamanic counseling, desperate for a long-term relationship, and when I read the situation psychically I see that her true longing is for a career advancement that she has been too fearful to make. Search yourself carefully; ask yourself what you expect love to bring you. Then appraise your expectations and see if they are reasonable.

Once you see a way your cup is empty because you are waiting for a lover to fill it, fill it yourself, whether your need is self-esteem, money, security, or whatever.

I am by no means expecting you to fill that gap in a week's time! If there is something that can be dealt with in a week, take care of it. If not, you needn't wait to move on to the final step of the love spell. Your intent to start filling the cup yourself, or maybe getting a tiny start—even such a start as having awareness of the problem—is probably enough. Judge for yourself how much headway is needed.

Filling the vessel can happen in innumerable ways. Much depends on what is missing from the cup and who you are as an individual. The following are a few examples of how you might fill the vessel yourself.

If the problem is that you are expecting a lover to give you the self-love or self-esteem that you need to give yourself, you might build an altar honoring your own self-worth.

If you are the proverbial woman of whom I spoke, looking for love instead of work, you might ask a friend for encouragement to risk writing that job résumé.

Getting support from friends to take care of yourself can be a very important way to give yourself love. For instance, if it is financial security you lack, ask a good friend how she gained hers.

Some people expect that they will be living the good life all of a sudden once they are coupled. If that describes you, it might be good for you to start living the good life now, on your own. Set aside time for more self-care. During this time do whatever makes you happy. Perhaps that is long walks on the beach, hot bubble baths, or trips to Europe.

Filling the Cup is a great chance to use The Spell Itself! For example, if you are lacking self-esteem, make gaining it the spell's goal, visualizing yourself filled with self-esteem.

If you have pinpointed what is lacking yet are puzzled about how to fill your needs yourself, you might ask for spiritual guidance either through a divination form, a simple prayer for insight, or a talk with a psychic. Asking your therapist how to fill yourself can also give you ideas, as can looking at the writing you did about power in lesson 7.

I have advised you that a week is the minimum time you'll need to spend on filling the cup before moving on to the next phase of the spell. However, when my friend who consulted the psychic asked about a love spell, the psychic told her that it was only once she felt more financially secure that she would be able to really open up to a mate. It took my friend several months to find a new job. She postponed her love spell until then; the new job filled the vessel.

THIRD RITE
Placing the Cup on the Altar

Tools and Ingredients

☾ A piece of paper

☾ Your red bag or cloth with its contents

☾ A red rosebud or a pinch of red rose petals

☾ A cinnamon stick. I don't mean the candy, but the actual spice in stick form, available where herbs and spices are sold.

☾ An amethyst. You can use a tiny rough piece or bead, quite inexpensive to buy. You can also use amethyst jewelry.

☾ A bit of dried orange peel. You can dry it yourself or purchase it where you find the cinnamon stick.

☾ Optional: A small piece of dragon's blood. Dragon's blood is a tree resin often used in incense. It has a dark, rusty appearance and a metallic odor when burned.

☾ Basil oil, dark musk oil, or amber oil.

Ah, the love spell! The term brings thoughts of fulfillment, intimacy, warmth, and good times. It tantalizes us with visions of a responsive mate, great sex, and healthy companionship. As it should, for within us burns a healthy Goddess-given desire for all these important things. Now comes the final step of our love spell!

Use The Magic Formula, including a pre-ritual cleansing. Yes, you have done a lot of purification work, but this is a powerful working, the likes of which have never been published! Because of a technical subtlety inherent in this spell, I want you to once again cleanse yourself of any notion of force in this rite. I'll explain:

This third working is wonderfully special; it is like putting on your sexy red dress, your red lipstick, a good perfume, and an open, warm, lovely attitude. It is like a peacock spreading his feathers. It is a calling out for love. This ritual is a natural human function, the psychic equivalent of courtship.

Most women are painfully aware of how intrusive some men can be when they're on the prowl. I always wonder why those guys don't wait for a smile or a come-hither before sauntering over, interrupting whatever I am doing, and assuming it's their right to demand my attention just because I am in the vicinity: "Yeah, I was just sitting here with twelve notebooks and a laptop computer because I thought it would attract guys." Those guys aren't courting, they're being inconsiderate. If I want a guy to talk to me, he'll know it. Even when a woman is walking down the street, on face value unoccupied, she might be meditating, or upset about a death in her family. "Look, Harry, a female! Any female will do. What do you mean she might be busy? How can you tell if she isn't pointing a shotgun at us?"

It happens the other way around, too. Even if a guy has an

interest in a woman, it is rude of her to push for attention if he has other things on his mind.

We are all well aware that no one should be forced to pay attention to another person on the mundane plane. It's the same on the psychic plane. The key word in both my examples is *attention,* and this is where the technical subtlety comes in: in your pre-ritual work, cleanse yourself of the notion that anyone even has to *notice* this call, this scent (I don't know exactly what to call it) that you are sending out. You are issuing an invitation, not forcing anyone to read it. Lack of courtesy pushes folks away on the psychic plane just as much as on the mundane.

In real courtship, when you put on your best clothes and makeup, fine scents and fine attitude, and spread your peacock feathers, when you call out for romance with subtle body signals, every person in your vicinity can choose whether or not he or she wants to even notice that. If someone else in your vicinity is deep in mourning because her father has just died she might not notice you, and rightly so. You wouldn't, in goodwill, go up to that person and say, "You darn well have got to notice me!" Have you arrived at a party determined that someone become interested in you? Ick! It wasn't pleasant, was it? It was misery and disappointment. And that is a mild example of what can go wrong.

And threefold return (the psychic law that anything a person magically does, good or bad, to another person returns to the doer multiplied by three) would leave you obsessed with watching everybody that passed by. If you were obsessed to begin with, you don't want it to get worse!

If your call to the universe for romantic love is meant to be answered, someone will really sit up and pay attention.

Step 1. On the piece of paper draw a heart. In this heart draw the male symbol (♂) and the female symbol (♀) overlapping. If you are gay, draw the male symbol twice, linked. If you are a woman attracted to women, draw the female symbol twice and linked. And if you don't know which gender of partner you seek, draw the symbol of your gender with a male symbol on one side and a female symbol on the other, the three linked.

Step 2. Add the paper and all the rest of the ingredients except the oil to your red bag or cloth bundle. Then anoint the bag with the oil. As you do all this, make the following prayer:

> *Mother, I have prepared myself:*
> *I am a cup of love.*
> *Mother, I have cleansed myself:*
> *I am a cup of love.*
> *Mother, I have filled myself:*
> *I am a cup of love.*
> *As your love now flows through me,*
> *I pray to you,*
> *so let your love flow to me:*
> *send me now my heart's desire,*
> *one who will love me of their own true will,*
> *with the fullest passion that only true will can bring,*
> *send me a lover who will love me as your reflection.*
> *Grant me the poet's dream,*
> *the lover's wish,*
> *the true mate.*
> *Mother, I now put myself on the altar,*
> *on the altar which is your universe.*
> *I am a cup of love.*
> *And, placed upon on this altar,*
> *I know without doubt*
> *that you who worked the first love spell,*

from which came all human love and passion,
will work your magic.
So mote it be!

That last line should be firmly and emphatically announced to the universe—a good, strong "So mote it *be!*"

Letting the Goddess pick your mate is not the same as saying, "God, you probably don't want anything really exciting and pleasurable for me. But since you are God you know best." Though no one's life is free from loss and tragedy, and though sometimes one must say, "OK, Goddess, I'll do it your way even if I don't like it. I'll trust that you know better than me," a witch also gets to ask for romance without thinking that the Gods have a staid, dismal picture of what that means. Remember, these are *pagan* Gods you are praying to!

Using the above prayer, you avoid asking for what you only think you want. Asking for the wrong thing can magically shove away the very thing that would fulfill our deepest hope. Our truest dream of love can be fulfilled when we leave the details to God. In fact, we can pray for fulfillment in any area of our life, leaving the details to the Goddess.

To my knowledge, no love spell as extensive, comprehensive, and witchy as this one has ever been in print. With all the power built up by it, you will have worked a powerful spell—yes, indeed! If the spell doesn't work, realize that only consistent effort produces the knowledge, skills, and polish needed to be successful in magical workings. Magic is a complex science; there are endless reasons a spell may or may not work. Whether you achieve your desired goal or not, you likely will be far closer to it. Below are some things to consider after the spell, to ensure success.

Don't assume that a spell hasn't worked just because you aren't seeing results as quickly as you want. Magic has its own schedule, and assuming your magic has failed can in fact cause it to fail.

A lot of energy gets raised in a love spell, so it is easy to fight with the beloved while or after doing the spell. This will be less likely because you have purified yourself of false expectations and ideas of force, but make a special effort not to indulge in temper.

Ever gotten all dressed up in hopes of finding the right guy and been surrounded by wolves? The same can happen in your *magical* attempt to find Mr. Right. You can send out the best energy, but you might still attract some of the wrong people. Just take it as a sign that the spell is working, and keep a positive attitude! You also might attract someone who, though perfectly lovely, is not right for you. Be discriminating.

Be open to a new friend: the Goddess might want you to get your love platonically for now. Or She might be sending you someone disguised as "just a friend."

Keep "filling the vessel." If you want to love someone, you must have love to give. Once you have found someone, even a permanent mate, you still must keep the cup full yourself.

The true mate might last a month or a lifetime. Treat any opportunity for love with respect and gratitude. You might even find that the Gods send you several lovers. If you are the non-monogamous type, enjoy!

The spell will bring you what is right for you.

Whether you make love with someone for a lifetime or a night, do so with love and respect. Sex and love must not be separated. A mystic knows this. Even a fling must be sincere and loving, a generous giving, and a pleasure shared in mutual respect. Sex is a sacrament. Just as witches do not differentiate between the mundane and the sacred, so any sexual act cannot be separated from the spirit.

If you want to do a love spell and my three-part spell seems wrong for you, consult the bookshelves of your local occult shop for a spell of your own choosing.

The Mother protects Her weak and mistreated children. Use any of Her magic with evil goals and She will revenge Her own. If you use a love spell with male chauvinist intent, you get really bad luck. Your woman will get stolen or a bad woman will lure you into a brawl. The powers of sex and love flow through the universe's most basic fiber, and are aware. If you use them to bad purpose, now or later someone or something or maybe even your own being will turn against you in the law of threefold return. The powers of the Old Gods are to be neither scorned, nor treated lightly, nor used for power over others.

Real power in life and true sexual potency means loving respect for the feelings of others, and tender care of the planet. Then courtship, on both the psychic and the concrete plane, is healthy and joyous, a part of our human heritage. Courtship should be relished with great pleasure. To do so, we honor our spirituality and our sexuality.

Everywhere You Go, There's Power to Be Had

A Witch Is Always in Control of a Situation

One of a witch's lifelong goals is to control all her situations. That is easily misunderstood. Being in control of a place or an event means *everyone* involved is in control. The assumption that if one person is in control no one else can be is nonsense! True power, true control, is a cooperative endeavor in which each person comes to power aided by the others involved, and is a mutual rather than exclusive concept—just like sex! This section might have been titled "More Ethical Uses of Power."

Herbal magic, candles, and incense are delightful ways to exert control over your home and other environments without interfering with the will of others. Any place can be made more the way you want it, just as you might decorate your home for a party because you like a warm, celebratory atmosphere.

Just as any herb, incense, or candle has unique properties visible to the average person, so each has unique psychic aspects. Burning incense or a candle, or placing herbs in an environment, sends a vibration into that environment. Depending on which kind of herb, incense, or colored candle is used, the immediate surroundings become more cheerful, or peppy, or healing, or. . . . Think of it as psychic decor!

As my candles, incense, and herbs release their specific energies into my home, I draw on their energy as naturally and automatically as I draw in the fresh ocean air at the beach. My visitors might also draw on that energy on an inconscious level, at which level they not only perceive the vibe, but choose to take it in or refuse it.

They might not have the same choice were I to cast a spell on them. I decorate my home pleasantly, and enjoy filling it with fresh flowers. My guests can draw on that effort or not, and if they so choose, they can feel more at home and relaxed. They are not being manipulated. The same goes for whatever incense and candle I burn in my home, or whatever herbs I have placed around: my visitors can choose to enjoy my psychic decor or not.

Using these tools at your workplace is a wonderful way to have more influence on your work environment without being pushy, or domineering. Again, the idea is to come to power without making others lose theirs. If others lose *theirs*, then in truth we have lost ours; we are not separate from that which is around us. All things interweave with one another, or as Martin Luther King, Jr., said, "None of us are free until all of us are free." And any high-earning businessperson knows that teamwork spells success.

Treat the following ways to use incense, herbs, and candles as you would a new cookbook: scan now, then apply when and if desired. The Magic Formula is not needed for the following work.

Herbs can be used by placing one or more containers in the environment, or by sprinkling a pinch in a corner, nook, or anywhere else. When it comes to herbal magic, some folks feel more is better; others believe that a pinch is plenty. Herbs can be disguised by being mixed into potpourri, and you then get to feel secretive and smug.

Harmony in the Home and Workplace

I burn a pink candle, and/or place lavender and/or peppermint about my house to create harmony. The herbs release an energy of peace. And in an open container, they add a nice decorative touch. Aren't I a domestic witch?

Domestic problems that this might improve include a teenager going through the typical crises of youth; fighting between siblings, mates, or roommates; and the stress of moving from one dwelling to another. Don't forget that you can also introduce a harmonious vibration into other environments, such as the workplace or nursery school.

Conflict in any environment may also be helped by burning frankincense, sandalwood, or sage. This purifies the space of negative energy, which helps bring harmony.

I place lavender and peppermint in my home even when there are no problems. I like peace and harmony in my abode, just for its own sake. Remember: stay free of beliefs that others in your environment *must* become calm and harmonious.

Stress Reduction and Healing

Blue candles are calming. I might burn one if there is a lot of stress in my life. Blue candles help folks who have deadlines, or who are involved in the hectic atmosphere of community service, to go calmly about their business. Also, they are good candles to burn when your baby has colic and you feel completely frazzled by it. Blue is also helpful when you are doing a meditation to bring about peace and serenity.

Blue candles are also spiritually and emotionally healing. I sometimes keep one burning when I am healing emotionally.

Sandalwood incense emits a lovely and gentle, calming influence, and spiritually uplifts you in your healing work. You could use it with the candle or on its own.

Burning frankincense purifies your surroundings of negative energy that may be upsetting your sense of calm or your mental health.

The mint and lavender previously mentioned are also calming. One of the nice things about lavender is that it doesn't look odd to your fellow workers; it just seems like potpourri on your desk.

Physical Healing

Green candles emit a healing influence. One can be burned when you, or someone you live with, is ill. Or burned at work if there are a lot of flu bugs going around. Burning a green candle is a prime example of using magic to help others without casting spells on them.

A Pepping Up

Burning cinnamon—you can put it on aluminum foil in your oven—or a red candle is excellent when you lack energy or enthusiasm about life. This also works for an elderly person who needs vitality. Is a job deadline discouraging you about your career? No one at the office will know that the red candle on your work desk is witchery.

Meeting a Deadline Midst Chaos

Burning an orange candle helps me concentrate when I am trying to focus amid a lot of activity. (Parents, take special note. Boisterous wee ones, no matter how beloved, can make it hard to even think straight, let alone concentrate.) Or you might prefer the following when you need to meet a deadline midst chaos.

Grounding

When you are "spaced out," or feel scattered all over the place, or just need to be more down-to-earth, burn patchouli or amber incense and/or a brown candle. This is also good when you need a more grounding or practical influence during a rite, event, or period of life.

Adolescence is a hard time, for both the teenager and the parent; everyone involved has so many emotions, needs, and issues flying around. It is nice to be in an environment that is grounded during such a time. A household with a teenager in it is also a good candidate for regular spiritual housecleaning.

Luck with Money

Burn bayberry incense to draw money. In addition, or instead, wash every morning with cinnamon soap. Remember what money *is*: an exchange for something you do. After you burn the incense or wash with the soap, you may need to do whatever is necessary on the mundane plane for financial gain, like looking for a job.

You might get more ideas about controlling a situation from the Occasion Candle material in the fourth week's lesson.

When, How, and Why to Use The Magic Formula

Now that you've been consistent in its usage, you needn't always use The Magic Formula. Once a karate block becomes automatic to the karate practitioner, it will stay so if he practices his block often enough and maintains his other karate practices sufficiently. In the same way, the proper ritual conditions and states— for instance, the dream coming into the waking mind—happen automatically on the unconscious level without use of The Magic Formula as long as you continue to use it often enough and sufficiently keep up with the rest of the practices in this book.

A shaman's magic is trained into her being, until eventually some things happen automatically on an unconscious level. For instance, anointing one's forehead with mud becomes touching one's forehead becomes the same energy drawn in with neither external action nor any conscious thought.

Use your common sense, and your knowledge of magic and spirituality, to decide if The Magic Formula is important for a given rite. You might decide that only part of the formula is relevant to a working you are about to do. Don't eliminate any part of the formula permanently.

How often is often enough to do The Magic Formula or any part of it, and stay in shape? That depends on you and your goals. As experience teaches the karate student, so experience will show you what keeps you in good enough magical and spiritual shape to automatically and unconsciously call forth the power of The Magic Formula without actually using it. You also want to stay in good shape for its own sake. I find there are times I can be lax in my magical and spiritual disciplines—above and beyond just the usage of The Magic Formula. At other times, I have to be more constant and exacting, and at yet other times I can be on a medium ground.

This training has asked you to think for yourself. There will be lots more of that before we are done. You will make mistakes. For instance, you will make the wrong choice sometimes when figuring out when, how, and why to use The Magic Formula. Sometimes you will make big mistakes while trying to live a Wiccan life. Any adult endeavor or learning process is filled with mistakes. If you want to apply something you have learned, whether about magic or about anything else in life, there is no way to avoid figuring out for yourself the best way to apply what you're learning. Are you all on your own in your efforts? Nope. You can always ask the opinion of others, and of the Gods.

One of the values of doing ritual without any rigmarole is that it can be done right when and where it's needed. Here's an example of such a rite, one that needs no magic formula, unless you so choose:

RITUAL
Changing Moods

This is a simple, quick spell, made more effective by all your training.

When you want to change your mood, imagine it so. Perhaps you are trying to write a letter and can't find the words you want. Right then and there, you can ask yourself what you would feel like if you felt creative, then imagine it so. Or perhaps you're on a date with your new sweetheart and suddenly you feel insecure. You can go powder your nose (what do men do to get a moment to themselves on a date?) and ask, "What would confidence feel like to me?" then imagine you feel that way. You can imagine you feel grateful, happy . . .

How to Create Your Own Rituals

Poetry—in the broad sense in which I have been using it—is an essential form of worship and magic. This is demonstrated through beautiful language in a ritual, storytelling as part of teaching, and the creative expression asked of my students.

I have asked you express your own poetry in any form it takes—dancing, cooking, hugging. For some people, this means rituals of their own making. This is what enlivens their inner poet and draws them close to God. Victor Anderson says, "Ritual is living poetry." If you want to be a bard, in the sense of one who creates ritual, this section is for you. Everyone else: you may want to read it anyway; you might find it surprisingly relevant. Here are some ideas about creating your own spells:

Let your imagination loose. Follow your fancy. Rituals can take as many forms as there are moments in the day. Being a bard doesn't even mean using words! A rite can be all the more powerful in silence. Ask yourself what seems a witchy means to a given end, then try that out. Be a magical researcher and experiment.

Celebration has power. In joy there is strength, solace, healing, and godliness. Besides, having a good time is a pagan thing to do! Strained, dour ritual can be unhealthy and not work as well. It can even cause problems. Celebration makes for healthy ritual and sincerely loving worship.

Sensuality is magic. Dressing in silks and anointing yourself with sweet scents has power. If you ever feel stymied when trying to invent a spell, consider creating one you will enjoy doing.

Small can be better. Short spells with small goals sometimes work best, because they can take less energy to create, prepare for, and execute. Also, don't try to make bigger or more changes than you're ready for. You can always do more later. Accomplishing anything, magically or not, whether it's the acquisition of money or personal growth, often happens at a slower speed than we want or think correct.

Ritual is living poetry. Art can be used ritually—your culinary abilities, sense of decor, humor, sewing skills. A ritual to gain confidence when speaking in front of others might consist of no more than making a dress to wear for public appearances, telling yourself each time you sit down to sew, "This is my robe of confidence." You needn't make the rite any more elaborate than that, or add any more details. Without adding a stitch more (pardon the pun) to the spell, you've got a simple and effective ritual, plus a new outfit. That's Faerie. The fetch understands art. Art brings your dream to your waking mind, in a way that is grounded. Art integrates you, which puts you in the proper state for ritual, and is healing and empowering in and of itself.

Drumming is a mode that speaks directly to your fetch and the Gods. And drumming helps people bring their whole selves into a ritual. It is also a natural and direct way to send power to your Godself during your Ha prayer—perhaps with a big bang.

A witch looks for useful role models. You might want to browse through other Goddess Spirituality texts, or even sword-and-sorcery novels, and use their spells as models. If you want to use mine as models, occasionally use the original form of any ritual you constantly vary. Also, check in occasionally to see whether you're in the spirit of The Third Road®: new levels of understanding are constantly revealed. Besides, often we don't even *hear* something the first time our teacher says it.

Calling on and talking to the Gods in your own words has no substitute. This is true whether you choose common everyday language in a relaxed setting or speak quite formally in an elaborate endeavor. Either can bring insight, power, and magic that is transformative and a joyous gift both to yourself and to the Gods. When a prayer is a request, and one is waxing eloquent, it can be good to ask yourself two questions before you use the prayer. Do you really want everything you would be asking for? Is there something crucial missing that you should add so that you get whatever you need to be safe, whole, and happy?

As long as you consistently use the basics in this book, you'll generally be fine exploring creative means to your magical ends. If you get in over your head, all you need to do is ask for help. If you don't know where to go for it, ask the Gods to show you where: they might direct you to the resource list at the back of this book.

In Simplicity Is Power

Simplicity is important in regard to creating spells. It is also so important in other ways that I here give a lesson solely about it. Faerie Magic is simple.

In 1996, on a camping trip in the middle of nowhere, I heard a violin playing. The music stunned me with its penetrating depth and beauty, so I was surprised to realize that the tune was the theme from *Sesame Street*. The hidden violinist—whom I later met, and she did exist on the embodied plane—played on, amazing me because she continued to move me with one simple child's song after another. It was her heartfelt expression, and fine technique, that gave her songs power and made for effective communication. Likewise, the simplest magical spell has power if you are sincere and trained. When creating rituals, choose content over fancy form; a simple spell created with a simple goal in mind is often the most powerful Faerie magic.

Simplicity is a primary magical technique. Who was it that said a witch takes the shortest route? A simple spell lets you be straightforward and to the point. Think of how tricky the Goddess is, and how mischievous the Fey Folk are. Part of their mischievous rep comes from their direct ways of getting things accomplished. Here's an example of a traditional Hawaiian spell whose power lies in its simplicity:

RITUAL
Complaining to the Gods

If you feel like you have a lot of problems, or have something you want to get off your chest, go to your altar and bitch to the Gods about it, like to a friend. It's not a matter of asking them to do anything about it; it just feels good to tell your divine parents,

"Ouch! Boy, am I having a hard day!" (or week, or life!) It makes you feel like you've got a sympathetic ear. Bang on a drum while complaining, if that helps. It may not look like much of a rite on the page, but if you ever need it, wow!

The Nonritual Ritual

Anything can be a rite—walking the dog, washing the dishes. When I got divorced, and needed healing, a friend visited and did a nonritualistic ritual healing on me: she read me a story that she had written just for me, making me feel loved and safe. Another friend also did a ritual healing: he washed my dishes, which had sat molding through three weeks (ugh!) of divorcee grief. Both acts healed me with love and magic. A shaman uses the most direct means to an end. (Highlight that last line with a highlighting pen or tattoo it on your lover's body so you see it often.)

The point of magic is not to wave a wand around, but to find the most effective, suitable way to manage the energy of any given situation. This is a keystone of shamanism. You've learned house blessings that were not in the least ritualistic: a straight-ahead party blesses a home. I once heard Victor bitch, bitch, bitch, then realized he was exorcising evil from his house.

And, to show another example, perhaps all that is needed to transform someone is a chat with them. The nonritual ritual is a great way to use your psychic powers for the benefit of others without casting spells on them. There are also people with whom one can't overtly work with energy, and the nonritual rite is a wonderful way to help them anyway.

A rite can be simple or elaborate, ritualistic, or a mundane action. The point is to deal with the energy in your life, or to touch God.

Another part of this is that spirituality mustn't happen only in ritual. Donations to food banks for the homeless, giving up the habit of littering, doing housework for an overworked mother—all are shamanic rites.

Assignment

Use energy in a nonritualist way. Pick your magical goal, then ask yourself: What is the best way to use—or change—the energy of the situation at hand? What are your mundane resources that might be used to do so? For instance, if you are feeling blue—energy you want to shift—and you have brightly colored clothes in your closet—mundane resources you have at hand—dress in bright colors. When a more formal rite will work better, one should use one, but often the nonritualistic ritual is a better use of time and energy. Perhaps, on a given day, your fetch will respond more directly to clothing than to chant. Or if your usually amiable fellow workers at the office are at odds with each other, planning to go to lunch with them might be the best way to change that. Breaking bread is a powerful act that smoothes ruffled feathers and makes for camaraderie. Some folks have jobs that would allow them to stand with everyone in a circle and chant, but odds are good that, to move energy with others on your work site, a hidden nonritual will be needed. There is nothing unethical about hiding your magic.

When planning a rite, find the most effective and appropriate means, one that conserves your time and energy. Often the nonritualistic ritual is a better use of time and energy. Such rites are very powerful! Hugs, hot tea, warm smiles, a birthday card—all are magic. A

nonritualistic ritual may still benefit from, or even need, part or all of
The Magic Formula.

Every Moment Has Unique Magic at Your Disposal

An acupuncturist taught his students that if a client has *x*, *y*, and *z*
symptoms, then the client has such and such disease. If the client
has *s*, *t*, *u*, and *v* symptoms, he or she has (a different) such and
such disease. The teacher taught one set of symptoms after
another, with the corresponding diagnosis, until his students had
worn themselves to the bone studying. The teacher then said,
"Your patients will have none of these sets of symptoms." A student demanded, "Then why did we study so hard to learn all
these sets of symptoms?" The teachers explained: "Each set of
symptoms I gave you was like a point on a grid. But each patient
you have is unique, so will be on their own unique point of the
grid, with their own unique symptoms and corresponding disease. Having studied hard, you are now acute enough to recognize
the unique grid point that each of your clients will be on."

I can't think of a better analogy to Faerie Tradition. Faerie
magic is simple—training to perceive, use, and move the energy
that is present. Simple but not easy. To name the moment can be
hard. It is tempting only to look for things that confirm your pre-
conceived notions, instead of perceiving what is really going on.

Name the energy through either psychic or mundane means.
A witch doesn't forget to use mundane modes of perception.
Otherwise she can get really flaky, or be talked out of what her
common sense tells her.

A Celtic shaman's training was complex only so the shaman
could eventually act simply with great power. This sort of simplic-

ity could take years and years to perfect. This is one of the main goals of the training in this book. For instance, the lesson on understanding darkness, the visualization work, and endless purification all combine to help you perceive your life with a clear mind, sharp psychic vision, and pure heart. When you name and use the power at hand in a down-to-earth nonritual, or in a ritual I taught you, or in whatever you deem best, be proud of yourself for excellent magic.

Serving the Cosmos and Keeping the Stars in the Sky

The ancient Celtic shaman kept the earth spinning on its axis, the stars shining in the sky, and the cosmos healthy. As a priest was aligned within self and with others in love and harmony, so the Gods became aligned in love and harmony. In the same manner, the cosmos was set right. With spiritual health and purity, the shaman could do this work through an act of pleasure, one that might also be offered up to feed the Gods and to help them in their work and play. The offering was also sometimes made with the intention of keeping the earth fertile and pure. You can do all this, too.

RITUAL
Healing the Cosmos

It is imperative that The Magic Formula be used with this spell. As one lets the Gods pick the ideal mate in the love spell, so one lets the Gods define health in this rite. In your pre-ritual cleansing, purify yourself of all control as to what healing *is*, so that you do not subtly choose an agenda, which is not the point of this spell, not the style of this book. For instance, you might think, "Well, doesn't everyone need prosperity to be healthy? And isn't prosperity defined as . . . ?"

To believe that anyone, in *any* situation in life, has to act in the way that you think is best is not only unfair but self-defeating. If you think your husband would be happier and able to keep the job he is about to lose if only he would stop sulking and being so irritable, and you have the mental attitude that he *must* change his ways, you are making the statement that he has no choice as to how he lives his life—and are very likely to get into an argument with him that just makes things worse. This spell could backfire in the same way. You must let others follow their own destiny, whether you think it right or wrong.

This does not mean a witch would let her husband hurt her with his sulking and temper. It is any woman's right and duty to herself to live safely, in dignity, and with respect from others.

Step 1. Choose an activity you would enjoy: sex, going to a movie, giving a sick friend a massage.

Step 2. Offer up what you are about to do for the healing of all things with this simple prayer:

> I *offer all I am about to undertake,*
> *the pleasures and the pains,*
> *for the healing of all things.*

Step 3. If there are any specific people or things you want to aid, use the following line, filling in the appropriate name: "May [*person or thing you want to help*] be blessed by the Gods through my pleasures and pains."

Step 4. Enjoy whatever you have chosen. It's that simple. You needn't make it ritual-like in any way, shape, or form. Pleasure is sacred in and of itself. When you have an orgasm, our Mother Gaia, the earth, smiles, and in Her joy finds health.

Although no one should cause themselves suffering, if you must undertake something that is of necessity difficult, you can apply the ritual as it is to that instead of to an act of pleasure. You might find great joy in the selflessness of your offering.

Finishing This Leg of Your Shamanic Journey

With only one visit left, it's time to put some finishing touches on this leg of our journey together.

How to Make the Most of What You've Learned

You have many tools for growth in your repertoire now; you don't have to stop growing just because you've finished these lessons. I've taught you tools for full living. Apply them to your daily life. Now that you have tools, use them! Even if you don't further pursue the road to Faerie, you can continue to use the potent, life-giving tools you have learned.

As part of applying this book to daily living, do the Ha prayer every morning or three mornings a week. This is a lifelong discipline.

You can also thumb through this book in times of stress, looking for solutions. And you can use the text as a cookbook on an ongoing basis to keep your life going well. Keeping this book on or by your altar will cue your fetch to use the book's spells when they are needed. You have worked hard at your shamanic training;

honor that work instead of tucking the book away on a shelf where you might forget about it. The same goes for your Book of Shadows. It can be a valuable asset.

Assignment

It is easy to be puzzled about how to apply one's knowledge to daily life. One day over the next three weeks, look through this book for a tool, myth, story, or lecture relevant to that day's events. Then apply at least one of the things you have discovered. Do this assignment again, maybe a week afterward.

Celebrating the End of Your Lessons

A friend of mine had a teacher in college who said that at the beginning of any semester the parking lot is full, and by the end of any semester it is nearly empty. The teacher added, "If your car is in the parking lot at semester's end, chances are good you were successful in your academic pursuits. Most of being successful is just showing up."

Congratulations for showing up! Your car is still in my parking lot, so chances are good you have been successful. To end this week's visit, read through the following ritual, which celebrates your efforts.

RITUAL
A Simple Rite of Celebration and Praise

It is easy to be blind to your own progress. When I told you that merely showing up likely made you successful, did you respond, "Naw, I could have worked harder"? If so, you discounted all the growth you've achieved, and the hours you put in.

Almost all my students succeed in my classes. Usually I see real and important changes in three months' time, if not in three days' time, even when a student falls far short of his ideal when it comes to doing homework, following instructions, and everything else. Remember: anything worth doing is worth doing poorly. I trust that even if you have done these lessons poorly, most likely you have made a significant change in yourself just by showing up.

Step 1. Write about who you were when you started this workbook and what your goals were. Then write about how you have changed since you started this workbook, what goals you have achieved, and what progress you have made toward other goals. Likely you will see only a portion of your growth. Often a person is the last one to see all her growth. It takes a year for most people's self-image to catch up with who they have become.

Discount nothing you write by adding a "but . . ." at the end of your statement. Don't say, for instance, "My goal was to explore Goddess Spirituality and I have done that, *but* this isn't much of an exploration." I assure you it was a big commitment to have made your way through this process; it is hard to keep going with shamanic work without a teacher's physical presence. Growth and shamanic discipline are challenging. Even with a teacher's presence, one works hard. I tell prospective students not to work with me unless they want to work hard and grow.

Don't write, "My goal was to loosen up. I am a bit freer in my thinking, *but* it doesn't matter because I haven't changed my behavior." That disclaimer desecrates your accomplishment. Thinking more freely can be the first step toward *living* more freely.

Step 2. Reward yourself for finishing your training. Sometime soon, go out to dinner, take a long, hot bubble bath, take a trip to Scotland, or brag to a friend about your follow-through.

It would be ideal to do step 1 before ending this visit. You may also want to choose your reward now, so that the momentum of training ensures that the reward happens.

You might find that using all or part of The Magic Formula for this ritual is necessary for you personally. If self-validation is hard for you, do a purification on those things that will keep you from making this act of self-love.

Merry Meet and Merry Part

Farther Along the Road to Faerie

Some folks will complete this training, then decide they have studied the Faerie path enough and need only apply what they have learned. Other folks will want, now or later, to learn more about the Fey magic and move closer to the Fey Gods. This latter group is addressed in this section, which also contains a few last pieces of the training and some material anyone might find useful.

Wait at least a month before further study. Take a well-deserved break! Don't worry that you will lose steam; even trees rest, every year, falling into winter slumber. Yet in spring they unfurl buds of green, and in fall are laden with fruit. You have harvested your lessons; now rest for as long as it takes to be filled with the life force needed to bud again. By being in tune with nature's cycle of work and play and rest, you can keep blooming and working.

Before you take your break, you might want to finish the assignment to celebrate the completion of these lessons, and the other assignments I told you to finish after the visits ended, so that you don't lose momentum.

When ready to start again, remember that a college student on her first day doesn't just walk into any old classroom and sit down. She chooses a curriculum and registers for classes. The first step in any journey is preparation. Organizing yourself as to how, why, and when you are to work is invaluable.

Preparation is *work*. I suggest you not use your semester break to do this prep. Rest. Watch TV. Read murder mysteries. Bake cookies.

Even if you don't intend to continue studies on this path, part of finishing the training is to browse this book for practices that I said should eventually be added to your work. Take as little or as long as you need for this; you may want to do it after your break.

The rest of this section consists of suggestions about further pursuit of shamanism—use the suggestions most suitable to you—and some "musts" about further pursuit of shamanism. All these items can help you choose your curriculum as you prepare and organize. It may take you years (and years) to even consider using some of the items relevant to you. That is not only fine, but expected and appropriate. Pace yourself *very* slowly!

The first item is summed up by what I tell all who commit to traveling The Third Road: face the shamanic challenge: embrace contradiction. We exist for two reasons: to enjoy ourselves with purely self-seeking motives, and to selflessly serve others. Opposite ends of the spectrum? Maybe, but who cares? Besides, you know by now that I don't believe in opposites very much.

In freeing ourselves from the tyranny of organized religion, it is necessary to reject hurtful religious practices. For instance, faith is suspect because it's been taught to convince disenfranchised groups like blacks and poor whites to bow their heads to oppression. However, an alternative spiritual choice must be more than rhetoric that makes us only *feel* free. Don't throw the baby out with the bathwater: faith can also be used to overcome oppression.

There are many behaviors and traits suspect to alternative groups for similar reasons, like acceptance, humility, and surrender. For want of better terms, I call them right-hand traits, and traits like strong will, healthy pride, and self-determination left-hand traits. The Third Road® brings the right- and left-hand paths together; a shaman must eventually embrace this contradiction.

Earlier, I said you have the right to self-determined goals, only to later insist you surrender to the Gods' choice of a lover for you. I also showed you the importance of developing and using your will, then announced that you must nurture pliability and willingness. Throughout your lessons, I have espoused many contradictions, and embodied more without pointing them out. Now we will go deeper into the heart of the matter. Let's look at some of the so-called opposites of the right- and left-hand paths.

Here's one pairing. Left-hand priorities are ecstasy and the devotion to fertility; I taught you that the goal of life is pleasure and abundance. I will now add the right side of the road: we exist to gain spiritual lessons and growth for their own sake. These two views only seem opposed, and are equally important.

A letter from my sister, Patricia, wonderfully embodies the priority of lessons and growth. It reads, in part: "The pain people have makes them real and sensitive and lovable and loving. Without it—or awareness and acceptance of it—we are cold, bitter, hateful, truly despicable, and selfish in the greedy sense.

"So, though there are times when I wish to not have pain or to not have to deal with my pain, I realize I am who I am, what I am, because my pains and sorrows are part of my wholeness. Knowing this, I can try to float with my painful feelings rather than being drowned by them."

However, the term *karmic lesson* is often used to blame and shame a victim for what others have done. Counseling that rape— for example—is a karmic lesson brought about by the woman (or man) raped so that she can learn a spiritual lesson is cruel, and deeply injures someone already suffering and perhaps defenseless. But if tragedy does happen, it is a shaman's job to learn and grow from it.

Let's look at another pairing: right-hand transcendence and left-hand immanence. I earlier pointed out that some religions believe it's wrong to want good things for oneself, insisting that goodness means transcending the material plane. I have argued, "No, God is *in* the world, so material things are sacred." However, what is more true is that a shaman embraces both paths.

It's not easy. Transcendence might mean saying, "I am living in oppression and that's OK!" What a statement! I know a woman whose husband had beat her for years, and her Catholic priest told her to transcend the beatings, which was a fancy way of telling her to put up with the abuse. That priest committed a sin. But, applied correctly, transcendence is a means to authentic peace.

Misfortune is an inevitable part of life. And not just for the disenfranchised. Life is inherently cruel, unsatisfying, and ugly. No matter how hard one tries to change the world or oneself, life remains a terribly mixed bag. If one wants to be happy despite this, transcendence is a crucial spiritual discipline. No matter *what* life brings.

The right-hand practice of acceptance is just as vital. When we accept life on life's terms, meeting life as it is, we are then able to find the joy, love, and humor in life. What I am suggesting is a spiritual challenge, and not even always a good spiritual approach, for sometimes the left-hand counterpoint to acceptance—the warrior's stance—is the way of the shaman.

Two women made an appointment for shamanic counseling with me. They lived next door to each other, and each had lost a child to the same drive-by shooting. Both women are loving and committed to spiritual principles.

That didn't keep one of them, Alice, a devout Christian, from breaking into tears, confessing, "I know I should trust God, but this all makes no sense." Her voice got louder and fearful, as if she were afraid of her own feelings: "I get so angry sometimes that I worry I am going to kill someone myself. What kind of world and God is this, to kill an eight-year-old girl for no reason?

"I'm constantly furious, obsessed wondering why this happened. I'm so angry that I can't sleep at night or focus when I'm at work. I'll lose my job! But all I can think about is 'Why us?' and 'How could I have stopped it?'"

Ruth, the other mother, responded: "Alice, I know what you mean. Francesca, I'm not doing much better than Alice. Andy died, but I've got two other children to love and raise. I want to be a good mom for them, but I just can't be there for them. I don't want them living in the shadow of Andy's tragedy.

"I terrified that I'll lose them too. Just seeing their faces when they come home safe from school makes me petty and irritable. I came close to hitting one of them yesterday. It frightened me.

"It's not that I do anything mean to them, because I keep an incredibly tight lid on myself, but that keeps me so tightly wound up that I can't give them the support and love they need to get over losing their brother. Francesca, what can Alice and I do?"

Often we cannot respond to tragedy with our best self. It's only human, and healing takes time. If there's anything I want to teach you, it is to accept yourself and others, with our all too common and constant shortcomings. Instead of criticizing Alice and Ruth, I did everything I could to help them find peace and closure around these deaths—though, being a mother myself, I suspect that no mother ever fully reconciles herself to something like that.

Over time the three of us worked hard, until one day I happened to look out my window as Ruth and Alice were walking toward my home for their appointment. Ruth was grinning from ear to ear, practically dragging Alice in her enthusiasm. Alice was smiling in tolerance of her friend's exuberance.

When we sat down, Ruth, who is my student, explained that the morning before, during her Ha prayer, she had realized that she could heal only through trusting that the Goddess had a plan for her that surpassed human understanding.

"The Gods," Ruth continued, "didn't just give me an idea or theory. They changed me inside: I am actually able to really feel as if they have a plan, and a deep trust of their good intentions in that plan."

I had kept an eye on Alice during this explanation. She was fidgeting, and getting more and more agitated. Finally, she stood up in a burst of frustration, declaring, "Ruth, I don't buy anything you're saying! It's poppycock. God doesn't want me to lie down like a doormat."

I didn't try to convince Alice to feel what Ruth had felt. Everyone has to find the solution that's right for them. Instead, Ruth and I listened to Alice's understandable anger and despair.

A year later, both mothers had successfully met the same challenge with very different spiritual solutions. Ruth's peace was not a temporary delusion. It proved to be an enduring, strong example of faith for others who had grappled with tragedy.

But Ruth's humble acceptance wasn't right for Alice, who told me that one day in church she had heard the Virgin Mary say, "*You* can heal only by using your righteous anger to fuel political action for urban change." Alice became a strong, driven advocate for strengthening gun-control laws.

Alice told me, "I trust my religion again, but not to make life perfect. If I wear rose-colored glasses, how can I see what needs changing or have compassion for others? Instead, I trust God and the Virgin Mary to see me through the battleground of American politics. They stand by me when the going gets rough." She added with a mischievous grin, "Mary's pretty good at coming up with political strategies, too. I want to become more easygoing again, but all in all I have made peace with God and with life."

Both women had triumphed over tragedy and hardship. Both had learned that if our lives are to be our ritual, we have to apply our spirituality wherever we are and whenever we can. Ruth's solution was right-hand, Alice's left-hand. Another person's would have been a combination of the two. A shaman must use both, and learns when to apply which.

Moving on to two more so-called opposites: pointing a finger at an oppressor or perpetrator for what he or she has done is a sound spiritual approach to, for instance, politics. That's left-hand: not being cowed into self-blame for someone else's unfairness. However, the right-hand counterpoint—self-analysis as to one's own part in one's problems, *even when they are caused by unfairness of others*—is crucial.

Margaret is black, and racism kept her from getting a job she wanted. A wise witch, she told herself, "Denial that external forces can hinder and even seriously hurt me would be a way of blaming myself for forces and suffering I do not cause. My Gods do not harshly judge or condemn me like that. They support and nurture me when I strive through hard times."

However, though we do not cause all the grief that comes to us, we sometimes feed into it; Margaret realized that her internalized racism and fear of success kept her from applying for a job where she would be respected. She cleansed those blocks away. And got a job she loves. Despite the system, we can *beat* the system. Magic works!—if you take responsibility for your own life.

Of course, some people are so wounded spiritually, physically, and emotionally that self-analysis is not possible. Those of us who can look inward have the responsibility to do so, so that we are in shape to help those people who can't.

To be an effective magician, and a happy person, you must consistently ask yourself, "What did I do to help [*whatever bad thing you're upset about*] happen to me?" whether you think the question is applicable to you or not. Even external circumstances that are truly atrocious might not be overcome without this self-analysis. When you find your inner block(s), a prayer for cleansing can be used.

Let's move on to another pairing. By now, we all know I am a hedonist. But though self-gratification is my buzz word, I pursue it with caution. Amy Tan, in her best-selling novel *The Joy Luck Club*, tells the story of a greedy woman who died after her stomach got fatter and fatter. Her stomach was then cut open to reveal a large melon inside. The anecdote ends, "If you are greedy, what is inside you is what makes you always hungry."

When seeking self-gratification makes me unhappy, or—take note—I am tempted to be destructive, or otherwise troubled, I ask the Goddess for help, and what to do next. She tends to tell me either to do the dishes or to do a selfless act. Selflessness is the right-hand balance to self-gratification.

After my divorce, with my daughter away at college and my family of origin a continent away, I felt isolated. I dwelled on my misery until my loneliness overwhelmed me. I took myself in hand: "Stop feeling sorry for yourself. There are others with problems, too! Do something about *that*." I called up a close friend. She is a single mom without much family herself. I offered to do regular child care for her daughter. Years later, the side benefit is that I am that little girl's honorary aunt, enjoying her love and frolicking in my home. More important, I get outside of myself, gaining a peace and satisfaction I find in no other way.

Focusing on helping others without remuneration, instead of dwelling on what may be legitimate problems, is one of the best ways to help oneself. Selfless service is a keystone to spiritual health, and is what I have most enjoyed and found the most satisfaction in. Yes, even more than sex—and, darling, I am a woman who can have seven-hour orgasms, I kid you not!

My own life illustrates more pairings. I have a global intelligence. Everybody has a knack for something. Some folks are a whiz with math, others with cooking. Some folks can pick up any musical instrument and play it, others could do brain surgery in their sleep. But a person with global intelligence takes to almost any activity like a duck to water. Yet, with all these gifts, I couldn't choose a career. I was easily bored, wanted to do something really useful, and felt limited when sticking to one thing. I wasn't happy, and had no goal other than a dream that life could be exciting, important, and fulfilling.

When a child and teenager, I found my classes irrelevant to my dream. Then, when I was fourteen, my father brought home a guitar for himself, and I claimed it as mine through usage. Because my folks didn't have a lot of money, suitable lessons were not available, so I taught myself to play the guitar and—this was at age fourteen, now—auditioned at a club and was hired, the first of many performances in adult and professional venues.

Ultimately, music wasn't fulfilling. As I got older and my horizons broadened, I had more access to education, but it still seemed irrelevant to real life. I am avidly curious and love to learn, so I took what few classes seemed relevant, took lessons in the arts—practice, not theory—and continued to educate myself as I had done as a musician. I acquired skills in many areas—I even worked as a stand-up comedienne—before I was drawn to the magical realms.

I found I had a gift as a bard, in the sense of one who creates ritual. I created new spells to do magic and to self-heal. My primary research was not in books, though I am an avid reader. Mostly, I used my common sense to observe how people were and what might help them, and my psychic abilities to perceive what happened on the psychic plane during magical acts. I brought these observations together simultaneously with meditation, in which I checked my deductions with the Gods and, with their guidance, created The Third Road. (My methods make sense if you know that I was trained in shamanism—my training included my psychic skills—to the degree an M.D. is trained in medicine.) After all my searching, *this* work made me happy.

In 1986, everyone thought I was crazy to start a school of shamanism and personal growth: such an institute was unheard of, a one-person staff (me!) could never pull it off, and who could earn a living that way? Well, here I am, still doing it, and happy as a bubble coasting along the surface of a brook. Things have grown into an international community, in which I am aided by many volunteers.

I had found my most special gift; I was a bard, and loved the task fully. Through The Third Road, I could also use my other talents. My music, poetry, storytelling, jokes, and skills in communication were means to teach and heal. My organizational skills were needed to run my school.

I could have accomplished nothing in this story without my left-hand traits. Only a *strong-willed* fourteen-year-old can teach herself music, then work in adult venues. I *chose my own goals and means* instead of the limited offerings of the academic route, and thus *developed myself* fully. Otherwise I never would have discovered my talents in ritual creation, talents that would make me the happiest and help others the most. Without trusting my *inner authority,* I would not have created The Third Road school, nor have been able to acknowledge my odd research as a valid preparation for becoming a theologian and philosopher. And who ever heard of such research methods, or such goals? What is a bard anyway? I even made up that definition of the word *bard,* though now I have found that there was a time when the term *bard* was used in that way. Finally, there is no question that *a strong ego* drove me the whole time. (Yes, I'm smiling at that last line.)

There's a right-hand side to this story: the sacrifices of following one's own path and serving the Gods. As a child, I felt left out. Though I didn't find myself odd, everyone else did. I was ridiculed and laughed at for following my own star. The ridicule continued painfully into adolescence. My childhood independence placed me in adult music circles, where I constantly felt frightened and alone. To find my niche, I over and over chose a career, was successful, and then moved on, until my friends (and I myself!) told me I was dedicated to failure and incapable of commitment. Creating the material and school demanded seven years in trance and insane work hours, not to mention my whole focus, so that I was just like a hermit off in her forest hut; I basically stayed single the whole time.

Though I wrote earlier that sex is the essence of spirit and of utmost importance, it is sacrifice of all things, including sex, that is the heart of happiness—concrete happiness that you can experience, not something that you call happiness but feels miserable.

I have learned to pray, "Goddess, thank you for the solitude in which I found you, myself, and a path that helps so many people."

There is another sacrifice: the Buddhist belief that a person's life can be shortened if she is a spiritual teacher. After being a spiritual guide for about twenty years, I believe this is true. Upon hearing me say this, my student Gertie responded indignantly, "Well, I disagree. I left the Catholic Church to get rid of that sort of martyrdom. That's just low self-esteem on your part to think that you have to knuckle under that way."

I answered, "Gertie, riding a motorcycle gives you more joy than just about anything. Statistics say your life is really at risk to have that joy and freedom. Like you, I am willing to risk a shorter life to have a life worth living. Like you, I have freedom and joy; being your teacher, I am choosing my happiest possible life.

"I know people unable to risk sacrifice, who spend their lives in a miserable caricature of adventure and selflessness, running from one spiritual and social craze to another."

I have made other sacrifices—better spoken of face-to-face—to follow this odd path the Gods have asked of me. I let God show me the needed sacrifice, and I know She will help me carry it off. Self-sacrifice is the right-hand counterpart to self-development.

All my victories happen because I constantly *surrender* to

God's will, so that Her enormous power can lead me, blind and riddled with inner blocks, to where I need to go to be happy and useful. I try to trust that, since the Gods show me what chores they need of me, they will take care of me through my trials and confusions. Surrender is a right-hand counterpoint to the self-determined goals of the left-hand path.

It is hard to know which side of the road to walk on when. One solution is another of our pairings: internal and external authority. I have a good sense of my psychic gifts; I repeatedly see jaws drop when I tell a client personal information about herself that I could know only by psychic means. I'm as accurate as a psychic gets! In my personal life, I live my whole day drawing on my intuition. God is always whispering in my ear, showing me my next best gambit. I trust my inner authority.

But Ms. Madame Francesca Knows-All-Sees-All sees and knows enough to realize she is often blind to her own personal issues and needs the guidance of someone other than herself. And when unsure if my reading about a client is accurate, I consult with a peer. When I pray for guidance, I sometimes know if I am hearing the answer correctly only by feedback from a friend or elder. All the input I am talking about comes from someone embodied; if I am puzzled and confused, I might misinterpret advice from a spirit.

Whether you are novice or master, get input when you need it or you are headed for psychic and spiritual trouble. A willingness to admit you can't figure everything out on your own does not imply any lack on your part. It shows a intelligent assessment of the complexities and enormous powers of life.

Ancestor worship and elder respect create inner authority. To be in harmony with your ancestors is to be in harmony within yourself. An altar honoring your ancestors—you can use your imagination to create one—and food offerings are ways to do this. Respect for elders also causes harmony with ancestors.

Respecting elders means acknowledging your sources. The writings of Jean-Paul Sartre, the French philosopher, are quoted as Sartre's, and when a physicist writes about a scientific fact that, of course, existed all along, he credits the person who first had the insight to notice it. But wisdom and truths about life orally transmitted by a shaman, instead of being acknowledged as the work of a philosopher and researcher, are "just something someone said" and go uncredited. Much of the ancient wisdom I pass on came to me directly from God and through personal observation, the results of my having invested as many years of applying rigorous, precise methods as does a laboratory scientist. Most of the rest is from my elders, whom I gratefully acknowledge by name.

It does not diminish a shaman to honor his elders. A lot of my training with Victor was in the form of his considerable feedback as I created my tradition and this book. I instigated lengthy dialogues with him to ensure that he got credit for that. Thus I am able to acknowledge his remarks in this text as his, except for a handful of phrases. This handful consists of either sentences that are the result of Victor saying, "No, no, say it like this . . . ," his feedback given in much the way a hands-on editor would give advice, or traditional Wiccan phrases, about which he said that honoring him as my teacher was sufficient credit. The many dialogues I instigated to ensure he got due credit were tedious and demanding work—and embodied the nature of gaining power.

A teacher's influence is considerable. His research is sometimes a jumping-off place for his students. When I say that I feel honored to have had Victor for my teacher, I am not giving him credit for my work. For instance, we disagree, as any two thinking adults might. The theories and practices about right- and left-hand paths in this lesson are basically mine, and I imagine he wouldn't agree with all of what I wrote if he saw it. To acknowledge that Victor taught me a few of the rites in this book doesn't deny that I wrote the rest, or that the paradigms in the book are basically mine. Instead, my acknowledgment of Victor has helped him pass the torch of power to me.

A teacher needn't be perfect to deserve respect. Spiritual leadership does not demand sainthood. Except on the part of the leader's mate.

Obi-Wan Kenobi is a Jedi master in *Star Wars* who appears to his followers after his death. He's a calm, serene, see-through kind of guy (special effects), but though I am considered a spiritual leader, I identify with Han Solo, the *Star Wars* intergalactic pirate who really would prefer to save his own neck, is obnoxious about it, but finally rallies to the cause. When I got a death threat last year—my work is controversial—I was scared. I whined, complained, and was all-in-all difficult for my friends (as I called the D.A.'s office, got a witness to accompany me for safety, and went right on with my work).

Now that we've looked at some of the contradictions a seeker embraces, you can easily analyze and apply similar material throughout the text. A shaman employs the shamanic challenge in real life, eventually as a daily discipline. Endless purification is one way to do this.

The inner blocks that cause harmful acts toward others are usually not the traits of a monster. Betty unknowingly hurt a lot of people because of her low self-esteem: her shyness made others feel snubbed; and her fear of rejection kept her from showing her boyfriend affection. When Betty cleansed away her poor self-image, she became kinder. Fear does more damage than hate.

Willingness to see your shortcomings is also crucial. Darryl was so afraid of hurting women that when he did, he could never admit it, even to himself. So he couldn't stop hurting women. It didn't help that in his college days he had been browbeaten by a so-called feminist, and became ashamed of being a man. (Do I hate men? No. Am I a feminist? Yes.)

Darryl never realized that an admittance of failure could be met without cruel judgment. It became crucial to him to always appear perfect, even to himself. He learned the politically correct things to say but continued to hurt women, in subtler and subtler but more and more destructive ways. His dishonesty and fear of discovery isolated him, even in his marriage, which looked real good, and felt real bad.

Sometimes Darryl unconsciously justified his wrongdoing with feminist rhetoric. Any authentic spiritual maxim, or powerful spiritual system, can be misused to hurt oneself or others. This can be even more of a danger for adepts. An antidote is recognition of human limits—a human is not omnipotent and will always have many shortcomings—and endless purification. A quick aside about another shamanic contradiction: though it is one's right and duty to acknowledge oneself as a deity who is all-powerful, one must balance that by releasing the identification with God and omnipotence when it interferes with one's spirituality. For instance, when it keeps one from acknowledging personal faults.

The further one walks along the road to Faerie, the more it becomes important to walk both sides of the path. Otherwise one gets to be an amazingly self-justified ass who wreaks havoc in everyone's life with the best intentions. You can strive toward lavish satisfactions sexually and materially without being trapped by illusions, pseudo-lusts, and addictions if you apply the shamanic contradiction and keep up your other shamanic disciplines. This will keep you from desperately seeking the ecstatic but never having *any* fun, just being frustrated and miserable.

The stronger a witch makes her will, the stronger her healthy ego gets, the more sure her inner voice—in other words, the stronger her left-hand path—the more she must be flexible, acknowledge her limits, and face humbling feedback—in other words, the stronger her right-hand path has to get. This not only keeps her ethical and safe, but gives the ultimate fun, in the most mundane sense: a picnic at the beach with Brie and fine wine; a ride on one of the carousels at the foot of the Eiffel Tower (there are two there); a Bruce Springsteen concert; and seven-hour orgasms!

A few nominal stabs at acceptance or open-mindedness about other people are not enough; I need a balanced and ongoing weaving of a right- and left-hand path, the right-hand spirituality having a disciplined, structured practice the same way my left-hand spirituality does. In the same way that visualization skills are built up and maintained with practice, spirituality is strengthened and then maintained through an ongoing daily discipline. A daily way of life!

Don't be discouraged by the amount of material in this chapter. This week's lesson will provide you with a reference section to draw on for many, many years and in many life situations. You can proceed with a healthy confidence in your knowledge. The following rites are an example. Because I am giving the right-hand rituals below to you all at once, do not think they lack power. Rituals such as these, substituted for my daily Ha prayer, form the basis of my work for weeks or months at a time.

If you want to continue along The Third Road, add each rite to your repertoire in sequence; if possible do each rite at least three times a week for about three weeks, then move on to the next exercise. Then do them all in sequence in one sitting. After that, experiment: use them in any order or combination, as suits you.

RITUAL
Buddhist Breathing

Watch your breath without judging or trying to change it. Just observe. When thoughts or other distractions come to mind, note them and let them wander away instead of following, fighting, or otherwise being caught by them. Do this ritual for one second to a zillion minutes. Ditto for the next two rites.

RITUAL
Resting in the Mother's Darkness

Adapt Buddhist Breathing: after each exhalation is a natural pause. It is the Mother's womb. Instead of watching the inhalation, rest in that pause. I return to this practice often. After years of teaching and counseling, I know enough spiritual tricks to fill a three-ring circus. But what I keep returning to is anything that helps me surrender to God. It is a remedy to almost anything.

RITUAL
Honoring the Father

This rite, and the next prayer, bring both sides of The Third Road together. The empty quiet gained by watching your breath is not better than the thoughts and worries that distract you. Adapt Resting in the Mother's Darkness by respectfully acknowledging your mental and physical "itchiness" as God, our Father, before you let it melt away. Though we focus on surrender and inactivity in these three rites, at other times we need to focus on the fire of thought and activity. We, as a culture, have ignored the feminine, dark pause and surrender. Let's not swing to the other extreme. That feminine matrix is impotent without the birth of the sun coming from it. The goddess Diana pulled the light from Her own darkness and fell in love with Him, for He is Her own self, and other half.

A Prayer for Grace and Surrender

Grace is the state of moving toward your desires effortlessly on the wings of the universe; instead of struggling, you can ride the currents of the events in your life toward your goals. The entire universe is the Mother, and with the hands and arms of this universe we are embraced and cared for by Her; within the embrace of this universe we are carried toward our desires by Her, if we are willing to go along for the ride. The laws of nature are simply the desires of the Mother, and it is Her desire that we gain that which we seek.

To gain your goals through grace demands trust, purity, and a belief in miracles coupled with enough common sense to get the rent paid. Finally, grace is living both desire and surrender. When using this spell, keep in mind that the desire spoken of in the prayer is not necessarily what you think is your deepest desire.

By the universe, I am held and moved toward my desire.

Like a leaf floating on the heated current of a summer's dusk,
I am held and moved toward my desire.
Like a rock nestled in a green meadow,
I am held and moved toward my desire.
I surrender to this.

Like a shiny placid bubble floating in the clear river's current,
I am held and moved toward my desire.
I surrender to this.

Like the shimmering heat the fire pushes upward,
I am held and moved toward my desire.
I surrender to this.

Like a rock fixed on the earth,
I am held and moved toward my desire.
I surrender to this.

Like a wolf carried by hunger, lust, and love,
I surrender.

Like a woman driven to the menstrual hut,
I surrender.

Like an atom blown by the breath of the Mother,
like a prayer blown within the breath of the Mother,
I surrender.

Before the closing lines below, you might want to imagine and/or state internal or external challenges to which you need to surrender.

By the universe I am held and moved toward my desire.
I surrender to this.

The shunning of menstruating woman in early societies perversely echoes the earlier menstrual hut. It was once understood that the powers of the Gods were upon a menstruating woman, calling her with an almighty force. She was driven away not in ostracism, but by the sacred menstrual force within her, to the hut where she would vision-quest and do ritual. It is this sacred drive—of a woman's power—to which I refer in the prayer.

Contemporary scientists have agreed that menstruation is indeed a time of power for a woman, during which she is more productive internally and externally. There is within a woman at this time a pressing, driving need for self-expression of the deepest, most spiritual sort.

This week's lesson on embracing contradiction is a simplified view, which serves as a jumping-off place for you to reach, through your own life experience, the deeper layers and complete picture of the shamanic contradiction. As you do so, remember: the exact opposite of any spiritual truth is also true. I think Mark Twain said that.

Logic, whether it be politically or psychologically based, might tell us that the right-hand approaches are not productive. Have you ever noticed how much cartoons and sound spiritual practices have in common? Neither of them makes much sense if you analyze them, but both make you happy.

Here are a few last pairings to contemplate when you wish (I list the left-hand attitude or goal first):

building of ego and pride / ego reduction, humility, shunning false pride

"As I will so mote be it." / "God, *your* will is my command."

On to more thoughts about further travel along the Road to Faerie:

Listen to the trees. And the ocean. And the sky. And an ant. And your house cat. Listen.

And watch. Watch the sand get soaked by ocean waves. Watch the sun fall into the ocean in the west. Watch the trees wave their leaves in the breeze.

Touch. Touch the velvet leaf of a rose. Touch your own face and know it to be the face of a God.

Nature is a teacher. The ancient shaman learned about magic and self by watching and interacting with the natural world. That is what any scientist does—observe and relate to the world about himself in order to learn truths.

Take up an exercise program. Paganism is a physical way of life.

You can honor the gift of the material world the Goddess has given you by using it to its fullest capacity. Health is a primary goal of shamanism. Spiritual health rests on physical well-being. Your body is the body of God. I do not mean it is the *temple* of God, it *is* God. The spiritual and the material are one and the same. Since exercise is an important part of being healthy, it is an important part of spiritual health.

Tai chi, walking, kung fu, and karate are particularly suitable forms of exercise. As is dance. If you want to be a pagan, one way is to learn to dance. Your body is God. God is happier when (S)he is dancing. Especially good are contact improvisation, and folk dances—for example, belly dancing and morris dancing. Folk dances are earthy, sexy forms that help you be in tune with yourself and nature.

Continue endless purification. It is absolutely necessary to integrate Fey power, however deeply you pursue it, with an equally deep pursuit of purity. Your work must not become one-sided—all spells for the good things in life or for positive traits like courage, and none for purity—if you want to be happy and a competent magician.

Start a daily purification regime. You can use this to move out of the major life patterns that keep you from being happy and of service. It can also be used in the evening to remove the fears, resentments, grief, unhealthy beliefs, and other impurities that accumulate on a daily basis.

For the evening check-in, simply tune in to see what must be cleansed to give you a good night's sleep and a better tomorrow. Are you carrying a grudge about something that happened in the morning, and trapped in the dark cloud and helplessness that so often accompanies resentments? Cleanse the grudge and impotence away. If the only thing that will heal you is taking action to change the situation about which you got resentful, you might also do a spell for that, perhaps by simply praying for the power to take action in your life, or by using The Spell Itself, in which case you might imagine yourself as completely able to do what you need to do.

Cleansing away unhealthy major life patterns as well as the daily accumulation of inner blocks is crucial, allowing a healthy flow of the Mother's love to pour through us and giving us the health, vitality, and pleasure we seek. Purity also prevents spells that are unintentionally destructive and harmful. Cleaning also helps avoid the pitfalls that challenge a spiritual master. In proportion as magical skill and spiritual mastery increase, so must purity.

You may want your daily cleansing to focus on major life blocks for a while, before you place much emphasis on the day-to-day fallout from present-day trials and tribulations. Though not a hard-and-fast rule, adding one new discipline at a time makes each step effective and not overwhelming. Also, I became better able to honestly appraise how I fall short in the present once I had cleaned up some internal blocks from the past.

Anyone who follows the Faerie path eventually needs to consider daily cleansing rites, though often not for years. It can have an invaluable effect on your personal life and your magical prowess, whether used as a lifelong practice or as a temporary measure during crisis or life change. And if your pursuit of the Fey Gods goes far enough, there will come a time when daily evening purification is a must, along with your morning Ha prayer and other daily routines. If a daily routine seems too much, yet you have the need for such a discipline, three days a week is excellent.

Read. Haunt the bookshelves of your local occult or metaphysical shop. Also haunt ordinary bookstores to find folk tales and science-fiction fantasy; important glimmers of the Old Ways are contained in such tales.

Pursue an art form, in the broadest sense of art, which includes quilting, carpentry, pottery, architecture, skiing; any way you can express yourself and feel close to the Gods develops your inner poet.

Continue to meet with the partner or group with whom you did this training. Here are some suggestions:

Meet once a week, or once every two months, or whenever the spirit moves you. (Boo!) Decide what's right for you. It can become staid to spend an evening just talking. Perhaps spend some portion of any meeting in ritual, even if it is a tiny ritual at the end.

Support while pursuing a spiritual discipline is invaluable, and can be gained by discussing magical-journal entries or recounting inspiration you have gotten from books. Reading folk tales to each other, and discussing them in terms of magic and the Gods, is a great education.

At some meetings, you might focus on one member with a pressing issue. Perhaps that person is thinking of leaving a marriage partner. Or maybe she wants to return to school and is afraid to do so. Dialogue and a ritual from this book can help solve the problem.

On a given evening, plan to do a *bardic circle.* Have everyone in the group bring a poem, story, song, dance, or thought on any theme the group chooses, such as ecology, spirituality and politics, power as women, power as men, and helping the Gods. Use of The Magic Formula would of course be optional, but it adds a surprising depth and magic to such an event.

This rite offers the chance for sharing and self-expression central to loving community. The bardic circle creates a powerful magic so unlike anything in contemporary society that a person might not even know it was missing from her life until she had experienced it, unless she had seen it in her dreams. I strongly suggest you try it.

Learn a divination form. There are endless books on divination available. One will be suitable for you.

Find a teacher. The primary form of learning shamanism is by sitting with a shaman. For most people, there is no substitute. A book can only be a start.

Faerie Tradition is a body of techniques and theory that takes years to learn and master. It is hard to find a teacher of the Faerie Tradition, and the different branches of it are so unlike as to be totally different systems of science and religion. But there are worthy teachers of Faerie and Wicca systems different from mine. The Goddess will guide you to the right teacher. See the listing of resources in appendix 2.

It is a common practice to pray for a teacher. When you are ready, that teacher will appear. In the meantime, listen to the trees.

Create your own rites. If it feels right to you to create your own rites, do so, as well as developing your own sense of magic. While one rightfully imitates one's teacher, having been drawn to that person because one wanted to be like him or her in some way, the most important way to imitate that teacher is to be yourself.

Don't try to be just like your teacher. You needn't be like me by see-ing spirits all day, coming out of the broom closet, being a driven person, teaching Goddess Spirituality, or in any other way. I am *very* Fey blooded, and so I practice a very Fey form of magic, at a heavy cost that I suggest no one pay unless they must. Everyone has a bit of Fey blood; all magic of The Third Road is Fey touched, to greater or lesser degrees. But the primary point of that Fey glimmer is that it helps you be yourself.

If you're basically Fey blooded, do Fey magic; if you're tree blooded, do tree magic instead. If the blood in your veins is like a rock's, do rock magic. Finding your style of magic is simple: be yourself, and follow what calls to you. Don't be caught by the Faerie glamour: it will lead you away from your destiny, and you can wake one day from your dream castle and pockets of gold only to find yourself living in a dumpy hotel room with naught to show but a pocketful of leaves and mud.

Honor the planet through ecology, in whatever ways seem right for you. Clean a beach. Take political action to save rain forests. Shop organic. If you want, use magic to implement your goals, but you must be part of nature through mundane acts if you want to fully serve the Goddess and come into full power.

Add your own ideas to this list. How do you think you should pursue your path? If you ask the God and Goddess for guidance as to where to go from here, they will grant your request.

I have given you a lot of material about going further along the road to Faerie. Don't overwhelm yourself by trying to take on too many new things all at once. Note how I paced you throughout this training, and then decide if you need to go slower, even at a snail's pace. For example, different times demand different paces, and besides, if you take on something like an exercise routine or a daily purification regime, that might be plenty of additional work for quite a while.

Merry Meet and Merry Part

"Merry meet and merry part" is an expression used to end a ritual. The Gods have been good to me, giving me this chance to write a book for you. It has been a rite unto itself. I have truly been merry met.

As my merry parting, I offer a few last thoughts to see you on your way:

No matter how great our strengths, they are naught compared to Hers. As Her priests we should command great power with pride and confidence. As Her children, we must turn to our divine parents, relying upon their resources instead of our own. She will always be there for us.

Be patient with yourself whether you walk the road to Faerie or choose another path. Growth is a slow process. Some people expect themselves to grow ridiculously faster spiritually or technically than is possible.

Any seekers worth their salt inevitably let themselves down ethically. Why? Mistakes are the inevitable result of really living your life. Hopefully it takes only once for the mistake not to be repeated. (Hah!) An error can be an invaluable lesson in ethics. Mistakes seem to be a necessary part of the growing and learning process. If you are a slow learner, repeatedly making the same error—like me—be persistent in your effort to change. The Gods will reward you.

Be yourself, be all the things you are, and trust your own observations.

Use your magic as often as you want. Magic is for living, for using as part of your real life.

Cast as many spells as you want for life's goodies. I myself am thinking of diamonds.

Risk living fully. Magic is a chance to do that.

Life is worth living, a celebration, even with all its problems. My goal has been to give you spiritual tools to create bounty and to meet the challenges of life. Remember that any spiritual path takes a lifetime to apply. Spirituality is often a drug in this culture: "Do what I tell you—it only takes five minutes—and all your problems will go away. You will be free of *all* fear and worry. I also sell heroin." I support you to work hard and face your challenges. My prayers are with you.

Magic is a plant growing, a prayer made, a dance danced, a lesson learned, a cup of love, a person who is Glory, a song to the Gods. Magic is a pleasure taken, a spell cast, a service given, and a thank-you to the Goddess at the end of the day.

The ancient Celts learned the Old Wisdom from the Faeries. As you have learned now, for I have been merry met, and now merry part, as

your own Fey Sorceress,

Francesca De Grandis

Francesca De Grandis

Appendix 1

Certificate of Completion

Most folks congratulate you when you graduate from college or get married. When you accomplish something unusual, no matter how consequential, it is harder to get recognition, yet perhaps more important to do so. The following certificate acknowledges your shamanic accomplishments, can bolster your ego, and adds more power to the work you've done. Simply photocopy it and fill in your name and the date. Put it on your wall if you want!

THIS DOCUMENT RECOGNIZES THAT

_____

HAS COMPLETED A SHAMANIC TRAINING THROUGH

Be a Goddess!

A Guide to Celtic Spells and Wisdom
for
Self-Healing, Prosperity, and Great Sex

Francesca De Grandis

Francesca De Grandis

DATED _____

Supplementary Magical Resources

Shamanic counseling (a psychic reading) can magically improve your life inside and out. My psychic readings also provide professional support for your work with this book, are suitable to people of all religious denominations, and can include psychic healings and rituals. I offer in-person counseling in San Francisco, and long-distance readings by phone. Exorcisms can also be done long-distance. Call (415) 750-1205, or go to www.well.com/user/zthirdrd/psychic.html.

For daylong Third Road® shamanic seminars, longer shamanic intensives, and ongoing classes in the San Francisco Bay Area, contact me at P.O. Box 210307, San Francisco, CA 94121; (415) 750-1205.

Information about my events outside the San Francisco Bay area is available at www.well.com/user/zthirdrd/index.html.

The *Wiccan and Faerie Grimoire of Francesca De Grandis* is to be found at www.well.com/user/zthirdrd/WiccanMiscellany.html. It provides general information about Wicca—for example, Wiccan networking and magical reading lists, as opposed to my professional services—or has links to Web sites that might. The Grimoire also has lots of information about Faerie Tradition.

If you are looking for resources that supplement this book, such as a Wiccan-friendly therapist, my on-line Grimoire has links to sites that might help you. You may find a group in your area that can give you referrals.

Or try *Circle Guide to Pagan Groups and Resources*. In its tenth edition, *Circle Guide* offers an extensive listing that includes networks, centers, stores, periodicals, and cyberspace resources in the United States and other countries. For current price and ordering information, contact Circle, P.O. Box 219, Mt. Horeb, WI 53572; (608) 924-2216; circle@mhtc.net.

To purchase magical incense and oils, and ritual accouterments, write to Astral Sea, Ltd., P.O. Box 228, Salem, MO 65560. Ask for their catalog.

My new music CD is called *Pick the Apple from the Tree*. I was blessed with amazing musicians for this project, like Bruce Smith, dubbed by Frank Zappa "a great guitarist." It was exciting: recording music with clear, fun lyrics about spirituality. Terrific listening for pagans and lovers of Celtic music and the blues! The album is deeply personal, but celebrates universal experiences. I left the music business to be a shaman, then discovered that music could be used ritually. I've used these songs in rituals and performances throughout the United States. Use my music: heal, sing, dance, and make your fondest wish come true. I worship the threefold Goddess: blues, jazz, and Celtic music. And *She* loves Her bardic brat! The Muse welcomes us to the primeval garden where apples hang on the tree of life. Innocent white pulp hides dark seeds of immortality. Pick the apple from the tree.

You can order copies of *Pick the Apple from the Tree* for $16 each CD, $11 each cassette, plus $3 shipping for the first item, $1 for each additional item (U.S. funds only); California residents please add 7.5 percent sales tax.

Checks, Visa, or Mastercard payment accepted. Use mail, phone, fax, or email to send your order to: Serpentine Music, P.O. Box 2564, Sebastopol, CA 95473; (707) 823-7425 (phone); (707) 823-6664 (fax); annehill@serpentinemusic.com.

Acknowledgments

I got tremendous support from many folks, who accept that, as a shaman, writer, and artist, I need a lot of solitude and neglect my social calls. Without Frederic Lamond's encouragement I wouldn't have written this book. Deborah Grabien, Starhawk, Sara Shopkow, Joy, Leili Eghbal, Daisy Anarchy and Anodea Judith also supported me. Mary Ann Murphy and Cristina Salat edited the book proposal. Victor Anderson proofed the manuscript for spiritual or magical flaws. His feedback and guidance as my mentor were invaluable in the writing of this manual. My students loved me through the writing and publishing process; I really needed that. The following readers let me know when the manuscript was confusing, obnoxious, or otherwise problematic: Alison Harlow, Achilles Gaubert, Tom Haney, Beverly, Anith, Jen Turner, Richard Goering. My spell to get the perfect agents and in-house editor worked: my agents Elizabeth Pomada and Mike Larsen, and my HarperCollins editor, Mark Chimsky, showed vision, bravery, creativity, and shrewd business sense. The HarperCollins staff jumped on my bandwagon, Goddess bless 'em. I thank the hundreds of people who, trusting in my vision, studied with me. Many, many of them also volunteered selflessly to keep my classes running; of special note are Sara Reeder, Geoffrey Cohen, Vanna Z. Red, and Dawnwalker. I want to spend all my time trying to save the world, and Stephen not only puts up with this but is interesting enough to distract me from my mission. He also did everything from collate to wash dishes so that this book could finally get into your hands. I am surrounded by a plethora of friends (pagan and nonpagan) who keep me healthy and happy. I am blessed. Omigoddess, I know I forgot someone! I'll make it up to you in the next book.